Studies in the
Postmodern Theory of Education

Joe L. Kincheloe and Shirley R. Steinberg
General Editors

Vol. 162

PETER LANG
New York • Washington, D.C./Baltimore • Boston • Bern
Frankfurt am Main • Berlin • Brussels • Vienna • Oxford

Tobin Hart

From Information to Transformation

Education for the Evolution of Consciousness

REVISED EDITION

PETER LANG
New York • Washington, D.C./Baltimore • Boston • Bern
Frankfurt am Main • Berlin • Brussels • Vienna • Oxford

The Library of Congress has cataloged the first edition as follows:

Hart, Tobin.
From information to transformation: education for the
evolution of consciousness / Tobin Hart.
p. cm. — (Counterpoints; vol. 162)
Includes bibliographical references (p.) and index.
1. Education—Philosophy. 2. Learning—Philosophy. I. Title.
II. Counterpoints (New York, N.Y.); vol. 162.
LB14.6 .H37   370'.1—dc21   00-056397
ISBN 978-0-8204-5131-2 (first edition)
ISBN 978-1-4331-0591-3 (revised edition)
ISSN 1058-1634

Die Deutsche Bibliothek-CIP-Einheitsaufnahme

Hart, Tobin:
From information to transformation: education for the
evolution of consciousness / Tobin Hart.
–New York; Washington, D.C./Baltimore; Boston; Bern;
Frankfurt am Main; Berlin; Brussels; Vienna; Oxford: Lang.
(Counterpoints; Vol. 162)
ISBN 978-1-4331-0591-3

Cover design by Nona Reuter

© 2009 Peter Lang Publishing, Inc., New York
29 Broadway, 18th floor, New York, NY 10006
www.peterlang.com

Printed in the United States of America

FOR MAIA, MAHALIA, AND MARY

CONTENTS

ACKNOWLEDGMENTS

Thanks to my colleagues in the Department of Psychology at the University of West Georgia for their support of this project.

Excerpt from The Essential Rumi *(1996). (Coleman Barks, trans.). New York: HarperSanFrancisco. (Originally published by Threshold Publications) Used by permission of Threshold Publications*

CHAPTER 1

INTRODUCTION

This book is about remembering what matters in education and in life. In many ways, it concerns who we are and how we know.

Our lives are full of moments when we have a choice between going a little deeper or moving on to the next item, person, or task. When we pass by someone familiar and hear "How are you?" when do we say "Fine" and move on without missing a step and when do we allow the question to linger within us for a few moments? When we eat a morsel of food, how much do we allow the taste and texture to wrap around our tongue before bringing in the next mouthful? When an idea comes before us, in which moments do we open to it, and in which do we let it just pass by? In the times when we do go a little deeper, experience is not measured by quantity but is perceived as quality or intensity. Both experiences have value but our lives are most significantly shaped by the intensities, the moments of greater depth. Entering into depth is actually an opening or awakening of ourselves that enables an expanded perception. Through opening we travel past points of certainty and meet both the world and ourselves in fresh ways; and, as Martin Buber (1958) writes, "all real living is meeting" (p. 11).

Education is no different; the choice to open more deeply or to move on to the next bit of information is always present. In contemporary practice, it is too often the case that curricular expectations, looming standardized tests, and general anxiety push us toward *moving on* rather than *moving into*. On the educational surface lives information and we tend to skim along at this level and accumulate what we can, assuming this to be the goal. But elevating information acqui-

sition to the goal of education glazes the surface of learning and ob-
scures information's potential as a portal into depth, presence, and
intensity. And where do the depths actually lead?

Drawing largely from the sages and mystics of our world, from
ancient wisdom traditions and contemporary research, I have constructed a map of the depths of knowing and learning that move
through six interrelated layers. As the surface layer, *information* is
given its rightful place as currency for the educational exchange. Information can then open up into *knowledge*, where direct experience
often brings together the bits of information into the whole of mastery
and skill. Knowledge opens the possibility of intentionally cultivating
intelligence, which can cut, shape, and create information and knowledge through the dialectic of the intuitive and the analytic. Further
down lies *understanding*, which takes us beyond the power of intelligence to look through the eye of the heart, a way of knowing that
serves character and community. Experience then has the possibility
for cultivating *wisdom*, which blends insight into what is true with an
ethic of what is right. Ultimately, the depths lead to the possibility of
transformation. This learning process might be thought of as microgenetic development, meaning the series of developmental changes that
occur even in a single thought, feeling, lesson, or moment. It is a
process that can happen in an instant or over the course of an assignment or course. Opening to the moment and into these depths does
not take away from the information exchange but makes it richer,
gives it context, and brings it alive.

Entering these depths offers an education that is both practical
and remarkable, one that replaces radical disconnection with radical
amazement. It includes the education of the mind and the heart, balances intuition with intellect and mastery with mystery, and cultivates wisdom over the mere accumulation of facts. This is an
education where growing down, embodiment, is the means to growing up and where the focus is on the dynamic process of knowing as
much as on the accumulation of specific knowledge. Ultimately, it is
education designed for us to assist ourselves in our own evolution,
enabling us to align with the rising currents of creation.

My motivation for this work is, in part, very personal. I have two
daughters in public school and I have seen the marks of education
being etched into their fine spirits. These marks are not all bad. Some
good things are happening, to be sure, and I honor the tremendously
difficult work that their teachers are confronted with each day. Too

often, however, the malaise of mediocrity and of compliance creeps in like some dulling narcotic fog. The fascination with the world that characterized my daughters' years before schooling becomes overwhelmed by a predominately modernist approach to education that, in actual practice, tends to treat information as commodity, education as industry, and students as either products or consumers, where standardized testing born out of fear becomes the tail that wags the dog, and where "getting through" overwhelms much opportunity to linger and "get into." This is a land where education is too often stunningly mediocre; where the promise of education is often unfulfilled and thus betrays both students and teachers. And what is worse, in order for teachers and students to fit in and adapt, they must betray themselves by remaining on the surface, ultimately missing the sustenance that lives deeper down.

I work mostly at the other end of the education line and I worry that I am seeing my daughters a decade down the line in the eyes of many of the university students that I teach. Too often there is initially a distance from our course material and from themselves. Many appear to be dazed, passive consumers who have stayed too long in the mall of education. Relevance and interest are shriveled into the inevitable question: "Will this be on the test?" Education is often seen as something to get through in order to reach the checkout with the grade or degree rather than recognized as a clearing for deep experience.

I also recall my own formal education. While I know people who have had good educational experiences, mine felt as if I was living on Novocain; I knew a vibrant world was out there. I just couldn't really feel it through education. Schooling seemed mainly to foster a numbness that kept my own knowing and the immediacy of the world at a distance. The exceptions were those rare times when something or someone was so sharp as to break through the haze or when I was granted enough freedom and encouragement to meet the world firsthand.

In many ways, education has improved since my days as a student but most of us still sense fundamental inadequacies in the current system; we have known for some time that we are "a nation at risk." As the report with that title, from years ago, underscores, "if an unfriendly power had attempted to impose on America the mediocre educational performance that exists today, we might well have viewed it as an act of war. As it stands, we have allowed this to happen to ourselves" (National Commission on Excellence in Education, 1983, p. 5).

Many educators and parents have been making an earnest turn toward improvement; I am encouraged by many of these initiatives but I am frightened by others. As a society, we are only part way into that turn and it's not clear where we will end up. We all want our children to know more and to score better but the path that we take in making changes is not always guided by more substantial concerns that live under the surface of test scores. Often, "solutions" consider only incomplete and superficial pieces of the puzzle. The calls for higher test scores, more homework, a longer school year, "back to basics," increased standardized testing, and so forth do not acknowledge the underlying processes that invite deep learning. And does anyone really think that incrementally better test scores will help engender the kind of individuals and society that we are hoping for? The history of education is strewn with well-intentioned and well-conceived programs that did not stick. Long-term teachers are accustomed to the next innovative program; it has as long a shelf life as perhaps an assistant high school principal or a few years at best until the next good idea comes along. Historically, educational change often looks like a pendulum shifting back and forth from basics to progressive approaches, from student-centered to technique-focused and the like. Because we have lacked a more comprehensive vision to upgrade education, too many policies are predicated on outdated or simply faulty assumptions about the nature of the child and the learning process, and on a myopic view of our cultural needs. Essentially, much of contemporary education remains guided by a nineteenth century model of learning and an early twentieth century model of learners. We do not have an educational vision that is adequate for the twenty-first century; instead we are left with a kind of vacuum that gets filled with the next idea.

In spite of many positive changes, for the most part, contemporary education actually remains geared to downloading facts and factoids and fostering compliance. We seek to shape a populace for the marketplace and treat the child as a receptacle to be filled and controlled. This is certainly not reflected in the rhetoric or in our vision of education, but it remains, I suggest, the most typical practice of it. Now there are glorious exceptions to this, vibrant schools and innovative teachers who move past this status quo. But in general, educational systems are still bound to a modernist milieu that misconstrues information, the worthwhile and necessary currency of learning, as the goal itself. This focus on acquisition that is consistent with the consumerist zeitgeist of the age, has not led to students learning significantly more information, and the emphasis on higher test scores has caused more teaching-for-the-tests. The result is that "neither teachers nor students are willing to undertake risks for understanding; instead they content themselves with correct answer compromises. Under such compromises education is considered a success if students are able to provide answers that are sanctioned as correct" (Gardner, 1991, p. 150). Overemphasis on information acquisition has inadvertently worked against higher-order intellectual skills as well as the development of character, dimensions that create, shape, evaluate, and use information. Ultimately the result is a constriction of human consciousness. Without a deeper understanding of the place of information and the capacity of human nature, education not only becomes mediocre, it becomes "dangerous" (Gokak, 1975, p. 116), resulting in "arrested growth" (Sealts, 1992, p. 258), and it even threatens "soul murder" (Whitehead, 1929/1967, p. 57).

These are pretty strong indictments. But they are intended to challenge the taken-for-granted practices (which are based on inadequate assumptions about human nature) that flatten a human soul and a society, not all at once, but little by little, so that what we learn and teach best is how to shut down and fit in instead of waking up to life.

We are bigger than this. And our children deserve better than that. But without an upgraded vision we will list and limp along and be distracted from essential change by the next initiative, be it political, curricular, character, or management. The solution isn't a business model. The solution isn't vouchers, or school dress, a longer school year or more standardized testing. At best these are means to an unimproved end.

Education is preparation to walk into a future not yet determined. The speed of change–technological, social, and environmental–in this century makes this stunningly clear. From access to instantaneous global communication, to giant buildings collapsing before our eyes, to a hurricane that drowns a city, rapid and unpredictable change seems to define these days and presumably those to come.

Along with rapid change, one of the other hallmarks of this new century is the rise of a global society. Education for a global society is preparation not only to walk into an unknown world, but also to walk in multiple worlds, crossing cultures and time zones, traditions and values, worldviews and wealth.

Our current emphasis on information acquisition, basic literacy and numeracy are insufficient to prepare our charges for the world to come. It is time for an upgrade to our operating system. At the most fundamental level, education can be about two overarching goals: how is it to serve society and how can it help the development and potential of the individual. Public education in America and elsewhere was explicitly founded to train workers for the marketplace. This is a reasonable but incomplete goal that continues to drive much of our educational policy, even though the actual results are often disappointing to the workplace and to the worker. A more balanced approach understands that the well-being of the individual is essential for the health of a society and reciprocally, a healthy society invites the flowering of diverse human potential. I think we can find some real agreement around these two fundamental ideas and unpack an integrative vision. As part of that vision of the individual is the need to develop the inner life. This involves everything from self-reflection to emotional regulation, from imaginative expression to empathic understanding. These elements do not take away from the acquisition of information and the mastery of skills. Instead the growing evidence suggests just the contrary, that performance is intimately tied to emotional well-being, sense of community, sense of meaning and purpose, emotional regulation, self-reflection, and so forth.

So in order to establish a trajectory for the turn toward substantial depth in education, I have asked the question: "What would education be if we derived our practice from the deepest view of human nature and culture?" And this immediately raises another question: "Who has this deep view?" Teachers and students are at the center of the question and so they offer a close up look at what works and what does not. I have gathered firsthand accounts of the issues and opportunities that are within their classrooms and their hearts. This particularly helps us to see the deadening of student interest and the frustration and exhaustion of the teacher on the one hand, and the moments of inspiration and significant learning on the other. Somehow, successful teachers maintain genuine interest in their subjects and their students; in the midst of fear and institutionalization, they create a clearing that invites meaningful learning. They succeed not because of a technique or a universal style but through their own authentic and unique expression of the art of teaching, an art that requires constant learning, character, and imagination.

Teachers and students offer a close-up look at the immediate problems and practicalities in education. But where can we find perspective and depth to complement the intimacy of teachers' and students' voices? I have "asked" many of the sages, saints, and mystics of our world, those who have offered words about education, to guide this book. I have been surprised to find that their views are remarkably consistent and complementary, from Plato to Whitehead, William James to Krishnamurti, Aurobindo to Emerson, along with dozens of others. And so I have blended the voices of these individuals and those of teachers and students (along with many of the freshest contemporary writers on education and psychology) to offer a view of education as transformative. This work draws especially from the wisdom traditions, contemporary transpersonal and consciousness studies, research on learning and the mind, pedagogy, philosophy, and art. These perspectives help to describe what human consciousness is and how our education can encourage its unfolding. I hope the result is an education for the explicit development of human consciousness, character, and culture.

In general, our wise guides from across the globe seek an education of inner significance that provides an opportunity for "bringing forth" the inner person rather than simply "putting in" information; they speak of unfolding rather than simply molding an individual. This does not require that more information be added onto the contemporary curriculum, but it invites us to the inside of the subject matter and the Self. In this approach, the largest and most universal questions sit alongside the smallest and most personal, and all are fair game. Education then becomes not just transmitting a subject but bringing about a change in one's mind (Krishnamurti, 1974), an opportunity for "regeneration" (Swedenborg, 1771/1933), for the elimination of fear, "developing the sensitiveness of soul" (Tagore, 1961, p. 64), and for wisdom and liberation.

Transpersonal and psycho-spiritual studies have helped to integrate many of the perspectives of the wisdom traditions into contemporary disciplines. A transpersonal orientation presupposes that ego and rationality are not the highest attainment of human possibility, while it still acknowledges their essentiality. In other words, there is more to us than our small self-separate identity, and our knowing operates in complex dialectics that go beyond basic logic and reasoning.

But conventional education has not adequately drawn out this deeper nature. As Emerson (1972) writes, "we do not believe in a power of Education. We do not think we can call out God in man and we do not try" (p. 290). This work attempts to call out those deepest parts. And I should note that I do not see capacities for understanding and wisdom, for example, reserved for higher stages or ages of individual development; they can exist in children. Plumbing these depths creates transformative movement at every age and stage.

Chapter 2 begins by recognizing the rightful and essential place of information as currency for education but sorts out the confusion of regarding it as the goal. Information serves as the fire around which we gather.

In the information exchange, an opening in the form of receptivity or curiosity occurs when interest is engaged. Interest means that emotions have been activated, and we know that cognition and emotion are interdependent. Emotion awakens attention, which drives learning and memory. Relevance and resonance activate interest. Relevance implies that we are conscious that an idea or topic relates to us or something we are close to. Resonance implies that something vibrates us, moves us in some way. This chapter also briefly explores mind-based education, which considers what enhances the information exchange.

Chapter 3 sees knowledge as constructing patterns. Knowledge involves the development of systems of information instead of simply discrete pieces. Taxonomy of plants and the history of a world war constitute knowledge. Having knowledge means holding together patterns of information and implies the basic ability to use information. At the deep end, there may be comprehension and mastery over a domain or skill, such as occurs when we can perform algebraic equations, write a coherent paragraph, or repair a car engine. Acquisition is the motif at the level of information, but mastery, quality, and talent are the foci of developing knowledge.

One of the ways that information turns into knowledge occurs when we see a story in it. The tendency for reductionistic thinking flattens the world into component parts. But stories re-member parts into patterned wholes.

The process of developing knowledge exists in the dynamic interplay of the trinity of educational practice: teacher, student, and subject. In an infinite variety of ways, great teachers dance with method, student, and ideas to invite learning. The student's talents, interests, knowledge, and tendencies, such as learning style and cultural background, compose one part of the trinity. The teacher's person and practice represents another. And the third is the "great thing," as Rilke called it, the subject itself. Education involves gathering around a subject and the teacher's task is to show the student a way into it. This trinity of educational practice is sustained through the cultivation of community and culture.

Scientism has skewed our understanding of what constitutes truth and offers closed systems of "truth." As a result, a "consensus content" begins to shape a "consensus consciousness" as modernist education invites us to swallow the same content in the same way without question. But when the process of valuing is understood as integrated with knowing, closed systems of knowledge can be opened up and treated as living words. Four distinct kinds of truth (*social, cultural, subjective, objective*), together with the constructed nature of knowledge itself, brings valuing back to the center of the consideration of knowledge.

Chapter 4 explores intelligence, which cuts, shapes, and creates knowledge and information. Krishnamurti (1974) says that education is not just transmitting a subject but "bringing about a change in your mind" (p. 18). Training for intelligence involves cultivating thinking rather than mandating what to think. Part of training for intelligence involves a shift from accepting and amassing answers, as is more typical at the layers of information and knowledge, to raising questions. Education for intelligence particularly involves refining the mind through critical and creative thinking, analytic critique and synthesis, and the cultivation of imagination.

The way we use the mind affects not only what is known but also the knower. Overemphasis on a predominately logico-empirical approach to knowing has caused a distortion of both knowledge and knower. In considering the experience of the sages and mystics, inventors and artists, great scientists and leaders, we discover that the knowing mind operates not simply as a calculator and storage facility but also in a rich dialectic between the intuitive and the analytic. The process of this dialectic includes quantum leaps of understanding and creative synthesis that operate beyond the bounds of sequential reasoning. The intuitive and imaginative have been confused and distorted but return as a partner in an education that cultivates intelligence. As a way of developing the analytic in dialectic with the intuitive, we will consider the empirical-rational, the roles of multiple kinds of logic, the natural place of philosophy in the classroom, and the tools of observation and awareness. By intentionally cultivating intelligence, we not only give space to outside material, but we attend to the inside—we grow the mind.

In chapter 5, understanding takes us beyond the power of intelligence to see the world through the eye of the heart. The word understanding literally means to stand among or under. This implies crossing boundaries inherent in "standing apart"–the root meaning of the word objective–and moves toward intimacy and empathy. Standing among, or "heartfulness," provides a balance to an objectivist style of knowing and transforms both information and the perceiver.

Virtually all of the wisdom traditions speak of heartfulness in some form: the eye of the soul for Plato, the eye of the Tao, South on the native American medicine wheel, the Chinese *hsin*, the sensitiveness of the soul, the compassion of Buddha, the love of Jesus. The wisdom traditions suggest that the most essential knowing is not associated with the head but comes through the heart. The development of heartfulness begins to take us beyond self-interest and self-separateness.

Understanding requires a fundamental shift in the way we know. Whether an idea, a rock, or a person, understanding meets and accommodates the other directly instead of manipulating or categorizing it and the result can be appreciation, awe, and even reverence. Buber (1923/1958) describes this shift as a movement from an "I-It" relationship toward one of "I and Thou." Understanding can be practiced through empathy. Empathy has been described as the base for moral development and even as the trait that makes us most human. It serves as an active center for character and compassion. In one section, I report how simple meetings with an eye toward understanding changed both teachers and students.

One of the most direct ways to experiment with understanding and empathy is through service, ranging from tutoring another student to using servant leadership as a model of administration. Service also extends beyond people to include serving the task at hand. When we notice the artist, mechanic, or even the engaged algebra student absorbed in work we see a deep relatedness and intimacy at work; the line of self-separateness is crossed as we feel into the grain of the wood or the intricacies of the mathematical problem.

Concerns with violence at a variety of levels distort and distract education. The consequence of a failure of character and community is violence of one sort or another. Gandhi used the term *himsa* which can be translated as "the intent to do harm," as the basis for understanding the core of violence. While a particular action may be destructive, the willingness and desire to harm another powers violence. Who we are and what we do to one another is shaped most deeply by how we know the other. Knowing in isolation or illusory objectivity creates distance from the other and this makes violence easier to imagine and justify. On the other hand, understanding or heartfulness builds connections and closes the distance between self and other. Understanding serves as the centerpoint, the axis, of an education that turns the tide of radical disconnection. Character involves the development of wholeness, a self undivided, which includes the integration of the knowing heart.

Chapter 6 explores wisdom, which blends an ethic of what is right, with insight about what is true. Often elegantly simple, wisdom sees through the cloud of complexity to offer direction and discernment beyond the capability of the intellect. One does not exactly possess wisdom as if it were an entity; instead one acts wisely. Wisdom is distinguished from technical mastery or intellectual acuity especially by its integration of the heart of understanding.

Wisdom serves to dynamically expand and integrate perspectives. It involves the capacity to listen and translate the power of the intellect and the openness of the heart into appropriate form (action, attitude, etc.). Whereas the heart of understanding is universal and indiscriminate, wisdom is able to bring this broad unconditionality to the particularities of a situation. For example, the wise response is not always "Just love"; it may be strategic, disruptive, and confrontational. Jesus was said to have turned over the tables of the money-changers who were set up in a holy temple; Martin Luther King, Jr., organized a sit-in at a lunch counter in Montgomery; Gandhi's radical nonviolence confronted the authority of the British Empire.

These examples reveal another characteristic of wisdom; the wise person sees beyond immediate self-interest. In this way, wisdom does not simply serve individual growth but the movement of growth (evolution, transformation) in general.

We can open up the wisdom space within ourselves and within a classroom through a coordination of functions, a centering. This space is opened as we move beyond the modernist quest for certainty. Instead of demanding certainty, wisdom is able to hold ambiguity in an unending dialectic. In this way, "ambiguity potentiates learning"

(Bateson, 1999, p. 137). Instead of grasping for certainty, wisdom rides the question, lives the question. As physicist David Bohm (1981) argues, "questioning is ... not an end in itself, nor is its main purpose to give rise to answers" (p. 25). Harmony with the "whole flowing movement of life" comes when there is ceaseless questioning (p. 25). When the quest for certainty and control are pushed to the background, the possibility of wonder returns. Wonder provides a gateway to wise insight. We move near the wisdom space by defining ourselves authentically and spontaneously in relation to the world. We do this by finding what we love, uncovering our shadow, and listening.

Wisdom involves discovering the nature of the Self, which includes, as Rumi (1995) writes, "a fountainhead from within you, moving out" (p. 178). Wisdom involves finding access to this source, our wise Self. Even the young child has this fountainhead waiting to be tapped. The internal source allows us the freedom and power to dialogue and dance with external authority rather than simply resisting or succumbing to it. Interpreting the underground murmurs, symbols, and signs from the wise Self requires the art of listening, sensitivity, and practice.

The wisdom space can be opened through the aid of what the Dalai Lama refers to as MindScience, which involves inner "technology" designed to witness the subtleties of our consciousness. This provides the power to recognize and interrupt habitual patterns of mind and action. The nature of the mind and specific secular practices appropriate for the classroom are explored. Presence helps to activate the process of transformation, the focus of chapter 7.

Driving this whole movement toward depth is the impulse of transformation, an expansion of consciousness. Transformation is both an outcome and a process; it is the push and pulse that drives self-organization and self-transcendence.

To transform means to go beyond current form. When education taps the current of transformation it takes us beyond the "facts" and categories of our lives, the limits of social structure, the pull of cultural conditioning, and the box of self-definition. In this way, we gain the capacity not only to gather the facts of our life but also to transcend and transform them; this is where the deepest moments in education lead. In a moment, we are changed forever as we learn the magic of reading or take in an idea that sets off a shock wave within us.

Transformation is a movement toward increasing wholeness that simultaneously pushes toward diversity or uniqueness, becoming more uniquely who we are, and toward unity and communion, recognizing how much we have in common with the universe. In this way, self-actualization and self-transcendence are not contradictory but form part of the same process. We actualize our ever-expanding potential by transcending current self-structure.

Transformation within (person) and without (culture and society) takes us beyond simple adaptation to the status quo. While adaptation has its place, it is incomplete and confining: "if your ideal is adjustment to your situation ... then your success is likely to be just that and no more. You never transcend anything. You grow but your spirit never jumps out of your skin to go on wild adventures" (Bourne, 1977, p. 334).

The reaction of transformation often catalyzes growth that extends beyond the individual. Interdependence at all levels reminds us that social structures (e.g., slavery), cultural beliefs or values (e.g., prejudice), and consciousness of the universe as a whole may be changed as the ripple of individual transformation grows to a wave. In this way, the microgenetic development that I have outlined in this book serves both ontogenetic development (the development of the individual) and phylogenetic development (the evolution of the species and the world). Most personally and most directly, transformation is about waking up. Since personal and cultural awakening are intertwined, the primary constituent of education for transformation is neither culture and society nor the student but the consciousness that underlies both.

The question is not whether transformation happens: it does. We change and grow. Instead, the question is whether we can help transformation along. Can we create an education that invites, even nudges transformation? This involves a dialectic or "holding a space" between masculine and feminine, agency and communion, autonomy and interdependence. Will and willingness are the active or functional principles of autonomy or agency on the one hand and communion on the other. Will is the power of intention that throws (or holds back) our weight, our heart, and our effort in one direction or another. However, the power of will alone is insufficient to sustain transformation; surrender and communion counter-balance will. This dialectic (will and willingness) can be practiced through experiments with truth that involve facing freedom, fear, and responsibility. In doing this, we transcend information, time, space, and even self.

In the end, this book is intended as part of a discussion about education and human consciousness. It constructs an integrated view of the process of learning for the explicit evolution of human consciousness, culture, and character, and provides practical ideas for those moments when we find ourselves as teachers. It is offered as a prayer.

CHAPTER 2

THE CURRENCY OF INFORMATION

I am only going to school until it comes out on CD-ROM.
— A fifth-grade boy

This is the golden, or maybe the silicon, age of information. Information abounds as never before, and each time we take note, the amount seems to have grown exponentially. We now have access to information about everything from pipe bombs to prophecy. We no longer need priest, permission, or professor to gain access to the mysteries; they are available in the bookstore or with the click of a mouse. Not so long ago, we might have been killed for possessing, or even mentioning, the secrets. But today we have such a remarkable connection to and availability of information that we may even begin to wonder if the world-wide-web is becoming the world-wide-mind, the collective consciousness of the planet in digital form (see Gackenbach, 1998). Computer technology and the Internet represent the "second coming" in information access; the first was Gutenberg's invention of the printing press in the fifteenth century. Both have precisely the same effect of providing access to more ideas, more directly, for more individuals. But what are the implications for education? Education gathers around information. But in this expanding sea of information, how do we help students and teachers see what is of significance? How is the silicon or the ink alchemized into the gold of knowledge and more?

First, let us put technology in its useful but circumscribed place. Fantasies about the role of technology (fueled by truly remarkable breakthroughs) tend to overestimate its importance, especially for schooling (see Morgan, 1999, for a thoughtful discussion of how fascination with technology distorts education's aims). In the modern and postmodern era, technology has often been elevated to the status of a panacea or a virtual god, a power that will solve our problems, eliminate hunger and poverty, cure disease, and give us veritable seas of leisure time. However, with the rise of technology, hunger and poverty have not decreased, new diseases have replaced old, and life seems to have sped up not slowed. We are not wiser, more intelligent, or better people because of technology, although we are certainly more dangerous. For education, information technology offers a few very valuable but circumscribed functions; it provides (1) access to information and people that we would not otherwise have (e.g., distance learning in rural areas, conversations with significant figures in distant places, video records of deceased personalities); (2) the ability to store and transmit masses of information in forms that we can return to at our convenience (e.g., web pages, data files); (3) the ability to manipulate data (e.g., create graphic models that help us to visualize difficult concepts, create multimedia presentations, calculate quickly, spell-check this page); (4) immediate feedback (e.g., well-structured learning games, from typing tutorials to mathematics adventures, that provide an interactive environment for basic information and skill acquisition). These functions can add dimension and flexibility to information. At its best, technology can enhance access, retrievability, manipulability, and feedback, but it does not provide salvation. As former senator Bill Bradley has said of the Internet, it is an improved means to an unimproved end.

But what is information and what is its rightful place in the educational scheme? Information involves discrete facts and the most basic skills. Information includes the average temperature in Boise, the correct spelling of a word, the chemical formula for salt. It is the currency of education and will remain so. Most educational debate orbits around which and how much information should be passed along, and how and how well we are doing it. Should we concentrate on basic skills or more diverse subjects? How should the learning environment and teaching practice be structured to maximize information exchange? Tests for teachers and for students determine how much of the "right" information they have remembered. Up to a point, this is reasonable. As Aristotle notes, "it is clear that children should be instructed in some useful things–for example, in reading and writing–not only for their own usefulness but also because many other sorts of knowledge are acquired through them" (quoted in Baskin, 1966, p. 8). But we mistake the tree for the forest if we focus exclusively on information acquisition. What has happened is that the essential currency for learning, information, has become mistakenly identified as the goal. And as information grows exponentially, so does our educational anxiety about needing to absorb more of it.

Too often schools skim the surface of information at the expense of knowledge, intelligence, understanding, and wisdom. This may be parallel and related to the activity that occupies our society at large. Economic currency, money, has become not mere currency, a medium of exchange, but the goal in itself, even a kind of substitute moral principle that guides our actions, thoughts, and desires. This is not unique to our culture and time but it has reached an extreme in the contemporary West, the apex of commodity culture. The path to fulfillment lies in amassing the most money and stuff. Similarly, the goal of education lies in amassing the most, or at least the "correct," information. The dominant motif is one of acquisition. While information, money, and "stuff" provide practical necessities, they are neither the guiding light of human unfoldment nor the moral principle that we can trust to build a life upon; though sometimes our practice of education suggests otherwise. In the dominating educational focus on information acquisition, we remain shortsighted and obsessive. Ironically, we do not seem to be learning much more information.

The degree of emphasis on simple information exchange, as opposed to more integrated learning activities, varies from one classroom, even from one assignment, to the next. However, there may be a tendency toward a general relationship between the average socioeconomic class of the community, and the kind of education that takes place, not just in terms of better or worse performance on standardized tests, but in terms of the types of curricula that schools offer. In one study, Anyon (1980) found that learning activities in working-class schools were mostly mechanical, involving rote behavior and little decision making. She suggests that this is consonant with most working-class jobs. Middle-class schools tended to focus on right answers, good grades, and some basic decision making with creativity peripheral to academic activities, very much like the work of lower-level managers, which involves a degree of planning but exercises no real control over content. The schoolwork in areas with largely affluent and professional parents, like the work of professional groups and somewhat higher-level managers, involves more individual thought and expressiveness, expansion of illustrated ideas, and choice. In elite schools, in addition to basic knowledge and skill accumulation, there is an emphasis on the development of analytic powers. Children are asked to reason through problems, to think critically about relevant issues, and to produce high-quality academic work.

It is no wonder that students from lower-class schools drop out and underachieve in droves and middle-class students are often numbingly compliant or dispossessed and rebellious. The education presented is insufficient to hold their interest or to provide stimulation and liberation. Basic information and good grades are insufficient for a fulfilling life and for sustaining a truly democratic society that draws its strength from individual decision making, creativity, diversity, and responsibility. And part of the problem is the underlying assumption that the goal of education, whether in the poorest or the wealthiest community, is primarily to train workers for the marketplace. This book develops alternative and complementary goals.

In the wisdom traditions, we see that simply possessing information does not equal or even approach insight, enlightenment, wisdom, or compassion. To activate such capacities as insight, we need experiences that live deeper down. We will explore these in subsequent chapters. In fact, information alone is often dangerous and can easily be misused, distorted, or confused. For example, Hitler memorized masses of facts to impress and embarrass his questioners. "This information 'proved' his transcendence and disguised his lack of thought and reflection and his inability to hold a conversation. The demonic does not engage; rather, it smothers with details and jargon any possibility of depth" (Hillman, 1996, p. 225). Some alchemy is required to turn information into a more valuable form.

Information may be thought of as the surface appearance of compressed data. Words, ideas, even objects represent the tip of the iceberg; they serve as the symbol or marker that provides a point of focus. But the surface is not the essence; the explicate order, in Bohm's (1981) words, only hints at the implicate. The spelling of a word, "joy," for example, contains within it a host of meanings: a cultural history, a sound, reference to an inner state that is both universal and individual, perhaps a particular event, and so forth. Likewise, a gesture or facial expression is laden with depth; a concept from a textbook holds within it material about the writer, the culture, and much more. Ancient Sufi texts (see Khan, 2000) suggest that even mystical experience can be encrypted in words; and in Christianity the mystery of the faith is encoded in the symbolic blood (wine) and body (bread) of Jesus Christ. The words or the symbols represent compressed and encrypted data.

In computer information transmission, fractal geometry has enabled data to be compressed. While a computer analogy falls short in capturing the richness of human complexity, it may provide a helpful image for human information exchange. Just as we would find the compressed data of an email attachment of limited use until it is decompressed, information exchange at the human level consists of compressed bits of data needing to be "unstuffed" for full usefulness and understanding. To misinterpret the surface (the presentation of the information) as the full offering is to mistake the wrapping for the gift.

But compressed data requires decompression for it to be understood. How are depth, mystery, and meaning revealed? We form a dynamic system with information within a living universe; in order to decompress the data and open into layers of pattern and meaning, we must enter into relationship with the symbols and signs and allow ourselves to be opened by them. For the Sufi's, uncoiling the mystical data that has been encrypted in words comes from *knowledge by presence*, which involves critical introspection, that is, through examination of both the data and our selves. Similarly, in other traditions understanding is revealed only through a change in the perceiver.

Education can provide opportunity not only to gather and manage data, but to decompress it, to break its code, moving through layers of knowledge, intelligence, understanding, wisdom; ultimately this is the process of transformation.

Information can expand our selves and our perspective of the world, but typical downloading and regurgitation make little room for meaningful and enduring expansion. The assembly line metaphor of the industrial age has been replaced today by data downloading, but the emphasis on filling students up with bits of information and skills remains predominant. In such an approach, there tends to be a distortion and fixation of view instead of an expansion; the forest is lost for the twigs.

Plato (Baskin, 1966) tells us that when we focus so narrowly on information recall, we create "imitators" or "tracers" (p. 544), instead of artists. This acquisition motif creates a compliant and dull populace. Whitehead (1929/1967) says that "a merely well-informed man is the most useless bore on God's earth" (p. 1). Even at the university level, Whitehead notes the consequence of reproducing mere imitators: "I have been much struck by the paralysis of thought induced in pupils by the aimless accumulation of precise knowledge, inert and unutilized" (p. 37). The task of education is, in part, to help children think (and act) well, not to teach them what to think. However, in a climate that overemphasizes downloading and acquisition, we provide students with a list of what there is to see and instructions in the proper way to see it. The sages and mystics tell us that human life is about unfolding and growing through lived experience. Instead of working with an organic principle of unfolding, more akin to gardening, the downloading mentality engenders a mechanical practice of exchanging inert ideas. The organic and intuitive process of learning is reduced to a linear exchange of discrete, often out-of-context content. Too often there is no time for the appreciation of and attention to value and meaning; we must keep on schedule and accumulate the factoids as we go. This downloading is serious business and so learning to play with the information becomes a distraction from the curricular goal. The result is demotivation, and a loss of wonder and curiosity. *Romance*, as Whitehead (1924/1967) noted, is bypassed in favor of some modicum of *precision*. But, as he reminds us, we need both at each step in order to lead to *generalization* or what Hegel called *synthesis* (Hegel, 1955; Stace, 1955). Einstein (1979) tells of his own experience at the hands of dry acquisition:

> One had to cram all this stuff into one's mind for the examinations, whether one liked it or not. This coercion had such a deterring effect on me that, after I passed the final examination, I found the consideration of any scientific problem distasteful to me for an entire year. (pp. 16-17)

This is not to imply that we should expect students to learn only that in which they find some immediate pleasure, but that information grows arid and pleasureless and rarely takes root unless we can find relevance and resonance with it.

The efficient measure of acquisition has become multiple-choice and standardized testing, which has become an institution unto itself, one that serves to concretize the flatland of acquisition. Such testing is convenient and simple, with a single number used to represent everything from history comprehension to overall intelligence. Its seductive convenience has reinforced downloading and memorization as the main educational goals and actually shapes curriculum, which, in turn, shapes what we do in the classroom. Stepping back, it is remarkable to see how our educational system orbits around standardized and multiple-choice testing. While tests have their place in providing feedback, an important aspect of the learning process, these tests have become the tail that wags the dog. Teaching discrete facts for an exam and training for the exam increasingly becomes the *modus operandi* for education, and curricular goals and educational practice have been geared to what we can measure simply and numerically. The rampant and often fear-driven priority given to increasing these numbers may cause an incremental rise in test scores but results in a profound distortion of the learning process. We certainly should expect our students to know information, but when the ultimate goal becomes the measurement of this on a multiple-choice test, the surface of education is barely scratched. The incessant question from our students, "Will this be on the test?" underscores the fact that the goal has become achieving the test score for its own sake, not for learning and understanding. Politicians, teachers, parents, administrators, and parents collude in this testing mania by emphasizing test scores at the expense of meaningful learning. The recent overemphasis on standards-based education (e.g., "Goals 2000") and proposals for increased accountability to test scores (e.g., holding teachers' salary hostage to these numbers) will result in more fear and more teaching for the tests. As Hillman (1989) writes, "multiple choice scoring as a test of comprehension—has produced illiteracy" (p. 170). We deaden students' innate hunger for knowledge by stuffing them with inert information. If we adapted goals that moved beyond mere information acquisition, then the role of multiple-choice testing would decrease. When we stop exclusively focusing on evaluating students in this way, we see how the meaning of the word evaluation can change. We can help *students* learn how to evaluate, that is, to discern value, for themselves.

Keeping in mind the liabilities and limitations of an acquisition orientation, I still want my daughters and my students to explore a lot of information. We all do. And they often hunger for this exploration. When the moment is right, they gobble up information; when it is not, they gain little. Information can be the current and the currency activating an internal and external dialogue that is the beginning of deep learning. The next section of this chapter offers some ways to enhance the information exchange.

Relevance and Resonance

Nothing interests us which is stark or bounded, but only what streams with life.
—Ralph Waldo Emerson (quoted in Sealts, 1992, p. 246)

If we find interest or meaning in something we pay attention and tend to learn it. Few things are more straightforward in life. Interest enables the three-year-old to know the names of dinosaurs, including which ones ate meat. It allows the child who struggles with simple mathematics to interpret and memorize baseball statistics; children who have trouble with basic written language skills have little difficulty memorizing and writing down the words to popular songs. Finding points of interest, the student becomes a partner and the learning process becomes self-sustaining. Interest means that emotions have been engaged and we know that cognition and emotion are interdependent. Emotion drives attention, which drives learning and memory. Emotions are integral to the learning process but largely excluded from contemporary educational concerns. Without the emotional pull of interest, learning often becomes inefficient and tiresome, like trying to swim against a strong current. But once interest is engaged, intrinsic motivation and even inspiration may follow. Interest is cultivated through relevance and resonance.

Relevance implies that we are conscious that an idea or topic relates to us or something we are close to. Sometimes relevance is apparent. For example, my daughter devoured books that she liked (often ones about adventurous girls close to her age) and pushed aside the ones that she could not find connection with. Asking students to follow their own lead through independent, self-selected research projects is a fairly reliable way to activate interest. At its steamiest, relevance may evoke passion; even a sense of calling that emerges from some mysterious origin. Passion means falling in love with something. It creates a magnetism that pulls us forward. We may or may not have extraordinary ability or background in the area of our passion, but the love itself is sufficient for us to organize ourselves around it. While relevance and passion can emerge spontaneously, at other times we may have to work at exposing relevance. We do so when we shape the curriculum with the concerns of students' lives, from their neighborhoods, or from a point of view that might be close to theirs. For example, a history lesson for junior high school students might be offered from the point of view of a twelve-year-old who lived at that time. When we work toward relevance we partner with the student to build a bridge between them and the curriculum and we, as teachers, meet them on that bridge. When any information passes before us, some part of us asks: "What's in this for me?" "What does this have to do with my life?" "What meaning does this have?" Making these questions explicit helps students to discover how the material relates to some present concern or future goal and thereby nourishes meaning and interest.

In her first day of class, one middle school teacher asks students to write down two questions that they have about themselves and two questions that they have about the world. After collaboration in small groups, they organize and rank the questions and arrive at some degree of consensus. These questions (e.g., Will I live to be a hundred?) serve as a point of relevance for the entire curriculum and lessons are regularly organized around them (Bransford, Brown, & Cocking, 1999). Relevance means keeping students' abilities, interests, and passions in view.

While relevance means that something may be useful to us, this is not just a self-serving awareness. When students use information to make an impact on others such as when they give a presentation outside of class or tutor others, especially in their local community, their motivation often increases dramatically (e.g., McCombs, 1996; Pintrich & Schunk, 1996).

Interest can ebb and flow. Some days, for whatever reason, the "mojo" of the classroom is just not working. This is the time to take a break, refocus, address immediate concerns, and maybe address the big picture: "Why are we doing this?" "What is the relevance?" If we simply push through in these situations in order to fulfill the requisite "time on task," little learning takes place. When we are not engaged or interested, an hour on task will accomplish little; on the other hand, if interest is present, quantum leaps in processing information and absorbing material can occur in a few moments. Considerations of "time on task" should be entirely subservient to issues of interest, motivation, and meaning. (Of course, there are times when teachers must just stand their ground and maintain high expectations of students that push past the surface of the material and past the student's premature frustration so that the material has a chance to awaken some interest and challenge.)

Resonance is subtler than relevance. The word literally implies that something vibrates us. For a kindergartner this may occur in directly engaging the felt world of the senses through a nature walk, for example, or singing about, coloring, and writing a newly learned letter of the alphabet. The older student may confront a suitably challenging problem, such as, "Why is there so much violence in our society?" or a brainteaser that stimulates curiosity. Challenge, curiosity, rich sensory experience, and juicy information wake us up, producing an echo or resonance within us. As with art, it is not just the superficial outline, contour, or shape of the information; "there is something additional, a breath that draws your breath into its breathing, a heartbeat that pounds on yours" (Davis, 1992, p. 16). When material is presented with enough depth and richness, we often feel its pulse within us. When it is not, we leave numbed; as one student remarked, "most of my teachers taught in a way that their subject resembled a dead corpse or a petrified dummy. They taught directly from the text and to the test. As a result, I lost all passion and interest."

The source for resonant exchange is the information and its particular form of presentation (e.g., through a lecture, a book, a game). Superficially presented information or information out of context is less likely to resonate within us. As Emerson writes, "Nothing interests us which is stark or bounded, but only what streams with life" (quoted in Sealts, 1992, p. 246). Great teachers know their subject deeply enough to bring forth its presence and vitality, its streaming life. They serve as artists and explorers who create a picture for the student to see and meet. Great teachers give a glimpse of the soul of a thing or idea, each in his or her own unique way. It is not just that they know content but they also understand the particular epistemics and aesthetics of their discipline. That is, they understand what constitutes knowledge, verification, degrees of validity, quality, and even beauty. The historian knows in ways that differ from the physicist or the English literature instructor. There may be significant overlap, but each domain has its own truth claims, principles, presuppositions, and style.

Great teachers also remain open to learning from and exploring the material in new ways; information remains unbounded, without preset limits, and available to flow into new forms. If material is only superficially understood or is too tightly bound, it will be insufficient to resonate within the student or the teacher. Material offered with depth is like a wonderful meal, sensuous and embodied; it makes us want to lick the plate and ask for more. This is what great art does, what a powerful song does, and what juicy information offers. Students are hungry but we must give them something that they can sink their teeth into. If we are simply asking for the memorization of a factoid for a test, they will learn that school is not a place to find real sustenance.

In many ways, contemporary schooling treats curriculum material as if it were not substantial or sustaining on its own. Of course it is not sustaining when we do not scratch beneath the surface and instead simply ask for recall for some examination. When we have only a superficial meal prepared for a test, we may need outside rewards and threats. But ultimately carrots and sticks may actually ruin the opportunity for direct relevance and resonance. Like most children, one of my daughters entered first grade with a natural drive and a sponge-like desire to read and be read to. She was thoughtful about her choice of books and really seemed to fall into the stories with the amazing fascination and capacity for deep pleasure that children have. But her relationship to reading changed in one day, probably in one moment, when she was told that she could win a gold medal and a pizza if she read (or had read to her) five hundred pages over the next few months. This motivational gimmick, though well intentioned I presume (and perhaps initially helpful for some students), assumes that the reward for learning cannot be the experience itself; instead, children should expect a material payoff, a bribe. So that very night my daughter began choosing books not by interest but by how quickly she could get through the pages so that she could add that number to her list. When I read to her I did not get the same kind of interesting questions and ruminations about the story (e.g., "I would never do what Jane was doing, I would..."; "I wonder what it was like for the prince to live on his own planet?"). Instead, I consistently heard: "How many pages is that book?" This was a stunning change from quality to quantity. What was diminished was the chance for resonance and real learning. I has literally taken years for her intrinsic motivation toward reading to recover from the programming that leads children to believe they are to get some "thing" for learning. At its best, this cultivates performance-oriented motivation, which is useful but limited, and tends to obscure learning-oriented motivation, which is the deepest and most self-sustaining orientation. Performance-oriented motivation is reinforced by a variety of typical practices from the structure of the grading system to daily rewards. Upon her return home from school one day, one of my daughters reported, "I got to go to the treasure box and picked out this [toy or candy] because I finished all my 'must dos' in my learning centers." "What did you do at the learning centers?" I said earnestly. "I forget," she responded honestly. I saw her losing contact with the object of her learning, the thing she is contacting, and the place in her where it connects, where it resonates.

Behavioral management and manipulation, rewards and punishments, have a valuable place in the teacher's toolbox. When the intrinsic value or interest in the material is not apparent to the student it is appropriate to build a temporary bridge between the object of learning and the individual's interest. Times tables did not seem to get learned during the hustle of the school year and so we thought this a good task for the summer vacation. We were traveling and my daughter asked if there was some work she could do during the trip to earn some spending money. The mighty dollar worked as the bridge to get this learning moving, with little prompting, as evidenced by her question from the back seat: "Can we do sixes now?" In the classroom, extrinsic motivational techniques, positive recognition, playful competition, learning games, gold medals, and treasure boxes, can build a temporary and precarious bridge of contact between student and task. But they should not replace the deeper efforts to motivate from the inside out by cultivating rich material and interesting applications, and matching student concerns and capacities, which make learning relevant, resonant, and lifelong.

Mind-Based Education

Acoustical resonance is a phenomenon involving a source and a receiver that connect through a particular frequency; for example, when a string on one violin is plucked, a second violin in the same room will sound the same note. The sound waves connect one to the other along a particular frequency wave. In education, the subject may be thought of as that first instrument, and the student as the second. In order for resonance to occur between subject and student, the material and the mind of the student must resonate with one another. This requires two things on the part of the educator: first, an understanding of the range and nuances of the students' minds; second, an ability to offer rich, varied, and multiple tones in the presentation of the subject so that there is a greater likelihood of resonating with many students. I will simply note several key aspects of mind-based orientation below. I present only a cursory examination of this material since the main purpose of this book is to present some ideas about moving beneath the surface of information.

Over the past thirty years, significant attention has focused on how people learn; recently, so-called "brain-based" approaches to learning have become popular. Despite some popularity, brain (neuroscientific) research actually yields little information that can be directly applied to education (e.g., see Bruer, 1997). Most often Neuroscientific research is necessarily too specific and atomistic to generalize to the complexities of human learning. For example, the measurement of synaptic densities at certain developmental periods (these are measured in monkeys or other animals and have been theoretically extrapolated to humans) probably has little to tell us beyond what we know already: enriched and varied environments are beneficial. This is not a criticism of neuroscientific research itself. This research has boomed with the aid of increasingly sophisticated technologies (e.g., fMRI, PET scans) that allow the functional tracking of the brain, that is, the brain in action (see Murray, 2000, for an overview of research strategies on brain scans and learning). The problem comes when extrapolations to education are overstated. These leaps are generally too great and too far because this kind of research is by its nature focused on minute changes in the brain that can not directly be applied to more multidimensional interactions like learning and teaching. So when we hear the term "brain-based," claiming neuroscience as its source, it is generally a misnomer and usually an overextrapolation of the original research. Instead, a "mind-based" approach is a more useful and honest orientation for enhancing information exchange. A mind-based approach considers the human being as a functional whole, including the neurological level but not limited to it. Consciousness is neither confined to nor adequately understood exclusively through brain-based approaches, valuable as they may be. Mind-based education can include in its consideration sensory style, cognitive style (e.g., Morgan, 1997), multiple intelligences (e.g., Gardner, 1983; 1993), areas of intensity (e.g., Dabrowski, 1964), brainwave patterns (e.g., Lubar, 1991), relational style (e.g., Gilligan, 1982) and social mediation (e.g., Vygotsky, 1987), contextual understanding (e.g., Bruner, 1963), cultural context (e.g., Freire, 1974), learning rhythms (e.g., Wood, 1998), movement and the body (e.g., Dennison, 2006), and so forth.

The discoveries in these areas lead to the general conclusion that in learning, one shoe does not fit all. That is, each child is an individual matrix of learning and cognitive style, various abilities and interests, backgrounds and experiences, values, goals, and unique callings, and these affect how each student meets and captures information. Therefore, no singular teaching or curricular approach will suit everyone. Generally, the more individualized the learning approach the better, and thus anything, especially the reduction of class size, that permits individualization is consonant with what we know about enhancing learning. In addition, the more multidimensional the approach to conveying information, the more likely it is to reach a greater number of students. Tone, pitch, range, and rhythm of material affects what is retained. A description of the class of one sixth-grade teacher provides an example. Jane begins the lesson by asking her students to close their eyes and imagine a scene from their history assignment, read the night before. After a few minutes, she asks them to silently draw a picture, then to list the sounds that they imagine, then to list the feelings associated with the event. She next asks them to free-write a paragraph as if they were in the scene or observing it from a distance; she then asks them to break into groups of three and talk about what stood out to them regarding this historic event, what was important about it, and how it might be relevant to life today. One person from each triad is asked to present a list of the most significant events as well as key facts that are important to remember; the class is then asked to arrive at some rough consensus without restricting alternative views. An acronym is developed for the five most significant themes, and key points within each theme are generated and written on the board. Students may receive feedback through a quiz the next day; perhaps this time Jane will ask questions such as who, what, where, how, when, and why? Answers to the quizzes may be graded by a classmate and explained in class; additional quizzes or assignments are available to provide feedback on learning for both student and teacher. An independent research project may be offered on some subset of this material (e.g., architecture from the period, religion, famous figures, music, natural resources and technology, and so forth).

Many teachers are successfully applying their own versions of such multidimensional approaches that both engage more students and engage more of each student. Mind-based models of the learning process provide guidance in formulating such applications.

Just as the "receiving" violin in the acoustical equation may be freed from its case and tuned, in order to better receive the sound of the sending violin, students' minds may be invited to unbind themselves and tune in, as a prelude to the learning exchange. "Get a good night's sleep and eat a good breakfast before the exam." "That last period class is just wild." "Johnny just can't seem to concentrate." "I put on a video to calm the class down." These familiar remarks reflect the commonsense recognition that consciousness varies from moment to moment and from one child to the next, and that these alterations can drastically affect the efficacy of the learning/teaching process. Research is hardly definitive or complete on how or how well the mind can be tuned to a particular task. However, we have for some time been trying to regulate this receptivity in one way or another. For example, the use (and overuse) of Ritalin and similar medication, neurofeedback and biofeedback, meditation, and imagery in mental rehearsal are specific attempts to help the "receiver" (the student) actively (or passively in the case of medication) tune himself or herself in order to improve learning or presentation, to bring himself or herself into an individualized "zone" of improved performance. As both inner technology (e.g., meditation) and outer technologies (e.g., neurofeedback equipment) become increasingly accessible and valued, their educational application will become more commonplace. Currently, top athletes use positive mental rehearsal and visualization to enhance performance and it looks as if neurofeedback training may provide one alternative to medication for some with so-called "attention difficulties." (Of course, the whole consideration of this book is to alter the classroom norms so that many who are currently labeled with "attention difficulty" can find an environment that is more deserving and engaging of their attention.) I will refer to this further as MindScience in chapter 6. Again, this has not yet been synthesized adequately for education but the teacher nonetheless can safely experiment with it. For example, music represents one very tangible and practical way to shift consciousness. Recent popular attention regarding music's ability to improve intelligence, "The Mozart Effect," has highlighted the value of listening to music; work such as Don Campbell's (e.g., 1997) approach to music and the mind have been extremely welcome and insightful. However, definitive data on the effect of the intelligence of babies who have listened to classical music do not exist. Rich and varied stimulation in infants does seem to add neural density, at least in animal studies, but evidence to suggest that classical music has unique properties in brain development is not clear. But rather than getting bogged down in this simplistic cause and effect question, we can instead think of music as a precursor, primer, or lubricant for learning. Music does affect consciousness (emotion, visual imagery, relaxation, excitement, awareness, etc.). We have only to play a favorite song to recognize its power to literally shift our awareness, mood, or thoughts. Music can be used to help bring consciousness into alignment with the task at hand; rhythm, tone, and emotional evocation can all be used to help entrain the mind. Shamanic cultures used particular types of rhythm and chanting to shift levels of consciousness; rhythmless Gregorian chant opens a particular spaciousness of mind; music that approximates the resting heart rate helps to calm us down. If I want a class to interact and loosen up, I might play Bob Marley; if they seem placid, more complex African rhythms seem to bring us to life; if the class seems out-of-synch, we stand up and tone a note together for a minute (an "Ah" or an "Oh"). I might play jazz if I want us to think "outside the box" in problem solving, or some "New Age" composition if I want students to creatively imagine an idea for a story. Mozart and Beethoven create a certain focused concentration, particularly if we are intending to bring precision to the discussion of our classroom material. The teacher can safely and simply experiment with helping students to entrain with the task at hand. Mozart probably will not directly make us more intelligent, but he may help us to entrain our minds in particular ways that enhance learning and performance. And, of course, beyond this utilitarian purpose, music adds depth, texture and beauty to our lives beyond measurable or easily reducible comprehension; it embodies the range and depth of our humanness.

Inner Teacher

Aurobindo, like so many of the sages and mystics, tells us "the mind has to be consulted in its own growth.... He himself must be induced to expand in accordance with his own nature" (quoted in Ghose, 1924, p. 3). Consulting the mind and one's own nature is aided by understanding how development unfolds over time. Developmental understanding gives us some general clues about where to look and what to look for when considering who the student is and how he or she learns. Essentially, this helps the educator to see through the eyes of the child.

As with an acorn, there is an innate drive in the growing student. In Aurobindo's educational model, "the child, with the tremendous motivating potential within, is his own teacher. The nurture of the child means this actualization of the inner motivating potential through the careful nurture of the developmental urge" (quoted in

Joshi, 1975, p. 52). The person tends to unfold in a sequence, not a rigid or simply linear one, but one in which new capacities build on and integrate previous ones. Stimulation from the environment activates and enhances this development. For example, language development requires exposure to language in order to maximize potential. Development moves toward increased complexity and integration, which means including and transcending each previous stage or capacity as we grow.

A single line or thread of development, for example cognition, psychosocial growth, moral reasoning, or empathy provides only a partial map; development is multilinear, and these threads intertwine. The weaving is often asynchronous, meaning that different threads (capacities, abilities, etc.) emerge at different rates; this is particularly noticeable in gifted children (see, e.g., Dabrowski, 1964; Silverman, 1994).

There is some agreement that the child progresses through some general or basic structures of consciousness (e.g., Piaget, 1977; Wilber, 1995), although it is important not to take a stage model too rigidly or allow it to overwhelm the less linear development that also accurately describes the child's unfolding. Developmental implications range from the value of sensory-motor activities like art and movement for young students to the recognition that children develop capacities (e.g., reading competence) at different ages and in different ways. Since many excellent books on development are available (e.g., Kegan, 1982, offers an excellent integration; Crain, 2000, and Goldhaber, 2000, provide rich surveys; Marshak, 1997, thoughtfully summarizes the developmental implications for education of Aurobindo, Rudolf Steiner, and Inayat Khan; Wilber, 1995, offers an evolutionary theory), I will avoid reiterating these ideas here; however, I do want to highlight the point that developmental theory provides a central component in a mind-based approach to learning that fosters resonance and relevance.

Once basic information acquisition is bumped off its pedestal as the primary goal of education, information can return to its rightful place as currency and as the portal into deep learning. As resonance and relevance are enhanced, we develop richer relationships to information that can catalyze the growth of knowledge and more.

CHAPTER 3

THE PATTERN OF KNOWLEDGE

What we want is to see the child in pursuit of knowledge, and not knowledge in pursuit of the child.

—George Bernard Shaw (Maggio, 1997, p. 134)

Knowledge involves the development of systems of information instead of discrete pieces. Gaining knowledge means constructing patterns of information and implies the basic ability to use information. The deepest form of knowledge involves comprehension and mastery over a domain or skill. The debater can make a reasoned and measured argument; the mechanic diagnoses a car problem; the writer shapes a story. Whereas the motif of acquisition dominates when information is seen as the goal, mastery, in the form of skill or comprehension, dwells at the deep end of knowledge.

As systems of information, we generally conceive of knowledge as external content (e.g., the botanist's taxonomy of plants) held passively in our minds for application when needed. Beyond knowledge as an entity, it is also understood as a skill or competence. Instructions to assemble the new bicycle serve as information, discrete and inert; we gain knowledge or "know-how" when we succeed in putting the pieces together successfully (with or without the directions). Know-how may involve a mental operation like using a mathematical formula, or a mental and physical activity like riding a bike or repairing a car. Internally, this involves transforming and integrating information into larger patterns or meanings. When we are able to do something consistently with precision, we say that we have mastered it. This is what we hope for by stocking classrooms with computers, by drilling mathematics, and by encouraging reading.

The age-old class assignment to "compare and contrast," for example, a particular Civil War battle and one during World War II uses information and organizes it to demonstrate or highlight particular dimensions; it builds knowledge because it asks us to uncover and create patterns and schemata with the information in our own minds. Analyzing sentence structure (e.g., "Underline the noun, the verb"), solving a mathematical problem, reading or writing a sentence are all knowledge-building activities. For some, teaching fellow students (i.e., through tutoring or presentations designed to actually teach material, not just to be performances) stretches knowledge to a deeper level of mastery as we are required to construct internal maps of the material and then translate those representations to the learner in a fashion that matches the learner's level of understanding and particular need.

Mastery most often equates to efficiency, accuracy, and precision. The master carpenter knows how to build the stairs effectively, the successful algebra student can match the formula with the problem and "do the math." These serve as appropriate and reasonable appraisals of mastery. In addition to precision and efficiency, mastery can also involve particular quality. For example, some stairs are just stairs, but others are works of art or ingenuity. Just one example comes from the famous spiral staircase leading to the choir loft at the Loretto chapel in Santa Fe. Built by a wandering craftsman, who disappeared upon completion of the staircase as mysteriously as he had first appeared, this magnificent wooden spiral defies conventional building wisdom and manifests remarkable quality, not to mention mystery.

Quality is a universal characteristic of humanity. We recognize it; we talk of it; we live according to an intuitive sense of its meaning; and it guides most of our actions and attitudes. And while it is difficult to pin down precisely (we can't measure it exactly or hold on to it), we do recognize it. Whether expressed in evocative artwork, in story, dance, or invention, quality requires an unusual intimacy with the task at hand.

Sometimes quality emerges as a talent, a kind of innate knowledge or capacity. My eyes widened when I saw how well my daughter danced after a lesson or two and how easily she was able to pick up new steps. She has a talent; I find her sprinkling something a little extra, quality, into her dance, and notice how natural it is for her to experiment and be inventive. My thirteen-year-old friend pushes his own limits on the piano and creates new music; one of my college students crafts prose with riveting depth and power. Some lives may orbit around a talent; for others, the talent may fall into the background as other interests, demands, or abilities take precedence. Mastery, especially of a talent, can provide fulfillment ("It's my best thing") and a kind of yoga or meditation that gives one the opportunity both to perfect and to be in the "flow" of the talent.

The ancients often considered the source of talent as one's personal genius, Daimon, or familiar spirit, and it seems that "education works to either close or to open the channel between children and their genius" (Gardner, 1996, p. 115). However we conceive of talent or genius, it is important to provide opportunities for its expression and indulgence. Otherwise, the "vision" offered by that Daimon may not find its way into the world and the innate knowledge may never provide real sustenance. Native American elder, Black Elk, says, "a man who has a vision is not able to use the power of it until after he has performed the vision on earth for the people to see" (Neihardt, 1988, p. 204).

Beyond the basic love of family and friends, few things come close to influencing how we think of ourselves more than the development of mastery; and nearly any kind of mastery will do. My very young friend learned to tie her shoe recently. Each time she comes to visit, she asks whether I want to see her tie her shoes. This know-how inherently satisfies and clearly provides a source of pride. She can do this thing called shoe tying and if she can master this, she assumes rightly, she can probably master other things. Self-esteem in school emerges largely from self-efficacy ("I am able to do this or that"), which in turn comes solely from experience at doing it. Positive affirmation can provide a gradual correction to internalized criticism, but the heart of self-esteem in school is a combination of self-efficacy born of mastery and a sense of communion and community; both involve tapping the deep contact with the world.

Rather than metaphors of banking or downloading as our goals of education, upgraded notions on the nature of knowing may be more helpful goals to focus on in this century. From computing and biology to physics and neuroscience, we are increasingly describing how the world works with words like *networks, webs, fields and streams,* instead of simply individual parts, bits, and components, reduced to their lowest independent nature. Some general examples may make the point. The forward edge of technology isn't bigger computers, its better networking–ways of tapping into webs of information. In biology, interactive field (e.g., Sheldrake, 1995) and systems theories (von Bertalanffy, 1968) are more complete (than atomistic "component") explanations for understanding the mechanisms of biological organisms, from cellular to social levels. In physics, field theories explain the subatomic world (e.g., non-local influence and electromagnetism) in a more satisfactory way than, say, Newton's description. The flourishing field of brain science tells us we operate as a neural web, one that even networks with others, underlying our interconnection in the field of consciousness. This has come to be understood as a neurological reality through the emerging field of *social neuroscience* (e.g., Goleman, 2006). And as William James recognized, with just a little self-awareness we come to notice that consciousness itself does not exist as chopped up bits, but instead as a constant flowing stream of experience. These terms and phrases give us some descriptions about how education might better match reality.

A banking metaphor of education is not wrong; we do amass information. But it is incomplete. And it is inadequate to explain the sonnets of Shakespeare, the inventions of Da Vinci, the declarations of liberty or how to tackle the perils and possibilities of the twenty-first century. Information and skills help us to frame questions, interpret and compare data, and expose us to new ideas and ways of thinking–absolutely central to be sure. But other qualities of knowing are equally important. This is why, in the work of great minds, we hear descriptions of intuition, imagination, intimacy, opening, and even love (see, e.g., Root–Bernstein, 2001).

The task of schooling for the twenty-first century is not just to load us up, but also to open us up. That is, to give us the skills to open and expand the range and reach of the mind so that we can see more and more richly. As opposed to merely amassing more, how do we move toward attuning to fields of knowledge and tapping streams of consciousness?

Making Contact

Education must pass beyond the passive reception of the ideas of others. . . . The second-handedness of the learned world is the secret of its mediocrity.
—Alfred North Whitehead (1929/1967, pp. 47, 51)

To move information toward knowledge and activity toward mastery, we must play with ideas, use them, and make them our own. When we make deep contact, a change takes place within us that allows us to accommodate to ideas, taking them into us and creating spaces and structures to hold them. The activity of schooling too often provides only superficial and sterilized encounters with ideas. Information remains uprooted from context, soil, and flesh, without relevance, immediacy, presence, or a sense of being part of lived experience. We wait for the mediation of the mental to tell us the meaning and value of the encounter, but we are rarely invited to listen to the subtle meanings sensed in our body, our breath, as well as in our thoughts. Making contact implies, in part, reconciliation between our selves and the context within which we operate. Contact forces the recognition that we are embedded in a relationship with the world.

In the early twentieth century, Harvard philosopher Alfred North Whitehead protested against what he called "dead knowledge" or "inert ideas." "Ideas which are not utilized are positively harmful. By utilizing an idea, I mean relating it to that stream, compounded of sense perceptions, feelings, hopes, desires, and of mental activities adjusting thought to thought, which forms our life" (Whitehead, 1929/1967, p. 3). Firsthand knowledge comes from engaging the world; "the second-handedness of the learned world is the secret of its mediocrity" (p. 51).

Information must be utilized, applied, integrated in one's mind and life in order for it to move toward knowledge and mastery. We actually have to "do math" in order to learn it: learning formulae is insufficient; we must practice reading in order to master it; and so on. And often, mastery comes only when knowledge is applied in our life beyond the schoolroom. Sebastian, a graduate student at a premier engineering and science research university, never understood basic fractions until he began to experiment with woodworking in college. Only when he needed to use the math to solve problems, to measure, cut, and calculate in order to build his ideas, did it click for him. Mary remembers the pleasure and sense of accomplishment in learning fractions as a child by making reduced-sized recipes, a single cream puff or cupcake after school. Both of these students turned information into knowledge by applying it in their world.

Krishnamurti (1974) says, "learning is doing, so in the very act of doing you are learning" (p. 82). Progressive educators have a long tradition of attempting to provide a more immediate relationship to the object of learning. Rousseau (1762/1957) advocated learning "naturally" and by doing; his call was taken up by Pestalozzi (1951), who focused on learning through direct concrete experience. Dewey (1938/1963) emphasized learning by experience and through cooperative endeavors; Bruner (1963) focused on problem solving and emphasized intrinsic rewards; and Freire (1974) suggested critical dialogue that addressed immediate real-world concerns. Some of this insight has certainly been incorporated in the mainstream. For example, in science education, we see initiatives to bring teachers and students into the "field" of their subject by experimenting and solving problems firsthand. They may work on a problem of erosion in a nearby river by visiting the site, taking measurements, constructing models, and so forth. And many enrichment programs emphasize problem-solving experiences. This gives immediacy to abstract information and necessitates its use in practice. However, this voice of direct contact too often gets overwhelmed by curricular demands, scheduling limitations (e.g., the forty-five-minute Carnegie unit), and primarily by the assumption that we can download material into an empty vessel or memory bank and adequately evaluate knowledge through a multiple-choice exam.

Not only do ideas remain inert without firsthand contact, but students can easily remain inert themselves, listless or mechanical, partially asleep;

> It's not that we want to sleep our lives away. It's that it requires a certain amount of energy, certain capacities for taking the world into our consciousness, certain real powers of body and soul to be a match for reality. (Richards, 1989, p. 150)

Those powers of body and soul awaken when we make contact below the surface of information and recall.

My then fourth-grader had science homework some time ago. The assignment was to read several pages about the solar system and moon phases and answer in writing the questions at the end of the section. This is a standard and valuable way to practice reading comprehension and was allegedly intended to explore science. My daughter's book had pictures of moon phases with explanations. These seemed abstract, a little over her head and, in fact, I found myself unable to get much out of them. I glazed over, yet I enjoy astronomy. On the other hand, the moon looked spectacular that evening; what phase was it in? If she and her classmates had compared the sky over several nights with the book information they might have gained a real foothold in understanding. But I suspect few, if any, in the class made the comparison between what was overhead and what was in the book in any meaningful and lasting way. It was just homework to get through, and the trick was to memorize and repeat only what the text was asking for.

One part of her assignment asked her to "name four systems." The student had to simply repeat what was said in the text (basic information recall, valuable but limited). However, the assignment entirely missed the opportunity for developing knowledge and intelligence. We may hear that students cannot tackle more complicated questions until they have the basics, but the basics are often mastered when applied and contextualized. In this particular assignment, the concept of a system is really a linchpin for understanding a pattern of knowledge. But what is meant by a system is not brought down to earth. Why are the planets part of a system (i.e., gravitational influence on one another)? Are there other systems that we can think of (e.g., your family, you and a classmate working on a project together, this class, the biosphere, the school)? What makes them a system (a kind of relationship that could be explored in class)? While my daughter can copy the words "solar system," remarkably there was not even any explanation in the assignment that the world "solar" means sun. By going just below the surface we discover that the solar system is a sun system and planets are operating in a relationship to the sun because of gravitational influence. With the comprehension of these patterns my daughter could turn the information into knowledge. There was no time—I checked—taken in the classroom for any exploration of suns, systems, moon phases, or the sheer beauty of the moon. No mention or explanation of the solar eclipse that had just occurred. Recalling the basic facts was the goal, and it missed the chance for developing the patterns of knowledge. An approach that skates along the surface of information provides little time or support to dig in deep enough to make substantial and meaningful contact.

What if part of the assignment had been to "hang out" with the moon a while that evening and perhaps for the next few nights, just before bedtime? "Sit alone in silence under the moon, and simply take note of your observations, as well as your own experiences including feelings and thoughts (e.g., curiosity, fear, convenience of the light, mystery, beauty, fascination). The great scientists find a way to meet the object of their inquiry, and they regularly describe their fascination, wonder, and deep relationship with the object. We invite fascination when we open to direct contact with knowledge. "Imagine traveling to the moon." "Write a story or a poem about the moon." "Make a picture." "What is the system of you and the moon?" "What poetry is there about the moon?" "What can we find out about the moon landings?" "What would happen if there were no moon? How would our planet be different?" "Interview each other about your moon experiences." A solar system/ moon lesson could easily have cut across all content domains: spelling, math calculations, history (e.g., the space race, the shift to a heliocentric worldview), and so forth. But curriculum teams rarely talk across disciplines, and so the curriculum becomes fragmented rather than naturally integrated. Teachers are required to push on with the flood of curricular demands and the pressures to teach toward a standardized examination. The surface treatment of a subject can change when learning asks for more than memorization, integrates rather than fragments knowledge, and shifts from a culture of fear, forced to teach for recall on a standardized exam, to a community that invites students to make deep contact with their world.

Growing Soul

The acquisition motif that characterizes most contemporary schooling, grown out of objectivism and industrialism, measures value by efficiency, which involves comparative quantity (more is better), speed (faster is better), and economy (least cost in resources is better). In the classroom, how much and how quickly we "cover" material becomes the primary measure of success. For the individual student, how much and how fast he or she can remember and repeat is generally the measure of achievement. This certainly has merit. However, in overemphasizing these goals, education becomes directed by the values of the machine age that name efficiency as the highest good. When this dominates the educational enterprise, we miss the opportunity, as scientist and mystic Emanuel Swedenborg termed it, to "grow soul."

Sharon was a young, accelerated college student who was taking many more credit hours each term than she needed, managing "A's" in nearly all her courses, and eager to get finished. She had mastered the game of schooling. She would sometimes complain that she would like to do more projects in one course or another, but it never happened. She was so locked into the fast track of accumulating courses and grades and heading toward degrees that she seemed to lack intellectual depth and the emotional color that comes from meandering about, digging into the landscape, and taking the material into one's life in some way. Like a hydrofoil, she seemed just to keep skimming along the surface of information. Then, in one term she decided to take an internship working with incarcerated adolescents, in part because she could get more credit for it and it would look good on her graduate school applications; but this internship began to "grow her down." Gradually, she began to shift the balance away from fast-track information acquisition to the less mechanical, more meandering direction and pace of a world built around meaning and intensities, not only efficiency. She did not learn less or more slowly, but instead she began to learn more deeply. Instead of simply accumulating information, she began to grow knowledge by applying and experimenting with information. She tended more toward application and critique, rather than simple recall. She also seemed to grow in a way that is difficult to describe precisely; she became more reflective, lingered longer in ambiguity, and was both more confused and more playful as she seemed to flesh out and color in the contours of her soul. The depth and meaning of her experiences took on new dimensions, moving from the relatively narrow path of her classes to the streaming of life. Whenever we take the time to help students explore the connections between their experience and some material, we make contact and "grow soul."

Somehow we have constructed a system in which the student rarely understands that the point of education is knowledge and growth. Instead, acquisition, recall, and movement to the next item, class, grade, or degree become the goal. Students often become enculturated into dazed, passive consumers who look as if they have stayed too long in the mall of education. Education becomes something to go to and get through, rather than a clearing for deep experience. I see this in my college students, in high schoolers, and even in elementary students that I interact with, especially when they ask the inevitable question: "Will this be on the test?" "Do we have to know this?" "Did I miss anything important yesterday?" (Translation: "Will it be on the test?") Rather than wondering where an idea touches them or challenging the validity of some authority's comment, mine included. The fearful push for higher test scores "or else" (we will fire the administration, rewrite the curriculum, hire a private management team, be held back, fail a course, etc.) does not result in better education but in "teaching for the tests." Test scores are useful for providing feedback on individual students, but they are being used as sticks to heighten a climate of anxiety and fear. This creates the opposite of an environment that fosters contact, embodiment, and ultimately, deep learning. Such simplistic information-oriented approaches will entrench our problems even further and shrivel rather than grow soul.

Stories

Perhaps the most universal way of moving information into the patterned wholes of knowledge is by offering material in the ways that we live and understand our lives, through stories and metaphors. Stories and metaphors offer patterns of meaning that may be interpreted at many different levels. They weave bits and pieces into patterned wholes located in time and space, with history and direction, just like our lives. Stories, whether about biology or philosophy, connect ideas and events to the stream of life, to the "pattern that connects" as Gregory Bateson (1980) named it. Inevitably, we act according to our stories (e.g., "I am a good student." "The world is round." "I am unlovable."); "we think and see in terms of stories because we are stories" (Feige, 1999, p. 87). The story defines us as humans:

> The first sign that a baby is going to be a human being and not a noisy pet comes when he begins naming the world and demanding the stories that connect its parts. Once he knows the first of these he will instruct his teddy bear, enforce his world view on others in the sandlot, tell himself stories of what he is doing as he plays and forecast stories of what he will do when he grows up.... He will want a story at bedtime. (Morton, 1984, p. 2)

Teaching the "story" of a discipline and setting that story beside the students' own stories brings resonance, waves that intersect and connect. This offers a way of presenting and knowing the world that comes closest to our lives and reminds us that we are living beings in a living universe (Bateson & Bateson, 1987). In practice, this means that when we teach the history lesson as a story (or if we are a student, turn it into a story ourselves) rather than as discrete dead facts, then the history comes to life. Of course, some metaphors are more effective at capturing the "story" of an idea or a discipline than others, precisely because an underlying pattern of the discipline or the idea is congruent with the pattern of the story. Even corn plants and genetics have a story. Nobel laureate Barbara McClintock describes listening to corn plants, essentially allowing them to tell their story of genetics (cited in Keller, 1983). In its simplest application, we embed material more easily in long-term memory if it has a story. For example, this mini-story may help in remembering the order of the planets, or at least the pre-Plutonic solar system: My Very Energetic Mother Just Served Us Nine Pizzas. Even individual words have stories that go beyond common definitions. When we see the etymology of a word, we often find a description of its living experience (phenomenology) within us. For example, the word "enthusiasm" means to be possessed by a god; "inspiration" means to be infused with the breath of a spirit. These bring a story to the definition that helps us to feel the meaning within us. The tendency toward reductionistic thinking and discrete information flattens stories into component parts. But stories re-member parts into patterned wholes. Finding a story is finding or creating a pattern, a meaning. Once a pattern (story) is seen, it has self-sufficiency within us. We cannot "unstory" it or undo the pattern, although we can revise and alter the story. Einstein's story updated and overturned the immanence of Newton's, for example. A new perspective on an event in history may dramatically revise a previous story. The Native American story (e.g., the "Trail of Tears") during the European "discovery" and development of the New World brings another perspective to a one-sided story of European conquest ("Was this brave discovery, genocide, or both?"). Once we have found a story, we further flesh out knowledge when we can find alternative and diverse stories; the closest we get to truth may lie between these stories.

Bits and pieces float along in space; patterns, stories, and metaphors connect bits together and connect us to them. This not only helps students learn information but also helps information form patterns of knowledge and beyond.

The Trinity of Educational Practice

Real learning does not happen until students are brought into relationship with the teacher, with each other, and with the subject.
—Parker Palmer (1993, p. xvi)

Like a boat in heavy seas, educational reform has listed between student-centered, content-centered, and teacher-centered approaches. We find arguments for "back-to-basics," or for attending to the students' emotional lives, or for honing teacher's methods. But the sacred geometry of education is a triangle (or pyramid) of these three;

contact is made and knowledge is grown in the center of this structure.

Great teachers come in all shapes and styles: Democrats and Republicans, communists and capitalists, lecturers and facilitators, demanding taskmasters and gentle encouragers. Great teaching takes place as some unique alchemical mixture within the trinity of educational practice: the student, the teacher, and the subject. The integration of these three creates a sacred clearing or structure (the meanings of the term "sacred" include consecrated by love or reverence, and being set apart for a purpose) and invites a "trialectic" and a "trialogue." In an infinite variety of ways, great teachers dance with method, student, and ideas to invite learning.

The student's talents, interests, and tendencies, such as learning style and cultural background, are part of the trinity. Like a stuffed book bag, the student brings into the classroom the whole of his or her existence. He or she carries family, culture, passions, worldview, cognitive style, talents, dreams, and fears. These aspects are as much the curriculum as any external content, and perhaps more. Aurobindo tells us that education should work from the near to the far (Ghose, 1924). While the far implies abstract principles or broad generalizations, the near lives in the immediacy of individuals' lives including the conditions in which they exist (e.g., poverty or privilege) and the conditions that exist within them (e.g., hope, fear, interest). The deeply individual concerns, as well as the learning style particularities, of the student can be welcomed and addressed. Palmer (1998) suggests that the worlds of the student and the subject are brought together when the little story of our lives intersects with the large story of the topic of study.

Many students require a relationship or sense of belonging before their engagement in the material becomes effective. As one student told me, "Developing relationships with my teachers was so invigorating and encouraged me to learn more. Some really seemed to care about me and through this I was reminded that I was worth caring about." Welcoming the whole of the student can be facilitated by simply and genuinely asking and listening. As one former student mentioned,

> My teacher wondered what I thought, what was important to me; he actually thought this was important, that I was important. And after years of getting the message that what they thought was all that was important ... I began to trust and listen to myself.... It was like being reintroduced to someone I forgot was there all along.

Moving to another side of the triangle, we recognize the importance of the teacher's person and practice. Sometimes teachers are skilled at creating strategies or explanations that bring a subject to where the student is, or into a clear view that the student can approach. The teacher's method and structuring of the lesson remain important. Goals guide methods. If the goals include knowledge and mastery then methods must include the chance of direct experience, direct contact, as mentioned above. Structure is manifest initially in the form of our lesson plans, however formal or informal, and enacted through our techniques and spontaneous interactions. How much and what structure is appropriate? When does our design engender learning and when does it close it off? Structure brings us to a focus, asks us to look here or there, offers sequences and strategies, and asks certain kinds of questions. Groups who are immature in relation to a particular task may require more initial structure; groups familiar with a task are often able to create the structure themselves. But structure is always transitional and must not interfere with the freedom of teachers or students to discover and create spontaneously. As teachers who are supposed to be experts and authorities, our own fear of exposing our inadequacies as a person or an expert may encourage us to hide behind structure, information, methodology, or role, rather than using these things to open up space and engender authentic contact. It is normal for teachers to feel like impostors at times, to worry about being exposed or losing control of the class. The danger does not come from that vulnerability; it comes when we use structure to shut down vulnerability and limit spontaneity. When we do, the clearing of education shrinks and students, who hunger for vibrant, authentic contact, feel the walls closing in and may simply tune out or act out in order to cope.

This side of the triangle includes more than the method, it also involves the teacher as person. We teach who we are. At times, it is the teacher's fascination and deep connection with his or her subject, or the intriguing personal qualities of the teacher, that coax students into opening up to the teacher's interest. When recalling teaching that was of significance, one student remarks, "I had teachers who really seemed to care about what they were teaching. There was an enthusiasm that was contagious." I recall the feeling of mystery and intrigue each time I entered Mr. Simpson's sixth-grade science class. He was an environmentalist and naturalist well ahead of his time, at least in my little rural town. I would see this tall, respectable man walk home

from school and pick up all the trash between his house and the
school; he spoke of poison apples (pesticide laden) and the particularities of the coloring on birds; he developed a nature trail behind the
school. His room always seemed to have layers of fascinating stuff,
from a wasp's nest to a human skeleton, to rocks and minerals. While
I had some interest in these things, it was his fascination and slightly
eccentric personality that drew in many of my classmates and me.
There was mystery, and the most remarkable, the most important
thing was that he was still fascinated and did not hide it. He might
get "off track" for a few minutes speculating on the development of
some rock or just "thinking out loud," wondering. Most significantly,
this meant that we could be fascinated and wonder too. And amidst
the growing concern to avoid social stigmatization and be cool, we
did not have to be afraid to show our fascination. The teacher who
wonders right along with his or her students, who enters the mystery
rather than mystifying, who allows himself or herself to be authentic
and present in the classroom, opens the clearing.

The third side of the triangle is the "great thing," as Parker Palmer
(1998) and Rilke (1986, p. 4) have referred to it, the subject itself. In
education, we gather around a subject and the teacher's task is to
show us a way into it. Perhaps we are moved by a story and find our
way into the world of literature, or maybe the power of technology
attracts our interest and we find magic in computers. Palmer suggests
"the teacher's central task is to give the great thing an independent
voice–a capacity to speak its truth quite apart from the teacher's voice
in terms that students can hear and understand" (p. 118). The best
teachers can both practice a kind of detachment or freedom from the
subject and also express a passion or a subjective view born of intimacy with it. The word detachment is sometimes misunderstood as
meaning disinterested or distanced. Instead, detachment implies a
freedom from one's own emotional and intellectual reactions to the
material that permits a "clean" and clear representation of it. In addition, the teachers may also usefully bring in their own critique and
conscious biases, judgments, and passions, but to do this prematurely
may not give the idea a chance to take root on its own, or for students
to find their own way of connecting to it. The vivid presence and
richness of the "great thing" can set off a wave of resonance, fascination, and challenge when it is allowed a genuine voice. If a teacher
doesn't know the subject well enough or care enough to really do it
justice, it may not have enough depth to draw us in. The same is true

if the teacher is unable to translate the story of the "great thing" into language or experiences that a student can make contact with.

Often, in the climate of information acquisition, teachers feel obligated to cover so much material in a course that they only skim the surface. There is hardly a moment to dig in; but we take comfort in knowing that we have touched on as much as possible. However, developing knowledge requires more than touching the surface of facts and factoids. I have given up surveying a field during class time; my students are responsible for reading the text and I am responsible for bringing forth and exploring just a few dimensions, maybe just one example from a particular section of the book on any given day. This seems to bring main principles and systems into view in such a way that students can then apply them independently to the rest of the material. I know most will not remember much of what they have surveyed after the exam if we just skim the surface; but if we can dig into a few areas deeply, not only might they learn the facts in context, but it is also much more likely that they will begin to see the story, the method, the meaning, and the application of the discipline in a more complete way. In a single idea or concept, we can find the whole of the discipline and in so doing enhance the development of knowledge; "each discipline has an inner logic so profound that every critical piece of it contains the information necessary to construct the whole" (Palmer, 1998, p. 123). In moving toward knowledge, sometimes less is more. The text can effectively cover the basic facts because it is a resource that can be returned to again and again, and remembering facts is enhanced through repetition. The classroom is the place where we can dig firsthand into the particularities of the great thing. (See Palmer, 1998, for a thoughtful and more thorough exposition of this.)

It is not only the great or noble idea that is food for knowledge; it may also be some unexpected or even unseemly curriculum: the epileptic seizure that occurs in our midst, the fight on the school bus, the trashy novel. "There is no right food and no wrong food; the food must only meet the appetite, the appetite find its own kind of food" (Hillman, 1996, p. 160). What matters as much as the content is the quality of contact, the authenticity of the meeting.

Clearing and Community

The center or mass of the educational triangle (subject, teacher, student) is a space that may be thought of as a "clearing" (Heidegger,

1977/1993), as the "between" (Buber, 1958), or as the overlap of play areas (Winnicott, 1996) that engenders a community of learners. It is in a community that ideas are tested and our understandings challenged and debated, and this is fundamental to growing knowledge.

Communities represent a natural ecological structure of humanity. While we have institutions and organizations, nations and states, it is the quality of communities, and of our communion with one another, that helps give human life quality and dimension. A society dominated by institutions is not satisfying or sustaining; a culture of communities, evaluated by the quality of human relationships, is required for human fulfillment, and the deepest learning.

While a student can open a book or click on a website and access information, it is in a community that those ideas have a chance of being challenged, tested, played out, and discussed; and these are precisely the activities that help grow information into knowledge. Community is so central because it enables dialogue and creates a dynamic tension; we never know quite where the conversation will lead. Our own thought can be more easily examined when externalized in a conversation or heard in the comments of another person; ideas leap off the page and out of our minds as they take on life in a classmate. Dialogue allows our worlds to intersect and join with the content of our lessons.

Community not only serves the learning process but also is its own lesson. That is, it reminds us that the world exists in relationships and that knowing is always about a relationship. We may begin to recognize that the housing development becomes a neighborhood only if we know our neighbors; the workplace becomes a place we look forward to or dread, not only because of the work but especially because of the quality of relationships. The classroom becomes a community when understanding both the material and one another becomes our mutual responsibility. Unfortunately, community is not always valued as essential for building knowledge; "teacher and students gather in the same room at the same time not to experience community but simply to keep the teacher from having to say things more than once" (Palmer, 1998, p. 116). And it seems that institutionalization often occludes the essentiality of community. Institutions offer the trappings of community and sometimes leave us confused and longing for a kind of relationship and care that the institutional structure does not provide.

The earliest years of formal schooling (i.e., kindergarten) probably attend to community best because we recognize the tenderness of our youngest charges and our need to create a kind of "school-home." However especially against a backdrop of anxiety, materialism, hyper-competition, individualism, and objectivism, the need for the essence of school-home–community– extends throughout every level of education (see, e.g., see Martin, 1992). When an individual does not feel the basic sense of belonging that a community engenders, alienation and anxiety rule (see, e.g., Horney, 1950). In a classroom, this may leave both students and teachers wary, causing us to expend our energies on self-protection, on closing down rather than opening up. We may keep our distance from one another and the material, positions that are the opposite of those that develop knowledge. Students may comply, shut down, or simply make themselves less present, as if nothing mattered. As one student explained,

> I moved from a very good school to a very discouraging one between third and fourth grade. In the first, I was treated as a blossoming person; in the new school, I was treated as a child to be controlled. I felt like a head of cattle that better not stray from the herd. My education was marked by a fear of being disciplined or embarrassed. As a way of coping, I withdrew and became lazy, as if it didn't matter.

Wariness can also take the form of a lack of civility, and even aggression, which is a violent expression of self-protection. Do our schoolrooms and our schools engender wariness or a general sense of trust? Classroom management has become a big topic as increasing numbers of students are perceived as being less civil, and more bold and dangerous in their defiance of authority. Whether this results from poor parenting, superficial curriculum, shortened attention spans, violent role models, or other causes is difficult to determine definitely. But it seems clear that expecting children simply to be obedient to authority is inadequate and even disrespectful. Instead, successful classroom management is largely about fostering a community and this includes clear expectations and limits, fair enforcement of those limits, respectful explanations for rules of conduct, and creativity and authenticity on the part of teachers and administrators. The first days of school can be used to explicate a contract about the expectations that teachers have of students (from bathroom breaks to biology homework) and that students have of teachers. These expectations are most helpful when they are clear, consistent, and reasonable. And it may not be sufficient simply to state these expectations. If we assume that students are respected colleagues then it is easier to understand that students deserve a rationale for limits and rules. We would not expect a colleague to do something for us that seems unclear or without justification; we would explain the "big picture." In addition, we would not talk down to a trusted colleague. Heavy-hearted and heavy-handed messages shame, destroying trust, esteem, and community. Being honest and requesting students' help ("I could use your help today..." "How can I help you to help me?") fosters cooperation. We partner with students when we find out about their expectations, in addition to expressing our own. "How would you like to be treated?" "What do you expect from me as a teacher?" Answers: "If I have done something wrong please don't embarrass me by holding me up as an example, just tell me." "Don't talk down to me, and I won't disrespect you." "Be fair." "Challenge me."

Community is a big topic and I will limit the scope of this discussion sharply. The essence of community is an integration of the concerns of the individual (agency, democracy, individuality, diversity, rights, dignity) and the needs of the group (republic, membership, cooperation, responsibility, common good). Each side requires the other for its existence. The self is always a self-in-relation to something or someone; the community is always made up of individuals. Ultimately these two sides are embedded in one another. The challenge of community is to hold these tensions simultaneously without letting one overwhelm the other.

Overemphasis on individuality, the self, and individual rights can tend toward a narcissistic preoccupation, social Darwinism, and a sense of isolation. At its worse, it leads to selfishness and rampant competition, where relations with the world are distorted into opportunities to serve the self, to meet "my" indulgences. On the other hand, overemphasis on the collective, with its agendas and institutions creates not a community but a crypt or a cult, often deadeningly restrictive and intolerant of diversity. This creates a hive mentality in which individuality and diversity are seen as a threat, rather than as the impetus to evolution and growth. The challenge of creating community (classroom, school, and society) is in navigating between these two dimensions: the personal and the communal. The integration of these two is a necessary condition of meaningful community.

Here is a short list of some elements that we can recognize in a genuine learning community. Notice that in order to build community, the teacher rarely acts directly on the student but on the environment; this avoids coercion and instead emphasizes the invitation to mutually create the community.

(1) Relevance and interest is cultivated. As elaborated in the previous chapter, this means that the individual is attended to.
(2) Creative conflict, honest disagreement, and divergent styles and points of view are tolerated and welcomed.
(3) Honesty, authenticity, and goodwill, especially that modeled by the teacher, enable community. We can often smell inauthenticity, dishonesty, and hidden agendas that collapse trust into wariness.
(4) Respect for others' possessions, persons, and ideas is expected. Do we actually listen with an ear toward understanding others? Do we snub or exclude others? Can we share in responsibility for each other's learning?
(5) Autonomy and originality are encouraged rather than thwarted. But independence and rights require an equal amount of responsibility. We share responsibility for feeding the class bunny, maintaining appropriate behavior, and getting our work done on time.
(6) Communities allow the freedom to feel and express emotion, to celebrate with joy and feel the depth of sadness. In other words, they reflect the human condition and do not try to overly limit its range.
(7) Learning communities provide fair access to resources, rewards, and to expression. While not everyone is equally assertive, effective communities regulate the environment in order that a few do not close others off from the possibility of participation or access to resources.
(8) Mistakes and discipline are not failures but lessons. There is freedom to risk understanding, experimentation, speculation, and fantasy, and freedom to be wrong.
(9) Free and clear choice is offered whenever possible. This allows students practice at valuing for themselves. There is freedom of choice to be private, and even to avoid being an active member of the community. The best we can do is invite, not force.
(10) A community of learners remains organized around the pursuit of knowledge of self and subject, structuring itself around the learning goals.
(11) The most powerful communities leave no one behind and lead from a principle of understanding. I will explore this idea in chapter 5.

(12) Diversity of learning style, ability, point of view, culture, and so forth are attended to. Alternative means to the same ends may be creatively and individually adopted (e.g., a student may suggest an alternative assignment for himself or herself).

(13) Expectations for behavior are clear, discipline is consistent, fair and often creative; explanations and rationale are offered, consequences are seen as opportunities for learning. We strive to treat one another with the respect of trusted colleagues.

Knowledge, Truth, and Valuing

He who contents himself with pure experience and acts accordingly has a sufficient portion of the truth. The child in its process of maturing is wise in this sense.
—Goethe (1829/1949, p. 127)

The ideal of every science, and often of education, has become the creation of "a closed system" of truth (James, 1897/1956, p. 332). In contemporary educational practice, what we are to know is rarely treated as fluid; it is typically presented as prepackaged and complete. Through scientism and the quest for certainty, we confuse knowledge with truth and observation with fact. The risk is that this may create within us a body of knowledge that is understood as the Truth: proven, measured, and closed. As a result, this consensus content begins to shape a consensus consciousness as we are invited to swallow the same content in the same way without question.

The great texts of the wisdom traditions are often taken as inspired words. But most agree that these are "living words" requiring exploration and personal engagement. They need to be considered again and again so that new understanding may be discovered according to the quality of our awareness. The same notion of "living words" can be applied to the knowledge and information that students encounter in school. One of the great fears regarding public education is that students will be tainted and propagandized. We fear the imposition of someone else's values, especially religious values, hence the abolition of school prayer and the general separation of church and state. However, a data-downloading approach to teaching most typically presents a closed system of truths and values. The message is that this information is to be memorized and repeated as truth, often without opposing points of view, and without consideration of its significance within the student. Public education has fallen into an error identical to the error that some reactionary religious groups are accused of, that is, the presentation of a text (written or otherwise) as the literal and definitive truth. As educators (and educated) we risk becoming interpretive literalists who present dead, closed systems of supposed facts rather than giving students the tools, encouragement, exposure, and guidance to find truth for themselves and to use data as living words with the potential to open into new knowledge. Many teachers know better, but in light of current curricular demands, few teachers have the time and encouragement to engage the material beyond memorization (as truth) for the examination. What this does is create a system of servitude to certain abstractions, including the abstractions called institutions, and students (and educators) become their servants.

Even in the realm of science, we discover that it is not massive amounts of information but "freedom in the presence of knowledge" (Whitehead, 1929/1967, p. 30) that enables insight and discovery. Drawing conclusions about his research on the education of great scientists, Roe (1953) suggests "once intellectual independence was really tasted, nothing else mattered much pedagogically; bad teaching was only an irritation" (p. 53). Freedom in the presence of knowledge allows us to open up closed systems. As David Bohm (1981) writes, "After the mind is . . . freed of certain blocks that are inherent in its accumulated knowledge, it is able to operate in new ways" (p. 13). This does not imply that students should avoid mastering the formula or the material. But if we assume the material to be Truth, then we do not invite the freedom to dialogue, play with it, and create new knowledge from it; we make it into an untouchable idol and education becomes idolatry.

Valuing

The activity of gaining knowledge is defined as recognition or becoming aware, and this involves a process of valuing. That is, as an inherent aspect of the activity of gaining knowledge, one inevitably places priorities on one technique or one idea over another. The chef fillets the fish in a particular style because he has placed a greater value on a specific outcome, for example, speed, safety, visual or gustatory aesthetics. The student forms a perspective regarding her geography lesson because it has been valued in a certain way for very individual reasons (e.g., she wants a good grade on the test, or her family is traveling to the region of interest this upcoming summer). As fallout from the quest for scientific absolutes, knowledge (like information) is often understood as existing independently from values and the process of valuing, thus remaining "pure," "scientific," and "true." However, gaining knowledge is ultimately entwined with valuing. That which we select to learn or master is selected in a way that gives a certain value or priority to one view, or one approach, as opposed to another. When we gain knowledge, we co-construct content and worth through our presuppositions, or perceptual filters, and our intention. So knowledge, rather than being simply a static, abstract entity, is both laden with value and remains in flux; it is an "undivided whole in flowing movement" (Bohm, 1981, p. 9). "Knowledge is an *active process*, which is present not in abstract thought, but which enters pervasively into desire, will, action, indeed into the whole of life" (p. 11). The implication is that attention to the subjective process of valuing is integral to the development of knowledge.

By making the valuing processes explicit (i.e., unpacking the motivation or assumptions behind a particular choice), we begin to attend not only to how we construct knowledge based on our values but also to how we use it. Sai Baba suggests that information and knowledge by themselves are half-sighted; "politics without principles, education without character, science without humanity and commerce without morality are not only useless, but positively dangerous" (Gokak, 1975, p. 116). Bohm (1981) contends that the fragmentation of knowledge and the separation of knowledge from values has "helped to lead not only to a dangerously irresponsible use of knowledge, especially scientific, but even more to a general loss of meaning in life as a whole (p. 8). Knowledge and values "are inseparably interwoven in a single undivided process" (p. 22).

We will pick up this theme of values and valuing in chapter 5 (understanding) and chapter 6 (wisdom); for the moment and for the consideration of knowledge, it is enough to recognize that our own subjective process of valuing, which is in turn shaped by culture, shapes our selection, perception, and construction of knowledge. Therefore, values and valuing are central to an education for knowledge.

Four Kinds of Truth

Besides the elevation of knowledge to the status of Truth, contemporary education tends to teach as if the "objective" scientific fact provides the only valid source of information and knowledge. In this way, scientism has led to a tyranny of truth. As an alternative, we can consider four distinct kinds of knowledge, each with its own validity claims or requirements for truth. I will draw from Ken Wilber's (1995) synthesis.

Exterior-Individual

The empirical, behavioral knowledge that we are most familiar with comes in the form of observable, material events. This is the empirical investigation and explanation of what is "out there," including the construction of a taxonomy of plants or the investigation of serotonin levels in the brain. This approach gathers data through observation and often measurement (e.g., through a microscope or an EEG machine) and seeks explanation through theory (the "rational" side of rational-empiricism). When we study the observable world of individual objects, the world of nature, or human anatomy, we emphasize the observable parts and functions of the body or the bug, the *exterior* and the *individual*. This objective approach seeks explanations "conceived as the development of theories that identify lawful or law-like regularities and causal connections between variables" (Rothberg, 1990, p. 175). This is the familiar and dominant realm of conventional scientific method and rational-empiricism. When our concepts or maps of this observable world appear to match our observations, we find "truth."

The objectivist approach to knowledge not only includes individuals (e.g., a bug, a molecule), but the naturalistic approach can also consider whole systems.

Exterior-Social

When the inquiry as to what is "out there" considers interacting systems instead of focusing primarily on individuals, it explains individuals in terms of their functional fit within an objective network. This is the realm of systems theory, networks, holistic wholes, "empirical" web-of-life approaches to truth. Essentially, this approach understands the observable components as parts of a web or system and describes the behavior and structure of that system. So while it may be "true" from an individual point of view that a cell performs certain functions, it is also true from a systems perspective that it operates as a component of a larger system, a collection of cells, an organ, and this single organ exists within an organ system (e.g., the heart is part of the cardiovascular system), and this system coordinates with other systems in the functional operation of an individual person, a society, or the biosphere of the planet. This *exterior-social* view of knowledge and truth considers explicit structure and observable behavior, whether this is the economic structure studied by conventional sociology or the ecological structure of a watershed. In studying a school (or family, organizational, ecological, or political) system from this vantage point, the emphasis is on behavior, explicit rules, structural hierarchies, organizational charts, and so forth. Both the individual and the systems/social view of knowledge emphasize what is observable in the exterior world and ignore the interiority of life.

Interior-Individual

When awareness is turned inward, we find the world of subjective experience, consciousness, and meaning. From Freud to Buddha, this inward path inquires into the depth of what makes us human. While the objectivist inquiry studies the brain (e.g., neurotransmitters) and observable behavior, the inward focus studies the mind in the form of our interior states, dream content, thoughts, and feelings. When we look at a piece of art or a beautiful sunset, feel deep compassion or moral outrage, have a moment of revelation or disgust, we experience some quality of meaning and value within us that we cannot adequately reduce to a measurable quantity. While science most often claims objectivity, we understand that our perception of the objective world is just that, a perception, a representation or construction based on the perceiver and the perceived. What we see depends on what we are looking for, what we have seen before, and what we expect to see. The observer is a living perceptual "instrument" and our awareness of the capacities and limits of the instrument will enable us to be more trustworthy reporters of both the subjective and the objective world. A student's unfolding awareness and ability to sort out his or her impulses, projections, values, and biases is profoundly significant for the development of this kind of truth. One's unrecognized projection may distort the lenses of perception. Truth or validity in this domain involves how trustworthy we are as reporters of interior, subjective experience, how clearly we see it, and how well, accurately and sincerely, we can represent it. So the third kind of truth involves the *interior-individual* world.

Interior-Cultural

The subjective world of the individual exists within and is influenced by culture. When we consider the shared values and mythology of a people, we learn about their culture. Individuals are inevitably shaped by their culture including language, customs, and worldview. Therefore, in order to understand the individual, we need to appreciate the cultural context, or the *interior-social* world. One cannot "see" culture like behavior; it is subtle and interior. Worldview, attitudes, style, and so forth live "between the lines" of social structure. Inquiry in this domain attempts to understand how individuals fit together in acts of mutual understanding. This mutuality forms implicit cultural agreements about meaning. We may recognize the intersubjective agreement in our own family as we share ways of making meaning about the world, or we may notice a "generation gap," which is a gap in intersubjective understanding. When Western medical interventions are attempted in the Third World, one of the biggest obstacles is getting individuals to use the medicine or the intervention in the way prescribed because there may be competing value systems and incongruent worldviews. A culture may value large families for agricultural needs, status, and so forth while First World representatives may emphasize contraception to slow population growth. This is not a clash of individuals or social structure but a clash of cultures. The "truth," from this intersubjective perspective, begins in mutual understanding.

Integrating Four Kinds of Truth

Could we create an educational practice that regularly moves in and out of these different perspectives? A multidimensional approach to truth tells us that the world is not just a singular "it" to be measured, as scientism and reductionism have led us to believe, but that it also exists as a system and social structure, as individual subjective experience, and as cultural patterns. Honoring these different kinds of truth means recognizing that no one view can take in the whole picture. Multiple and integrated perspectives are essential in the approach to knowledge. Learning activities can be approached from any of these vantage points; borderland disciplines might overlap two quadrants or more. An integrative approach recognizes the validity of each kind of truth and moves from one to another or combines perspectives as is most relevant for the particular inquiry.

In our fourth-grade solar system assignment (mentioned above), asking about the empirical facts of the moon phase looks to the exterior-individual quadrant of knowledge and truth; considering various systems (e.g., solar, earth-moon) in interaction, including causal mechanisms (e.g., gravitational influence), touches on the exterior-systemic; inquiring about the student's subjective experience of sitting under the moon and perhaps asking for poetry, open-ended questions or fantasies touches the individual-interior; and digging into our shared attitudes about the moon, for example, by comparing cross-cultural stories about the moon and its mythology, we peek into the interior-cultural. Each has validity, each is true in its own domain, and each serves the development of knowledge. The development of structures such as the liberal arts curriculum is an attempt to respect different domains. However, the segregation of disciplines and the domination of a positivist orientation across most disciplines, lead to the undervaluation of a multidimensional approach to truth; the result is a skewing of knowledge and a constriction of intelligence.

CHAPTER 4

THE POWER OF INTELLIGENCE

'Educate' in the real sense of that word; not to transmit from the teachers to the students some information about mathematics or history or geography, but in the very instruction of these subjects to bring about a change in your mind.
—Krishnamurti (1974, p. 18)

Intelligence involves the ability to use information and knowledge and also the ability to create it; intelligence shapes, changes, and constructs knowledge. The capacities for critical examination and evaluation open up closed systems of knowledge. Through the use of intelligence, knowledge and information can be taken out of context, recontextualized, and constructed for one's own uses. As Krishnamurti (1974) says, "intelligence uses knowledge" (p. 29) and this involves the capacity to think clearly. At the level of intelligence, critical discernment overtakes mere opinion, and multiple perspectives help to disclose the world more thoroughly. Rather than seeing either/or binaries, intelligence progressively sees the multiplicity of the world as an endless succession of "either, or, or, or" along with immeasurable combinations and relationships. In fact, Swedenborg suggested, "the rational mind is primarily an instrument that consciously discovers relationships" (Blackmer, 1991, p. 47).

The Greek philosophers distinguished between "the fact that" and "the reason why" (Gray, 1968, p. 17). While knowledge and information deal with "the fact that," intelligence can consider "the reason why." And in this way, intelligence involves the way knowledge is held and handled. This, according to Whitehead (1929/1967), is the "art of the utilization of knowledge" (p. 6). Developing intelligence involves cultivating thinking rather than mandating what to think. Education, then includes supporting the powers of the mind in their self-development.

Developing intelligence involves a shift from accepting and amassing answers, as is typical at the levels of information and knowledge, to evaluating and often challenging answers. In a study of the education of great scientists, Zuckerman (1977) came to understand that the best mentors taught their students not only the words, facts and formulae, but also the "music" of science (see also Ochse, 1990). This involved looking below the surface of facts, dismantling and reconstructing answers rather than always being satisfied with what was given. Contemporary schooling leaves out much of this "music," because

> Neither teachers nor students are willing to undertake "risks for understanding"; instead, they content themselves with safer "correct answer compromises." Under such compromises ... [education is considered] a success if students are able to provide answers that have been sanctioned as correct. (Gardner, 1991, p. 150)

Intelligence has predominantly been equated with Aristotelian logic, problem solving, language, and mathematical skill. Through the work of Howard Gardner (1983, 1993) and others, the domains of what we call intelligence have expanded. Educators frequently recognize such capacities as music and interpersonal ability, for example, as expressions of intelligence and competence. However, the strict expectation that mainstream schooling should educate the masses for the workforce, developing "human capital" or "human resources" (along the lines of cultivating a pulpwood forest or mining coal, one might gather from this typical language), inhibits a genuine integration of these other intelligences in most classrooms. John Gatto (1993), among others, has argued that the development of intelligence beyond fairly rigid guidelines would encourage creativity and individuality beyond the degree that could be easily managed and co-opted for a corporate workforce. In the end, the idea that intelligence is largely innate and unchangeable may become a self-fulfilling prophecy precisely because there is not sufficient emphasis on improving intelligence.

Focusing so exclusively on basic information downloading has had a paradoxical effect: students have neither learned more nor learned to learn better; our typical practices rarely help students to grow intelligence. Of equal importance to the number of words cor-

The Power of Intelligence 61

rectly spelled or facts repeated for the test is the means by which students learn to use their minds, unfolding their potential for concentration, creative expression, precise analysis, and also (we will see in the following chapters) compassion, love, and wisdom. An education that fosters intelligence is one that refines the mind through critical and creative thinking, analytic critique and synthesis, and the cultivation of imagination.

The activity of knowing underlies all these competencies. Rather than emphasizing various narrowed forms in which intelligence may be manifested (mathematical, spatial, etc.), I will focus on the aspects of knowing that are common to all of them. Once knowing is freed, it is able to express itself in an infinite variety of integrated "intelligences."

One more bit of differentiation may be clarifying. This emphasis on the process of knowing also more accurately captures the actual epistemic phenomena. While concepts such as multiple intelligences have expanded our notions of pedagogy, it has also tended to compartmentalize thinking in a way that does not actually represent the process of knowing. For example, Einstein is held up as a model of logical-mathematical thought. But Einstein's own descriptions of his process of thinking speaks of flights of imagination and richly felt senses–his "thought experiments"–that do not look like prototypical logical or mathematical processing. His own learning as a child blossomed when his family moved to Switzerland where he was enrolled in a Pestalozzi school. In this environment there was a more holistic emphasis on the senses including observation and learning through concrete experience. His own process of knowing was hardly limited to an isolated expression of abstract, mathematical or logical thinking, but instead he would essentially form "concrete" imaginary experiments and internally observe and sense their processes as he tried various interventions and configurations in his mind with, of course, remarkable results.

The Shape of Our Knowing

> We have unlearned how to see, hear, and generally speaking feel, in order to deduce [what we sense]
> —Maurice Merleau-Ponty (1945/1962, p. 229)

The *way* we know affects both what we know and ultimately who we are, our state of being and well being. Our style of knowing may invite us to meet the world as a problem to be solved, as beauty to behold, or as a concept to categorize. I will explore the activity of know-ing first by examining the contemporary skew in knowing and its im-pact on the learning process and the learner. I will then describe the integration of the analytic and the intuitive as a dialectical activity that lies at the heart of cultivating intelligence.

Assumptions about knowing are shaped by, and in turn reinforce, the sociocultural context (Miller, 1992, makes this general case well). As a reflection and an agent of social norms and "consensus con-sciousness" (Tart, 1987), contemporary education institutionalizes this knowing in its curriculum and practices. That is, education not only teaches what we are supposed to know but also and especially how we know, the style of knowing that is considered acceptable and as-sociated with status and the search for truth. In contemporary mod-ernist culture, characterized by competition, reductionism, individualism, and assumptions of objectivity, the style of knowing invited in schools reflects these concepts, and it values such goals as control, predictability, and logical sequencing. Children are taught to recall "objective facts," report one right answer, and at the high end, think logically and linearly, often to the exclusion of other forms or sources of knowing. When a narrow form of the rational is all that is emphasized, we shift "the center of gravity of experience, so that we have unlearned how to see, hear, and generally speaking feel, in order to deduce [what we sense]" (Merleau-Ponty, 1945/1962, p. 229).

When one way of knowing, a limited expression of the logi-cal/analytic is emphasized, one would think that students would stand a good chance of successfully developing their reasoning ca-pacities. Mediocre test scores along with evidence that students can-not apply material and lack basic understanding tells another story. One reason for this situation is that we do not provide an adequate balance of ways of knowing that will enable the analytic to reach its potential. Too often, analytic processing becomes one-dimensional, an isolated, limited, and sterilized mental activity without context, meaning, foil, or mate. When we use only a slice of our knowing ca-pacity, ignoring or even dismissing other ways of knowing as irrele-vant or immature, we know, at some deep level, that the whole of our being is not represented. We have been betrayed by the promise of education and, in order to fit in, we must betray ourselves. One should in no way construe this view as an argument against the ana-lytic or even against such practices as basic memorization and rote learning, which are valuable and necessary; but they should not constitute all of what we do in schools.

While such measures as mediocre test performance send up red flags, more disturbing signs lie closer to the root of the issue. Gardner (1991) summarizes several experiments, ranging from physics to the humanities, in which even high achievers have proved unable to demonstrate understanding of the principles that they have memorized. While some students can recall sophisticated theories and formulae (information and knowledge), they remain unable to apply them outside a limited classroom context and instead fall back on mental explanations and strategies that they established in their preschool years. Their intelligence did not grow sufficiently to enable them to use their knowledge in working on an unfamiliar task. More testing, more homework, and more school days will do nothing to improve the ability to skillfully handle knowledge and information; it can only entrench "correct answer compromises" and further dry up intrinsic motivation.

Enculturation into one right answer starts very early and serves to constrict the development of intelligence. On her fifth day of kindergarten, the day after her fifth birthday, one of my daughters was given a very short homework assignment that required her to circle the two out of three objects on a preprinted page that were alike in either shape or color. There were six sets of shapes on the page. She handled all without ambiguity except one group that included a small green rectangle, a green triangle, and a red square. Which two were the same? She circled the red square and the green rectangle. When I asked her about this, she acknowledged that two had the same color, but she saw more value in the fact that two of them had four sides each, while the other had three. The next day at school this was marked wrong and returned. Obsession with the right answer misses the opportunity to see the question from multiple vantage points, in this case to understand that some shapes can perform certain functions. My five-year-old explained that rectangles and squares form "bottoms" of things like buildings, while triangles may form "tops." This homework assignment is a tiny example, involving a tiny kindergartner in her first days of school, but it will happen again and again and will teach her that there is only one "correct" way of looking at something.

Because of their enculturation into the world of "one right answer," students often balk at attempts to think critically or to apply material, as teachers at any level can attest. Most of the college fresh-men in an introductory psychology course that I teach initially have great trouble in doing anything but memorizing information. For ex-ample, applying concepts in order to design simple hypothetical re-search projects of their own choosing seems mind-boggling to most, and this is after several hours of discussion and reading and the pro-vision of plentiful examples. For them to then critique their own or another's work seems an impossible task for many. They are more concerned with asking for the facts that I think are important, because they assume that they will need to repeat them to me within the pre-dictable confines of a multiple-choice test. This is a common tale, one in which education and understanding "is sacrificed to knowledge-as-commodity" (Richards, 1989, p. 16).

Laboratory of the Mind

Part of what education lacks is imagination. When we build closed systems of knowledge, imagination is irrelevant, even a disturbance, and so it typically receives only token attention if any at all. Imagina-tion is not integrated into curriculum goals or practice, and instead it may be marginalized to the low priority area of the arts. The steady (but just as steadily dismissed) admonitions from wise educators to integrate the arts, music, and theater into the heart of the mainstream classroom remind us of the importance of invigorating the imagina-tion. However, the arts and imagination are merely frills if the goal is simply to bank information. However, cosmologist Carl Sagan (1980) understood this way of knowing as essential: "Imagination will often carry us to worlds that never were. But without it, we go nowhere" (p. 4).

Imagination as "the action or faculty of forming mental images or concepts of what is not actually present to the senses" (Webster's, 2001, p. 404) is a capacity of interior knowing. Einstein's thought ex-periments—"I imagine that I am on the head of a rocket traveling at the speed of light," Picasso's unusual way of bringing his unique per-ception and play to art, Martin Luther King's imagining a world of justice and equality—"I have a dream"—are forces of interiority which take us beyond the information given and beyond the status quo. Imagination has been mistaken as a colorful accent to schooling, and largely dismissed in an educational age anxious about meeting stan-dards and status. However, it is this rich interior way of knowing and playing with knowledge that is central to discovery, invention, synthesis, and application.

For our youngest charges and perhaps our wisest, an imagined world is often the means to figure out how the world works, address issues, work through difficulties, and ponder mystery. Imagination is like a laboratory of the mind where we can play out endless possibility. Stories like the Greek myths–the Gods themselves–were imaginary friends, we might say. These were explanations especially of the human psyche forged out of imagination (see Hart & Zellars, 2006, on Imaginary Friends).

Yet, there has been a tendency in the modern west not to take imagination seriously. The non-observable, non-logical nature of imagination renders it difficult to pin down and thus uncomfortable to take seriously in a modernist, materialist backdrop. With respect to education, the dominance of developmental thought, especially Piagetian maps, attempts to subsume imagination under the cognitive powers of the mind. It becomes an aid to symbolizing which is regarded as a transitional stage in a child's development and as such is denigrated as a mental activity not necessary in later life (Casey, 2000).

However, we do not outgrow imagination individually or culturally, as this process is fundamental to our knowing at any level of development. We hear, for example, that imagination is described as the source of insight from scientific discovery to artistic innovation.

Jonas Salk, most famous for invention of the polio vaccine, certainly had good training and skill but it was a particular process of imagination, something he even had his own name for–"inverted perspective"–that he described as the key to unlocking insight.

> I do not remember exactly at what point I began to apply this way of examining my experience, but very early in my life I would imagine myself in the position of the object in which I was interested. Later, when I became a scientist, I would picture myself as a virus, or a cancer cell, for example, and try to sense what it would be like to be either. I would also imagine myself as the immune system and I would try to reconstruct what I would do as an immune system engaged in combating a virus or cancer cell. (Salk, 1983, p. 7)

Through the insights gained he would then design laboratory experiments.

> I would then know what questions to ask next.... When I observed phenomena in the laboratory that I did not understand, I would also ask questions as if interrogating myself: "Why would I do that if I were a virus or a cancer

cell, or the immune system." Before long, this internal dialogue became second nature to me. (p. 7) I could manage to solve problems more easily because I could look at the problem from the viewpoint of subject and object at
one and the same time. (p. 10)

While imagination is often described (if it is considered at all) as a
mental cognitive vehicle or operation, that is, a function of the mind,
Hillman (1988) suggests that rather than the mind being primary, it is
imagination that is so. Rather than an operation of the mind, the mind
is a fantasy of the imagination. We do not need to resolve this in our
own minds (or imaginations) but it makes the point that our presuppositions about our nature are, well, imagined. The instantiation of
the mind as primary is a common description but not a proven fact, as
we tend to apply it.

Metacognition

In addition to imagination, intelligence also involves a capacity to
think about what we know, to think metacognitively. Arlin (1990) describes metacognition as an ability to engage dialectical thought, that
is, to use the interplay of opposing views in the thought process. Dialectical thinking is an enterprise that raises anxiety in the one-right-
answer world of most classrooms. And while I cannot expect my
daughter at elementary school age to operate at full dialectical capacity, this development is cultivated or retarded depending on our educational practices at every level, including the earliest years. Inviting
her to take another's perspective, to articulate and test her own hypotheses, to find what is wrong and what is right and to realize that
something may be both, opens the door to intelligence. In addition to
learning basic language and math skills, her broader and deeper
knowing capacity is invited when such questions are part of the
norm.

Metacognition involves recognizing the limits of one's knowledge. It enables students to ask questions of themselves in order to
assess and improve knowledge. For example: "Do I understand this?"
"Do I require more information?" "What evidence do I require to be
convinced of this?" "What strategies might be used to demonstrate or
pull apart this idea?" "How can I test my understanding and the validity of the idea?" "What does this mean to me?" These questions can
be engaged with the youngest as well as the most sophisticated students. A young learner may begin to recognize that he or she must
practice spelling words in order to remember them; an expert in some

field may recognize that his or her own presuppositions are getting in the way of seeing a problem in a fresh way. In problem solving, thinking about thinking can also be organized around managing one's problem solving strategies (see, e.g., Schoenfeld, 1983). For example, one might be asked to generate alternative courses of action, assess which one seems best, evaluate how much time the endeavor will take, assess whether an approach will yield the information that is being sought, and monitor one's progress both along the way and upon completion. Through coaching, modeling, practice, and analysis, students come to ask self-regulatory questions that expand intelligence and learning.

Unfortunately, too often "teachers [do not] pose challenging problems that will force their students to stretch in new ways and that will risk failures that might make both students and teacher look bad" (Gardner, 1991, p. 150). It becomes difficult for a teacher to teach beyond basic acquisition when there is little support or freedom to take risks whose goals are not immediate and quantifiable. Too often exhaustion, automatization of the learning process, testing, fear, and mediocrity win the day. Education for the growth of intelligence requires the energy and skill to wade and play in the worlds of information and knowledge.

The Shape of a Person

The consequence of the imbalance in how we know goes beyond poor performance and a lack of understanding to affect the person, their being or their soul, we might say. In our schools, we can easily find attitudes of coping, resistance, and alienation in a great many students, even (and sometimes especially) the brightest. If they learn to play the game of school well, they learn to be competitive, compliant, and "in their heads." Many students may feel the incompleteness of such one-dimensional and shallow knowing. Disappointment gives way to resignation or alienation, or to a twisting of the two. The result is mediocre education and a population of students who have spent so much time resisting education that they have poorly developed analytic skills and undeveloped alternatives.

When the innate drive (Weil, 1972) for intuitive or nonlinear consciousness is thwarted, it ripples into our psychological health in profound ways. The nearly exclusive emphasis on basic Aristotelian logic, objectivity, and acquisition becomes generalized to the way we know and talk to ourselves. Our internal dialogue becomes a constant stream of categorizing and calculating. At its infrequent best, this looks like analysis; at its most common, it becomes chronic brain chatter, a kind of obsessional thinking that reduces our ability to be present in the here and now. Some degree of this is inevitable. However, many practices, from meditation to the martial arts, recognize the limits of this preoccupied state of mind and specifically attempt to reduce internal dialogue in order to facilitate opening to other ways of knowing and being. (Contemplative practices will be considered in some detail in chapter 6.) I contend that many of our "practices," including alcohol use, excessive television watching, and so forth, are pursued, in part, because they dull brain chatter, although they do not necessarily open up awareness at the same time.

In addition to our internal dialogue, our "external dialogue," that is, our relationships with the world, also shapes our existence. As Buber says, "relationship educates." But what kind of relationship does a rationalist-positivist knowing invite? In this style we know the other by standing apart from him or her. This distancing has great value in that it enables reflection and representation; our minds can extricate us from enmeshment in the world. By its nature, this intellectual capacity reinforces a separation from the world. And without the balance of other kinds of knowing it tends to fixate that separation. In Buber's (1958) words, this perpetuates a distinct "I-It" instead of an "I-Thou" relationship. The consequences of such a detached worldview and the alternative to it will be discussed in more detail in the next chapter.

Anxiety, depression, alienation, and narcissism describe the vast majority of contemporary mental health concerns. My contention is that they are intertwined and invited by the way we know the world, specifically by an exclusive emphasis on low-order rational processing. Such incomplete ways of knowing do not provide the rich and natural sustenance that is essential to our well-being.

A Dialectic of Knowing

Our intellectual handling… is a retrospective patchwork, a post-mortem dissection, and can follow any order we find most expedient. We can make the thing seem self-contradictory whenever we wish to. But place yourself at the point of view of the thing's interior doing, and all these back-looking and conflicting conceptions lie harmoniously in your hand.

—William James (1909/ 1977, p. 117)

Here I will tease apart some of the subtleties of the interaction of the intuitive and the analytic and suggest that a recognition of the natural dialectic of the two is basic to the renewal of education and the cultivation of intelligence.

While often equated with a purity of linear logic, the activity of intelligence is multifaceted and operates as a dialectic of the intuitive and the rational (Hart, 1998a). The mind reveals leaps in pattern recognition, creative synthesis, and understanding that linear processing models cannot adequately explain. By itself, linear sequential logic reveals only a partial view. As William James (1909/1977) declares,

> It [logic] has an imperishable use in human life, but that use is not to make us theoretically acquainted with the essential nature of reality.... Reality, life, experience, concreteness, immediacy, use what word you will, exceeds our logic, overflows and surrounds it.... reality obeys a higher logic, or enjoys a higher rationality. (p. 96-97)

The analytic and the intuitive play off each other: the analytic grasps and holds, while the intuitive opens and embraces; the analytic has purpose, while the intuitive plays; the analytic measures and calculates, while the intuitive appreciates; the analytic builds, cuts, and controls, while the intuitive remains open-ended and is characterized by movement; the analytic is contained and directed by ego and the will, while the intuitive tends toward self-transcendence and arises spontaneously; the analytic is willful, while the intuitive willing; the analytic fosters self-separateness, while the intuitive sees interconnection; the analytic is bound to subject-object distinctions, while the intuitive transcends boundaries; the analytic tends toward linearity and moves step by step, the intuitive meanders and leaps. In dialectic, these ways of knowing generate a plurality of knowledge and a depth of intelligence. To what extent do we invite one or the other, both or neither, in our educational practices?

Intuition

Intuition is familiar but subtle. It is difficult to approach directly or nail down precisely but this should not diminish its value or validity. It has been called meditative thinking (Heidegger, 1966), spontaneously arising cognition (Washburn, 2000), pure experience (James, 1967), ontological thought (Tillich, 1951), and contemplative knowing by St. Bonneventure (Wilber, 1989), to name only a few terms. Out of this nonrational knowing arise the experience of flow (Csikszentmihalyi, 1990), empathic resonance (Sprinkle, 1985), noesis (Plato), creative and scientific breakthroughs (Arieti, 1976), ecstasy (Laski, 1968), revelation (Heschel, 1962), and inspiration (Hart, 1998b). Because the contents and results (e.g., actions, attitudes) of intuitive knowing vary tremendously, its underlying core has often been missed and its centrality to the learning process largely ignored.

Adding to the complexity, the meaning of intuition has included direct mystical apprehension, perception of limited basic truths, unconscious pre-rational processes, and mere irrational feelings. While I will not offer a thorough discussion of meanings, I will note the most salient issues for contemporary education.

Logical positivism assumes knowledge to be based exclusively on reason and sensory data; no possibility of intuition as a valid source of knowing exists and, therefore, education bound by positivist assumptions cannot overtly entertain intuition as part of the learning process. In this view, intuition is often dismissed as "a result of insufficient analysis or inferential process" (Westcott, 1968, p. 22). This probably does describe some instances of knowing, in which the knower simply remains unaware of the conventional analytic process at work and labels it intuition. However, to assign all intuition to this reduction ignores the evidence of the experience itself.

At the other extreme lies the idea that all intuition discloses truth. Yet, we know that some intuition, or interpretation of it, simply turns out to be wrong. If we avoid ascribing ultimate validity to the content and instead concentrate on the activity as one legitimate way of knowing that works hand in hand with the analytic, we place intuition in a position where we can integrate it into educational practice.

The evidence for the centrality and absolute necessity of a non-rational, intuitive process in learning, problem solving, creativity, and psychological well being is compelling. The non-rational activity of intuition in dialectic with the analytic plays an instrumental role in human creativity in all domains, from science to art, to daily existence. Arieti (1976) saw the interplay between rational and non-rational capacities as the source of creativity. Valett (1991) emphasized intuition in the development of creative imagination. Johnson (1992) suggests that intuition or "qualitative thought" precedes and makes possible logical thought and provides the source of creative thinking. And Nietzsche suggested that the non-rational mode has importance precisely because it "tears down the barriers that have been erected by excessive rationality and individuation and in so doing it opens the ways to the Mothers of all Being, to the innermost heart of things" (quoted in Vogt, 1987, p. 34).

This knowing takes form as a "glimpse" or "sense" of a direction for some and as a whole or complete "vision" for others. One does not experience this knowing in linear or typically linguistic form but as a more direct knowing represented in a variety of metaphors. It emerged as a birdsong for Milton, as a golden chain linking heaven and earth for Homer, as love for Dante, like a dream for van Gogh, a song for Goethe, a flash of light for Tchaikovsky, a beneficent power for Dickens. Vaughan (1979) differentiates intuitive content by level: physical (e.g., a shiver, a headache), emotional (e.g., hurt, longing), mental (e.g., a clear thought such as a solution to a problem), and spiritual (e.g., the recognition of the unity of all life). We might tune into our intuitive capacity by simply paying close attention to one or more of these levels. Each person has his or her own particular balance or constellation of intuition. One person may find himself or herself particularly tuned to emotional material, while another may recognize intuition through various physical sensations, images, or synesthetic experiences such as feeling and imagery merged. In addition to levels and styles, intuition may emerge in different functional domains such as discovery, creation, evaluation, operation, prediction, and illumination (Goldberg, 1983). For example, one may have a creative vision in writing a paper (creation or illumination) or sense the best path to take in evaluating two or more options (evaluation) or discover a previously hidden perspective while working on a problem (discovery).

For the most part, the analytic-intuitive dialectic has been described as a tension of opposites and as a shifting back and forth, an oscillation with an emphasis on the analytic as the ground or base and the intuitive as the experience of an occasional opening. This shifting may occur with increasing frequency and ease as the dialectic refines. As the activity of knowing develops still further, there may be less of a sense of swinging back and forth and instead a more immediate interplay as the analytic and the intuitive seem to fold into one another. In this development, egoic-rational consciousness no longer provides ground and perspective. Instead, a more deeply integrated and fluid process arises as "ground" from which one can maintain a simultaneous multiplicity of perspectives, perceive the unity of "opposites," and represent perception in a single "vision." This has been described as vision-logic (Wilber, 1995) and integral-aperspectival cognition (Gebser, 1991), as opposed to egoic-rational-perspectival cognition. Aurobindo offers this description: "[It] can freely express itself in single ideas, but its most characteristic movement is a mass ideation, a system or totality of truth-seeing at a single view; the relationship of idea with idea, of truth with truth, self-seen in the integral whole" (Wilber, 1995, p. 185). This idea represents an integration/dialectic of the rational and intuitive characterized as "authentic" (Puhakka, 2000), and possessing "presence" (Welwood, 1996, 2000) as well as having the capacity for revealing the knower as transparent to himself or herself (Feuerstein, 1987). If we assume that this dialectical knowing constitutes part of our intellectual potential, along with Aristotelian reason or empirical/analytic cognition, then integrating the intuitive takes on even more significance for the educational journey.

Several authors have offered suggestions for cultivating intuition in general (e.g., Vaughan, 1979) and specifically in education (e.g., Noddings & Shore, 1984). Essentially these methods invite a shift away from typical analytic processing and encourage receptivity to intuition. (The receptivity has importance since one might depart from normal analytic processing, for example, in a dissociated state, but not hold one's self aware and awake to the intuitive.) Intuition cannot be willed, as it arises spontaneously, but it can be welcomed or invited by one's attitude and actions. When we suspend our comparative judgments and our concentration on plans for using information, intuitions are more likely to appear. Our typically fast-paced, production- or achievement-driven existence does little to welcome this shift. Intuition does not depend on a universal technique such as visualization or meditation but may open up naturally through a great variety of activities. For example, we bring intuition close through the appreciation of great beauty, the intimacy of caring service, strong emotion, meditation, art, music, play, exercise, dreams, imagination, stories, a frustration of normal understanding, critical reflection that may rattle the ego and temporarily loosen ego-generated analysis, an alteration in routine, a creative visualization, or simply taking a vacation. Intuition-evoking moments tend to deautomatize our cognition and bring us into "presence." At times, this is a very intentional act, one in which we throw ourselves fully toward something. As Rollo May suggests, "The deeper aspects of awareness are activated to the extent that the person is committed to the encounter" (May, 1975, p. 46). We help students "commit to the encounter" by engaging their deep interest. This must be followed with an openness or receptivity, "holding [oneself] alive to hear what being may speak.... [This] requires a nimbleness, a fine-honed sensitivity" (May, 1975, p. 91).

Intuition may also be invited through a general style of openness. Literature on exceptional creativity (e.g., Richards, 1996; Montuori & Purser, 1995) understands the creative person as an open system, one that is open not only to internal processes but to surrounding spheres of influence; "the creator and the surrounding world of information are in constant exchange and in unstable equilibrium" (Richards, 1996, p. 54). Openness is encouraged when we no longer see the other (e.g., person, idea, object) as a threat to our identity or as an object to manipulate, but instead as an opportunity to encounter. The most important element for cultivating intuition in students is for the teacher to explore and develop it in himself or herself. In addition, the arts and other creative and imaginative activities (e.g., simply drawing a picture, inventing a story, or asking for as many questions or answers about an issue as possible) may help to initiate a shift away from exclusive reliance on linear sequential thought.

We have examined the consequences of an overly analytic epistemic skew, but what of the other extreme? I find students who, when given license to acknowledge and cultivate their intuition, especially after having been epistemically constricted, sometimes altogether dismiss the rigor, precision, and utility of the analytic. The result is sometimes a sloppiness of feeling, thought, and action–a kind of preoperational swamp. Reason seems unimportant and wanes while intuition never fully ripens, though dependence, even fixation, on "nonrational" knowing increases. When used in balance with the intuitive, the analytic sets up reflexive (e.g., "Is that feeling I'm having projection or insight?") and intersubjective dialogue ("Let's compare our hunches.") as well as tests of validity (e.g., "My intuition said they would have a car accident today, but it didn't happen; how did I misinterpret this?" or "How might I distinguish between literal and symbolic impressions?" or "What is my feeling and what am I picking up from someone else?"). The analytic can frame problems for the intuitive, translate vision into form, help to interpret and deepen results. Without such balance, the intuitive may simply operate as a flow of free associations and regress into pre-personal knowing, sometimes mistaken for transpersonal development. Even upon the high ground of mystical experience, one does not leave the analytic or the ego behind but is challenged to transcend and include, constantly updating maps, the way we make maps, and the mapmaker. Higher development begins to loosen identification with the ego, but there is no evidence that we lose ego and with it the rational mind.

The Rational

Whereas intuition implies some type of more direct knowing, the rational implies knowing mediated by conception and language. It is representative and calculative, enabling us to categorize, cut apart, verify, critique, deconstruct, deduce, and induce. It draws from memory and the senses (and intuitions) to form concepts. It generally follows a linear path and stands apart from the object or idea of scrutiny, operating at arm's length from experience. It may be considered agentic in that it is undertaken by the subject of cognition, usually called the ego (Washburn, 2000). Rationality can take as its object of focus the material world before us and even reflexively consider the source of the analysis, that is, the thinker.

The analytic can develop from simple representation and memorization to complex language formation, problem solving, synthesis, critique and critical dialogue, deconstruction of assumptions, and increasing sophistication of pattern recognition. It contains the capacity for understanding, but in contemporary education we do not encourage it to go far beyond its most basic capacity for cataloging and recalling memory. Bloom's (1956, 1981) "pyramid" of educational objectives (knowledge, comprehension, application, analysis, synthesis, evaluation) is hardly approached, much less scaled. I will briefly consider three interrelated analytic capacities below. Not only are these ways complementary to one another but they also open the door to and often rely on intuition, as I will try to demonstrate. This logical-intuitive interplay, while most easily recognized in higher-order knowing, may be incorporated into functioning at any level. The main point is that thinking and intuition can be improved and developed.

Empirical and Rational

The empirical/rational involves (empirical) observation and (rational) analysis. This way of knowing is the most enduring legacy of the Enlightenment and has enabled incredible scientific and technical advancement. In contemporary usage, this approach generally involves measurement, control, and predictability. As we cultivate the conventional scientific method, we develop observational capacities and techniques for forming and testing hypotheses. Technology, in particular, has been tied to the empirical/analytic and has extended our senses (e.g., the microscope) and our calculative capacity (e.g., the computer). In its most commonly taught form, it is positivistic and reductionistic, and it assumes the exclusive validity of objectivity. Since observation plays so central a role in this activity, training for the rational/empirical can naturally involve nurturing observation skills. When a four-year-old sees two pictures in her magazine that ask, "What is different in these two pictures?" or "How many birds can you find?" the task activates observational skills. When we take students of any age on a nature walk, ask them to try to appreciate a piece of art, notice body language, or listen to the layers of a piece of music, we invite them to hone their skills of observation. Simply listening to the content, rhythm, and tones of the words of another person provides a powerful exercise in the same vein. The focus of observation may be narrowed, for example, in a very intentional quest for certain items (e.g., a treasure hunt), or opened (e.g., "What stands out to you about your reading or a particular picture?"). When observation is combined with categorizing and measurement ("How many acorns did you find?" "What is the level of the rainwater today?"), empirical comes to mean mainly measurement. However, the word "empirical" originally meant "experience." When its meaning is restricted to "measured sensory data" we tend to constrict the world and our ways of seeing it. Measurement is valuable but simply incomplete. This sort of measurement and deduction does not lean so much toward discovery as it does toward verification, which is valuable but only part of the capacity of the rational-empirical. Seeing without measuring allows unexpected relationships, meaning, and beauty to be revealed. Whether through reading a text or taking a walk, the more open-ended seeing for discovery (instead of just verification) comes not from questions that quantify and truncate observation ("How many things can you discover?") but from more explorative ones ("What do you notice?" "What stands out?"). And when we compare and combine our perspectives with those of others, our observations are multiplied.

The child uses the empirical/rational in forming and testing a hypothesis about something ("If I stand on the chair, I may be able to reach the cookie"). In Kolb's (1976) description, the empirical/analytic recognizes different subcomponents or mental activities within this process: observation, problem identification, brainstorming, developing a means to test a hypothesis, testing it, and then going back to observation in a feedback loop. Each aspect represents a dimension that may be assessed and enhanced as we teach this method of inquiry. For example, one may have a great ability to brainstorm multiple possibilities but little skill in defining the most salient problem to solve or in testing a hypothesis. Identifying and teaching these strategies directly enhances intelligence.

The rational/empirical forms the basis of contemporary science. Science can be lively, personal, even deeply touching; at its best, its process begins with curiosity and leads to awe. Yet mostly we see this manifest in only the youngest children and the most remarkable scientists. Intellectual technology is often taught in a sterilized form and made distant and lifeless as the deeply personal search for empirical contact is replaced by the valueless search for facts. As linearly as this method of inquiry is assumed to unfold, the way we teach students that science and discovery occurs is not actually the way great scientists know in the scientific enterprise, precisely because it leaves out the intuitive. Polanyi's (1958) study of the process of great scientists describes the interaction of intuition and the analytic. We discover that the scientist's "quest is guided throughout by feelings of a deepening coherence.... We may recognize here the powers of dynamic intuition" (Grene, 1969, p. 60). As Einstein tells us, "Only intuition, resting on sympathetic understanding can lead to these laws, the daily effort comes from no deliberate intention or program, but straight from the heart" (quoted in Keller, 1983, p. 201). Ideas and insights come as pictures or senses consistent with a nonlinguistic process; for Einstein, breakthroughs emerged "as clear images which can not be voluntarily reproduced or combined" (Ghiselin, 1952, p. 43). Nobel prize-winning physicist Wigner says "the discovery of the laws of nature requires first and foremost intuition, conceiving of pictures and a great many subconscious processes. The use and also the confirmation of these laws is another matter... logic comes after intuition" (quoted in Grene, 1969, p. 45). For Bruner (1963), whose focus was on problem solving, "intuition implies the art of grasping the meaning or significance or structure of a problem without explicit reliance on the analytic apparatus of one's craft.... It is founded on a kind of combinatorial playfulness" (p. 102). So even the heart of the rational scientific enterprise is awash in the intuitive and imaginative, and therefore the development of the intuitive in dialectic with the rational is a "basic skill" of knowing.

Questioning and "Logics"

Questioning enables the capacity to unravel unchecked assumptions, identify and correct faulty reasoning, and uncover understanding through the use of questions. While this is often thought of as a more mature capacity, basic reasoning skills have been successfully introduced in elementary schools as "Philosophy for Children" (Lipman, 1993). As a means of developing reasoning capacity, this program invites questions such as "What is the problem?" "Is there evidence to support claims?" "What counterexamples or exceptions are there to challenge the claims?" These types of questions are easy to introduce at any level and provide a basic skill set that serves as a foundation for knowing across all disciplines.

In addition to using the tools of basic logic, questioning in the form of metaphysical reflection opens a related sphere. Matthews (1980) challenges Piaget's limits on children's cognitive capacity by suggesting that subtle and sophisticated reasoning, including metaphysical questioning, is possible in children of early school age. Such radical questioning may be even more likely to occur in young children because they lack the years of educational enculturation that tends to offer answers rather than creating space for holding such questions. Matthews suggests that a young child is particularly well equipped for philosophy because he or she "has fresh eyes and ears for perplexity and incongruity ... and a [high] degree of candor and spontaneity" (p. 85). In this way a child may be well suited to ponder not just the little problems ("How can I get my sister away from me?"), but also the big ones ("Are dreams real?" "What happens after you die?" or as my five-year-old asked the other day, "How were the first people born?") (see Hart, 2003).

The way questions are held may help to yield insight. For example, one may hold two incompatible thoughts together, in a process called bisociation (Koestler, 1964), or Janusian thinking (Rosenberg, 1986), named after the Roman god Janus who had two faces, each looking in opposing directions. The dynamic tension of holding opposing views simultaneously may produce a shift in our normal waking state, catalyzing the development of new schemata, and opening to intuitive insight or synthesis. If we can hold the tension of the incompatibility or discrepancy long enough, a new perspective may break through. We find a similar process when using a Zen Koan, for example, in which a question or paradox may absorb and then frustrate the normal chain of analytic thought, opening up the possibility for insight (deBono, 1985, also offers an alternative and practical set of teachable thinking skills).

Critical questioning can begin to challenge the logic and evidence of unchecked assumptions (e.g., "What is the evidence for your conclusions?" "What are the exceptions?"). When pushed further, the capacity for critical questioning may deconstruct the context and underlying assumptions on which ideas are founded. This involves a mental suspension of beliefs and assumptions in order to reveal influences beneath the ideas. Critical questioning helps to reveal and deconstruct the spheres of influence (e.g., economics, class structure, gender bias, scientism, etc.) that shape ideas and thoughts. Socrates and Plato apparently engaged such questioning through dialogue. When parents and teachers discuss and dialogue instead of simply downloading didactically, the space for questioning is open and intellect grows (e.g., see Sigel, 1993). Questioning proceeds by concepts and language and then may open to noesis, intuitive insight. "Initially questions might reveal our perhaps unexpected ignorance, thereby liberating our wonder and curiosity" qualities that are associated with a more direct, spontaneous knowing (Rothberg, 1994, p. 5). Such insight may be engendered by intention or thrust upon us as when we encounter radically new conditions (e.g., traveling to a foreign county, imagining we are visitors from Mars, or involving ourselves in a contrived situation such as that created by school teacher Jane Elliot in her experiment on the effect of prejudice known as "Blue Eyes, Brown Eyes" [Rodriguez & Hutchings, 1987]). Questioning helps to unravel the implicit values that shape knowledge. As David Bohm (1981) reminds us,

> When someone tries to achieve what he regards as knowledge that is free of values, this generally means that he has uncritically accepted either the tacit values that may happen to be current in the community in which he lives and works or those values that are implicit in his subjective fancies. (p. 22)

Questioning helps to disclose these implicit values. And this includes the questioning of the questions themselves, "for in the beginning these usually contain the very presuppositions that are behind the unclarity and contradiction that led one to question in the first place" (p. 25).

One of the ways to talk about these different aspects of reasoning and questioning is to consider them as different logics. Logic is normally conceived in the West as linear and sequential, dependent on three fundamental postulates: the law of identity (A equals A), the

law of contradiction (A cannot equal not A), and the law of the excluded third (A cannot be equal to A and not A). This kind of logic
moves in a straight line and requires a subject and an object. It cuts
the world into either/or binaries. However, there are other kinds of
logic that have been largely excluded from Western consideration.
From quantum physics to Indian philosophy there is an acknowl-
edgment of the multidimensionality of the universe and with it a multiplicity of logics. For example, Lama Govinda describes
multidimensionality in the roots of Indian philosophy, which postulates four possibilities: Being (or existence of the object), Not-being,
Being as well as Not-being, Neither Being nor Not-being (cited in Berendt, 1991, p. 45). Paradoxical logic postulates that A and not A can
both be predicates of X. While these ideas sound like gibberish to
those adhering to conventional Western logic, they begin to gain currency through descriptions of quantum mechanics (e.g., light behaves
as both waves and particles), or through practices such as the Zen
Koan that aim to expand awareness beyond the limits of conventional
reasoning. Eric Fromm (Martino, Fromm, & Suzuki, 1960) notes
"paradoxical logic was predominant in Chinese and Indian thinking,
in Heraclitus' philosophy, and then again under the name of dialectics in the thought of Hegel and Marx" (p. 102). The logic of both
quantum mechanics and Zen Buddhism reveals the difficulty with the
separation of subject and object. For example, Heisenberg's uncer-
tainty principle recognizes the interdependence of "observer" and
"event." They are bound to one another in ways that defy Newtonian
mechanics and perhaps Aristotelian logic.

As we will see in the next chapter, there also seems to be a logic of
the heart. For now, it is sufficient to recognize that non-Western logics
can take many forms and that Aristotelian logic may simply be insufficient to address the whole of our existence. It operates within a stra-
tum of human experience that has its limits. Our lived experience
begs for approaches that complement the geometry of the straight
line; we also live in circles, zigzags, wiggles, and spirals.

Phenomenology

Phenomenology represents another interrelated dimension of inquiry,
one that especially complements logic and rational-empiricism. Using
the subjective world of the individual as the basis for understanding,
phenomenology notes and brackets experience. It brings everyday
lived experiences, so often left out of the empirical/rational, to a posi-

tion of value. It serves as a means of inquiry centered on qualitative description and self-reflection, filling a gap that has been widened by the dominance of scientism with its emphasis on measurement, objectification, and verification of what is "out there."

In an effective and simple way, my daughter's elementary teacher used a phenomenological approach one day. The teacher returned the writing response journal in which my daughter had written brief comments about what happened in a book chapter that she had read. My daughter's responses had been mostly limited to recalling the events of the story. Her teacher's last feedback was: "What did you think and feel about Karen's haircut?" which was a radical and upsetting event for Karen, and "What would you do if you were Karen?" Such questions expand responses beyond recall and paraphrase to include the student's own perspective and experience.

Such questions have the potential to lead toward personal relevance and self-awareness; they also invite opportunities for intersubjective dialogue, such as might occur if other class members compared their thoughts and feelings about Karen's haircut or about an event at school. This dialogue in turn may help to cultivate communication, empathy, appreciation of multiple perspectives, and self-reflexivity. We may find that one student views Karen's haircut as a liberating event because, as she explains, her mother always insisted on her having long hair, and the more it grew, the more she grew to resent it. Another student identifies with Karen's pain; when that matter is explored further ("Have you ever felt like this?") the child reveals that the underlying issue relates not to hair, but to issues of injustice or powerlessness. This discussion could easily lead to a consideration of broad issues of justice and justness, of power and oppression, and of related universal human predicaments. (We could imagine questions that would help link these personal reactions with various lessons, for example: "How is your experience of Karen's haircut similar or different from the experience of women in contemporary society?" or "What do hairstyles tell us about cultural and cross-cultural values?" and so forth.) When education becomes deeply personal, that is, when it includes one's personal reflection or reaction, it opens up to the richest and most immediate curriculum.

When we identify and compare our experiences, opinions, and assumptions we do not become more self-absorbed or narcissistic but just the opposite. We learn that multiple views are possible, and as a result, we may loosen some of the rigidity of our point of view as we reframe our perspective or try on and test out other views. This helps us to move from opinion to considered judgment and can free us from unconscious identifications. I hear college and high school students who bark out their opinions on something as if the more conviction they have, or even the louder they say it, the more validity it has. They may tend toward a radical relativism in which the justification for an opinion is "What I say is right because I say it." This is because their opinions and reflections have not had a fair chance to ripen in the sun of open consideration and mutual dialogue. This subjectivity and the opinions that grow from it often remain in the shadows and stay puny and green; they are not necessarily bad or invalid, but they often lack the depth, subtlety, and refinement of understanding that marks a maturity of consideration. Everyone may be entitled to his or her opinion, but some opinions are simply better than others. Perspectives are cultivated and tested when they are invited as a regular component of education.

This kind of inquiry into one's subjectivity deepens not only through one's reflective capacity but also through becoming responsive to our experience or allowing more of our experience into our awareness, the subtle gut feeling, flashing thought, vague discomfort, and so forth. This moves toward a more open witnessing of events, allowing us to be increasingly "present" to ourselves. We will discuss this further in chapter 6 on "Wisdom," but the point for the consideration of intelligence is that this opening of awareness, along with the reflection on that direct experience, involves a dialectical activity of the intuitive and the analytic. At the far end of this process, we may even begin to open to a very deep order of seeing, even engendering transpersonal knowing (Hanna, 1993), transcendental phenomenology (Husserl, 1936/1970), higher reflection (Merleau-Ponty, 1945/1962), "phenomenological seeing," and "meditative thinking" (Heidegger, 1929/1975), all of which attempt to describe a more direct and penetrating disclosure of subjectivity. This points the way to a more spacious, direct, open disclosure of the world.

As I have tried to demonstrate, we can treat thinking, whether in the self-reflection of phenomenology, in the development of logics and questioning, or in the skills of rational-empiricism, as a skill that can be developed. In addition, intuition complements the autonomy of thinking and enhances its power. Thinking and intuition function naturally and optimally in a dialectic that lives at the heart of the activity of the knowing intellect.

Along with its power, intelligence also has a limit and even a danger. Krishnamurti (1974) tells us, "You have to be educated so that you become a really beautiful, healthy, sane, rational human being, not a brutal man with a clever brain who can argue and defend his brutality" (p. 62). Intelligence by itself can actually enable brutality. Clever arguments and self-serving manipulation abound among those seeking their own self-interest and the control of others. Avoiding brutality involves something beyond intelligence; it involves spiraling inward toward self-knowledge and toward the heart. The bud of the inward spiral takes form in intelligence, through the growth of the rational mind and intuition, and blooms in the heart of understanding and wisdom. The next chapter takes the turn inward toward the heart.

CHAPTER 5

THE HEART OF
UNDERSTANDING

*The day will come when, after harnessing the ether, the winds, the waves, the
tides, gravitation, we shall harness for God the energies of love. And, on that
day, for the second time in the history of the world, man will have discovered
fire.*

— Pierre Teilhard de Chardin (1975, pp. 86-87)

In daily conversation, we say we "understand" something when we
have a basic grasp of an idea, thing, or act. Usually this understanding implies a generally agreed upon meaning, a consensus. Thus, a
chair is, in most circumstances and for most people, a chair. This is
basic shared understanding. Understanding also comes to mean the
ability to apply information in ways beyond the limited context in
which it was acquired, for example, when we know enough about the
thing or idea to apply it in novel situations. The deep end of knowledge and the cultivation of intelligence address these meanings. But I
want to go past these to something deeper. The word "understanding" means literally "standing among or under." This implies crossing boundaries inherent in "standing apart from" and moves toward
intimacy and empathy. This opens the door to a richer perception that
transforms information and, along with it, the self who perceives. As
Buber (1923/1958) says, "All real living is meeting" (p. 11), and understanding of the sort I am describing comes in the activity of meeting.

Understanding requires a fundamental shift in the way we know.
Buber (1923/1958) describes this shift as a movement from an "I-It"

relationship" toward one of "I and Thou." Understanding comes when we empathize with the other, lean into the other, and suspend our distant self-separateness for a moment. As we do so, a recognition of interconnection may emerge. This way of knowing is as useful in science as it is in human relationships. Nobel laureate Barbara McClintock described a less detached empiricism, one in which she gained "a feeling for the organism," — she explored genetics through working with corn plants — that required "the openness to let it come to you" (quoted in Keller, 1983, p. 198). The other is no longer separate but becomes part of our world and our selves in a profoundly intimate way. Krishnamurti (1974) says, "To help him to be alive it is imperative for a student to have this extraordinary feeling for life, not for his life or somebody else's life, but for life, for the village, for the tree" (p. 176). This "feeling for life" comes through meeting instead of only measuring.

The kinship generated by understanding is captured in *The Education of Little Tree*. The narrator describes the meaning of kin, as his grandparents knew it:

> "I kin ye," it meant, "I understand ye." To them, love and understanding was the same thing. Granma said you couldn't love something that you didn't understand; nor could you love people, nor God, if you didn't understand the people and God. Grandpa said back before his time "kinfolks" meant any folks that you understood and had an understanding with, so it meant "loved folks." (Carter, 1986, p. 38)

Understanding makes the other "kin"; it makes the other "loved folks."

Expressed in another way, understanding is learning to see through the eye of the heart. All of the wisdom traditions speak of this profound knowing. For example, the eye of the soul for Plato, the eye of the Tao (Smith, 1993), South on the Native American medicine wheel (Storm, 1972), and the Chinese *hsin* which is often translated as mind but includes both mind and heart (Huang Po, 1958). "Both Matthew and Luke speak of a single eye which lights the whole body like a lamp and without which 'how great is the darkness'" (Smith, 1993, p. 18). Houston Smith notes that "in contrast to modernity which situates knowing in the mind and brain, sacred traditions identify ... essential knowing, with the heart" (p. 18).

Understanding moves beyond the rational and the sensory. As explained in the previous chapter, intuition enables understanding because it allows more spontaneous and direct engagement. No longer confined by linear logic or linguistic limitation, knowing takes up the "logic" of the heart, an experience not unlike walking into a world in which the learned laws of physics have been upended. Paradox and possibility open up. Old divisions of either/or move even beyond multiplicity to seeing with a singular depth, to the unifying heart of things; the loving heart is the bridge between worlds. Note the "Gospel of St. Thomas":

> When you make the two one, and when you make the inside like the outside and the outside like the inside, and the above like the below, and when you make the male and the female one ... then you will enter [the Kingdom]. (in Robinson, 1977, p. 121)

We could call this the development of heartfulness and this is the secret, the Holy Grail, according to the wisdom traditions, that will take our world, including the world of education, beyond where it is today; for the center of the world, the *axis mundi*, lies in the heart. This "secret" opens us beyond self-interest and provides a new centerpoint for knowing and being:

> The mind is a doorway through which you walk to live within your world. It has the capacity to make sense out of illusion. It is the tool you have chosen to keep you effectively and effective in your world. It walks you to its expected limit; then you must leap beyond.... Your intuitive heart is the doorway that stands between the worlds. (Rodegast & Stanton, 1989, pp. 27, 26)

The heart of understanding is cultivated through empathy, appreciation, openness, accommodation, service, listening, and loving presence. At its core, heartfulness involves a quite literal shift in our being. In the midst of a conflict or frustration, in the middle of a hurried day, or as a regular "tune-in," most of us can get a taste of our heart by simply sitting quietly for a few minutes, taking a deep breath, and gently bringing awareness to the area of the chest. There is often a felt shift involving a sense of tenderness, spaciousness, slowing down, and settling in. This process often changes our perception of the scene that is before us or the one spinning around in our minds. Few activities are so simple and powerfully beneficial yet so infrequently practiced. Listening to a particular piece of music, thinking about a loved one, appreciating someone or something, reading inspiring words, imagining a joyful or beautiful scene may all help engender the shift as well. Childre and Martin (1999) have demonstrated how this shift toward appreciative beholding entrains the beat

frequency of the heart and this in turn may entrain brain wave frequency.

What follows is an exploration of the activity of *heartfulness* or *understanding* in education. Various facets and approaches are examined
and one or all may be useful entry points to education for understanding. First I will consider how the eye of the heart has been
clouded by the domination of objectivism.

From Objectivism to Epiphany

*The beginning of our happiness lies in the understanding that life without wonder is
not worth living.*

—Abraham Heschel (1972, p. 46)

Standing Against

Much of contemporary knowing does not invite meeting or understanding. This is largely because of the domination of the assumptions
of contemporary science, which are based on objectification (Schrodinger, 1945, p. 140). The notion of objective knowing has led to a new
level of control (domination) over the natural world, and its presuppositions have flooded into educational practice. Cartesian subject-
object division provides the cornerstone. However, the maintenance
of this separation between observer and observed is artificial, justified
in the name of objectivity and reinforced by a cognitive repression of
the awareness of interconnection. I am not speaking of the valuable
arm's-length perspective that the intellect can provide; instead, I refer
to the inflation, distortion, and institutionalization of this method into
objectivism, which reduces the world to a collection of objects. The
opposite of objectification is understanding, which involves connection, relatedness, intimacy, even oneness; but education does not often permit this. Lisa recalls her early educational experience:

> I think of my own repeated attempts to reach out toward "oneness" being
> met with deleterious forces. My kindergarten and grade school teachers
> come to mind; their seeming desire to murder my spirit. Murder is a strong
> word and yet looking back it felt like their actions were attempts at annihi-
> lating any part of me that represented openness. Our openness to the un-
> known is violated when we are punished for accepting and playing with it
> by fear-abiding, control-invested adults.

What are we to make of this accusation of spirit-murder? Can a
well-intentioned first-grade teacher actually leave a child feeling so
betrayed and violated? Is Lisa's experience just an aberration, an un-

fortunate clash between a particularly tender child and a difficult teacher? The effect of objectivism is so pervasive and subtle that it is difficult to recognize its brutality. As Lisa said, it tended toward annihilating any part of her that represented openness to others and to mystery by punishing her for playing with the unknown. Instead she was told what to see and how to see it.

The root meaning of the term objectivism is "standing against" or apart from. Parker Palmer (1993) describes the consequence of this stance:

> This image uncovers another quality of modern knowledge: it puts us in an adversary relationship with each other and our world. We seek knowledge in order to resist chaos, to rearrange reality, or to alter the constructions others have made. We value knowledge that enables us to coerce the world into meeting our needs—no matter how much violence we must do. Thus our knowledge of the atom has brought us into opposition to the ecology of earth, to the welfare of society, to the survival of the human species itself. Objective knowledge has unwittingly fulfilled its root meaning: it has made us adversaries of ourselves. (p. 23)

With the distance between knower and known maintained and without recognition of their interplay, we remain separate from (above or outside) the world we perceive. The modernist objectification of the other, including the natural world (environment and body), contributes to difficulties in relationships and limits the experience from which to make ethical choices. At the beginning of the twentieth century, William James (1909/1977) recognized that "materialism and objectivism" tend to lead human beings to see their world as alien. And "the difference between living against a background of foreignness [i.e., treating the world as alien] and one of intimacy means the difference between a general habit of wariness and one of trust" (p. 19). The result of this habitual wariness and distance is anxiety, depersonalization, alienation, and narcissism. Unfortunately, we have ample evidence (e.g., from Columbine to Rockdale) from our students and our society at large, of how alienation grows into aggression toward others or ourselves. Coping and compensation take more subtle forms as well: students may simply comply, shut down, or make themselves less present, more distant and depersonalized, as they objectify themselves and the world. We will return to these difficulties at the end of this chapter.

Objectivism is an insufficient ground on which to fashion character or human values. Such objectivist knowing tends to invite self-separateness and a lived solipsism (Schroeder, 1984) in which we never experience the other or the other's subjectivity. Objectivity creates distance from the other; understanding invites dialogue, mutuality, and participation. Reinforcing self-separateness tends to overvalue ego, leading to a narcissistic preoccupation that fails to mature into social interest (Adler, 1929) or critical consciousness (Freire, 1974). The "other" remains an "it" for our distant examination and utilitarian manipulation, or an object either to possess or defend against. The capacity for mental distancing and self-other differentiation is basic and essential in human activity, but its overemphasis and distortion into a rigid objectivism makes it dangerous and incomplete.

Assimilation, Accommodation, and Appreciation

Understanding is directly affected by the particular way we take in the world. A modernist style of knowing is dominated by what Piaget (1977) called assimilation at the expense of accommodation, and the cost to our understanding, our meaning-making, our empathy, and our educational vitality has been great. Simply put, in the cognitive process of assimilation, new information is evaluated in relation to previously determined categories of meaning (e.g., me–not me, good–bad, animals–plants, etc.). This Aristotelian pigeon-holing is efficient for quickly discerning the potential relevance of new information (e.g., "Is this dangerous?" "Do I enjoy things like this?"). It enables evaluation of a potential experience or a piece of information without the evaluator having the experience, that is, without really meeting it. The trouble comes when we become overly dependent on rigid categories. When something does not fit (e.g., a new perspective that poses a challenge to existing knowledge) we often marginalize, ignore, or distort it to fit in our categories. As we grow in dependence on assimilative skill, we may come to see the world largely as we expect to see it, as a projection of our categories. And this is what was so damaging to Lisa (quoted above) as she was pigeonholed into preset categories rather than receiving encouragement to "play with the unknown." Postmodern deconstruction, critical questioning, and creative and divergent thinking, among other practices, help us to reconsider and break down some of our compartments. But, in so doing, they threaten the authority of knowledge and of those who claim to hold it. They challenge textbook, theory, and teacher as the primary sources of knowledge and we have often been unwilling to allow this to occur, much less to invite it.

As the balance and mate to assimilation, accommodation occurs when we no longer fit something into our categories. Instead, new schemata and new understandings are created and we are literally changed in the process. The self becomes less rigid, more fluid, "Protean," to use Lifton's (1993) term, through a strategy of accommodation. In this way, every accommodation becomes a potential revision of identity. In other words, when we are no longer able to translate or to insist on translating something into our schema, we are open to the possibility of transformation.

We can invite accommodation through making contact or genuinely meeting the object of our inquiry. Accommodation is a mechanism of knowing; meeting or making contact is the process or action that invites it. Categorization is encouraged by demanding one right answer, dependence on external authority, extrinsic motivation, and distance and alleged objectivity from the object of inquiry. Accommodation, on the other hand, is nurtured through flexibility and expectations of multiple perspectives, open-mindedness, valuing the authority of direct experience over the authority of a theory or an expert, practicing individual expression and interpretation (e.g., through art, music, writing, etc.), seeking personal relevance, and achieving a fundamental attitude of appreciation. As Heschel (1972) explains,

> Mankind will not perish from want of information; but only want of appreciation. The beginning of our happiness lies in the understanding that life without wonder is not worth living. What we lack is not a will to believe but a will to wonder. (p. 46)

When we assimilate a tree or a flower (or person or idea), we anchor our attention first in our concept of the tree as we categorize and calculate: "What kind of tree it is?" "How old?" "What is its utility (shade, hardwood)?" "How big a chain saw would I need to cut it down; will it fall on the house if I do?" "Is it healthy?" "Who planted it?" On the other hand, when we accommodate to the other we open our awareness rather than narrowing it. Instead of anchoring in the concept of the tree, we attempt to meet the tree itself. This may begin with an attitude of appreciation and develop into a feeling of affection, gratitude, understanding, and care.

The pressure toward assimilation and the stable self that goes with it have been maintained in part by a confusion. We have mistaken stasis for balance. Dynamic balance in our cognitive style involves flux and interplay between assimilation and accommodation.

Along with this, we can find comfort in the balance and fluidity of identity rather than needing to define and defend an unchanging sense of self and the world. If we assume that the world is something to be controlled (objectivism) and possessed (materialism) we tend to feel anxious when it does not neatly fit into our boxes. We reduce this anxiety by placing the world in categories, trimming what does not fit neatly, and marginalizing or repressing what does not fit at all, instead of meeting it directly. But what we lose by staying at a distance is the possibility of awe, wonder, and epiphany:

> Our systems of education stress the importance of enabling the student to exploit the power aspect of reality…. We teach the children how to measure, how to weigh. We fail to teach them how to revere, how to sense wonder and awe. (Heschel, 1972, p. 36)

Reciprocal Revelation

The great texts of the wisdom traditions are often depicted as "living words." They are in some mysterious way described as alive on the page. This is why in all of the traditions there is invitation to reconsider the words–the ideas–again and again in order to see what light might be revealed this time around. It is as if the words are encrypted and compressed. To gain access to the mysteries and reveal the deeper meanings we have to break the code.

The process of deep learning in secular education is no different. While our emphasis has become bits and bytes, the biology text, the notes on the board, the "text" that is the person or situation in front of us, and the world as a whole are living words–awaiting expansion in order to be more fully understood. Their richness and dimensionality already exists here and now but must be decompressed to be realized.

A secret to breaking the code lies in *knowledge by presence*, which involves looking not only at the outer data but also opening into our selves. Presence in this sense is eminently practical for learning and may be recognized by such qualities as: non-defensive openness, flexibility of thought, curiosity and questioning, a sense of wonder, suspension of disbelief, leading with appreciation over judgment, an emphasis on contact over categorization, a willingness to really meet and therefore be changed by the object of inquiry whether a new idea or a new person.

The code is broken, the words come alive, and the world is opened only to the degree that there is a corresponding opening of consciousness within us–a kind of *reciprocal revelation* occurs. In this sense we recognize that *what* we know is intimately bound to *how* we know. And that deep knowing moves paradoxically and simultaneously both inward and outward.

Such knowledge by presence reveals the intersection of our individual depth with a more universal depth. The universe lies not only about us but also within us; the outside can reveal the inside and vice versa. Emerson (1837/1968) knew something about this

> In yourself is the law of all nature . . . in yourself slumbers the whole of reason; it is for you to know all; it is for you to dare all. . . . Man is surprised to find that things near are not less beautiful and wondrous than things remote. The near explains the far. The drop is but a small ocean. A man is related to all nature. (pp. 47, 46)

A more intimate knowing balances the objective and detached knowing that dominates education today, with a participative, relational activity. Both detached and intimate knowing are necessary in the world of education, like breathing in and breathing out. Together they form a more powerful and well-rounded dialectic that opens the mind and through it the world.

The Sensitiveness of the Soul

Love is freedom: it gives us that fullness of existence which saves us from paying with our soul for objects that are immensely cheap.
—Rabindranath Tagore (1961, p. 57)

Most of us notice that when we pay attention and are simply open to the person in front of us, we come closer to understanding his or her experience. This is simple enough; although it can be easily forgotten when we are caught up in agendas and the hurry of daily activity. But when we really meet another, we begin to "feel into" his or her world; in other words, we empathize. When this occurs there is often a feeling of really having met the other person, "Oh, this is who you are. I didn't really see you before." The person in front of us begins to take on new dimension, like a cardboard cutout coming to three-dimensional life. They have depth and substance, meaning and complexity, value and beauty beyond what we had seen previously. And often, our own projections of who we thought the other person was or who we wanted him or her to be are revealed as the individual steps into an existence outside the gravity of our projections. In this way, empathy and understanding provide a powerful experience of self-knowledge as well as knowledge of the other. Because of the profound importance of this kind of meeting, empathy has been described as the basis of moral development (Hoffman, 1990), and it may even be the trait that makes us most human (Azar, 1997). It can assume its rightful place at the heart of education for understanding and character.

In order to cultivate empathy and understanding *in* students, teachers must first experience empathy *toward* students. How do we create opportunities to learn the lesson of understanding?

In one project, teachers enrolled in a graduate education course, taught by my colleague Tom Peterson, were invited to form an intentional relationship with a "difficult" student. Specifically, the assignment was to "connect with a student whom they see as especially disconnected." In response, most chose low or underachievers and students who particularly challenged or even intimidated them in some way. What teachers described, following their own initial reluctance and fearfulness and the understandable wariness of the student, is something quite important.

This intentional relationship may begin with the teacher asking a simple question (e.g., "Please tell me about something you like."), taking the time to sit with a student and see what conversation arises, or asking the student if they wouldn't mind being interviewed for the teacher's own class assignment. Instead of simply disciplining him yet once again, Lawrence decided to sit down with seventeen-year-old TJ, who is described by his teacher as "a loud, cocky, and obnoxious seventeen-year-old who I would regularly have to reprimand and remove from class. He had a way of just getting under my skin." As he pulled TJ aside and sat down to talk, Lawrence asked, "What can I do to help you and what can you do to help me?" He says, "I did not think any real progress was made but the next week I did notice that he was a little quieter in class and actually brought his book and a notebook to class." This next week TJ asked, if he remained quiet, whether he could draw a picture in response to a group project that required students to read and answer questions about their lesson on the Middle Ages. Lawrence agreed and it turned out that this unruly student communicated with clarity and virtuosity through his impressive artwork. TJ ended up drawing a creative and accurate solution to the question posed. Lawrence's simple attempt to make contact with TJ resulted in an opening and softening. In a subsequent conversation, Lawrence asked TJ to describe the most important person in his life. He spent several animated minutes describing his young brother. "He even said that keeping his brother safe and cared for is 'my only goal in life.' I asked him why he felt this way. 'My brother is the only one who loves me just the way I am. [My mother] loves me because I bring home [money]. My grandma loves me because I help pay the bills. Tommy, he just loves me because he wants to.'" In Lawrence's eyes, this hardened and "obnoxious" individual became a tender brother. His teacher began to understand him for the first time.

A relationship may shift through an unexpected opportunity. Megan, an elementary teacher, knew who the most disconnected and frustrating child in her class was, but she was uncertain as to how to approach him. When a dove got out of its cage in class, Megan specifically gave seven-year-old Kendrick, described as extremely disruptive and uninterested, the responsibility to capture, hold, and care for the dove before placing it back in the cage. She says, "When another student came up to my desk and tried to help he politely told them it was his job and he could finish it on his own. He had rarely spoken politely to adults before that moment, much less to his classmates. For the first time I saw a loving and caring side of [him]. Up to that point, when I had tried to hug him, he would freeze up, as if he did not know what to do. Now we can't get him to stop giving us hugs. At the end of the next day he approached me and said that he wanted to come back to school the next day. Previously he would only say: 'I hate school.'" She goes on to say that his school performance suddenly exploded. "When asked to describe his favorite teacher he wrote, 'Mrs. Partain I like.' I was amazed to have gotten that much structure since most days I just received a conglomeration of letters copied at random; often I could not even read them. Now, he had not only written words that were not displayed on the word list but had organized them into a phrase to answer the question. A few weeks later, after some help with a volunteer, he read his first book. I was so proud of him that I started crying as he was reading to me."

Through intention and effort to meet the student, a bridge is built, a new level of connection, compassion, even love and understanding can be created. This new connection often results in an improvement in a student's attention and attendance, learning and performance, as well as peer relations.

Kelly, an eighteen-year-old tenth-grader, did not attend school regularly, and when she did come, she laid her head on the desk, covered her head with a coat, and went to sleep. After a few brief "interviews" conducted after school in which her teacher simply tried to invite conversation and ask about Kelly's life and interests, her teacher says, "I noticed that Kelly began to take more of an interest in her studies. She started listening in class. She didn't go to sleep. She participated in class activities and discussion. When the six-week report cards were issued, she was passing all of her subjects for the first time. I feel differently about her. I have more compassion and a genuine affection toward Kelly."

Six-year-old David never spoke to or interacted with other children. He walked into class with his head down and responded to the good morning greeting (and nearly every other comment) with "I hate school." Terry, his speech teacher, decided that she would place David in a small group for their twice-weekly meetings. She also decided to pick David up personally from his classroom. "I made an extra effort to reach out to him in the hallways, as he was getting on the bus, and in our sessions. By the end of April, he began shyly waving and saying, in the lowest voice possible, 'Hi, Miss Davis.' He began eagerly wanting to do activities in class. He began interacting with the two other boys in his group. He began talking with them, asking them questions, even arguing with them."

Mary describes her experience with Jane, a hearing-impaired student from a family of ten children living in a federal housing project. Mary had attempted to make an effort to communicate with Jane (who seemed entirely isolated) first by speaking through her signing interpreter and then by learning some sign language herself. "Jane, who never communicated with anyone in class, started to come to my homeroom before the other students and talk to me about her family and her school work. She acted very shy in class around other students in the beginning, but as she and I began to communicate more she became more involved with the other students. One day, after we had been meeting for a few weeks she came into school quite upset and I learned that she was menstruating for the first time and had been unprepared for this by her mother. She was very fearful and upset. We talked about it and I assured her that it was normal and that everything would be fine. I hugged her. When she left she said, 'I love you. Thank you for caring about me.' When she left my room, tears rolled down my cheeks and I felt very happy to have had the opportunity to know this child. I felt a sensation of love vibrate through my body."

We know that these relationships are not magical cures; students may fall back into a disconnected life, one overwhelmed by poverty and violence, conflict and alienation, disappointment and dispossession. Students drop out. TJ says, "I can't quit work [forty hours a week] to go to school regularly or my little brother Tommy won't eat regular. Martha [his disabled mother] doesn't get enough money to support us on her own." Cultures like TJ's affect us to our bones, but often one real and dependable contact, a "leg-up" person, may be sufficient to catalyze success and resilience. The resilient child almost invariably has an adult who understands him or her in some way.

While we may have an impulse to scoop up a poverty-stricken child, or to make a project out of saving a gang member or a social outcast, the point of meeting is not to rescue but to understand; to care, not to cure (see Montgomery, 1991). Understanding or empathy implies knowing and may stimulate an impulse for mercy or service, but the center of what it does is to open our heart. This helps us avoid molding the student into what we think the student should be. Simply from this meeting, both lives may be changed.

As significant as the change in students can be (better attitude, cooperation, performance, social engagement), the change that the teacher describes in himself or herself is just as noteworthy. Mary says, "I began to develop closer and more meaningful relationships with my students as a result of this experience and I see students in a different light. I have also learned to be more patient with my own daughter." Katherine says, "This experience changed me more than it did [the student]." Teresa, who interviewed a sixteen-year-old, dispossessed, "counter-culture" girl, reports, "After being around Ann I realize that maybe I only take time with the 'good' kids, the students that seemed more like I was in school. I now wonder how many Ann's there are in my classes. How many children just want one person to ask them a question about themselves?" Terry, who met with six-year-old David, says, "I realize that I am in a position to change lives. On the other hand, I am in a position to have my life changed." Lawrence says, "I can never go into a classroom again without seeing TJ in the faces of each of my students. Each will have a story to tell from now on. When you start to see students as people with real needs beyond the sphere of typical education it becomes very difficult to stay focused on the task at hand. I felt that it was my responsibility to stay within the guidelines and focus on how I could help them through the curriculum. Now I have to rethink that position. The boundaries have become fuzzy and the zones of black and white have become gray. Maybe I am learning what good teaching and the truth really are."

When the heart opens, boundaries do grow fuzzy. No longer are we left with subject versus object, task versus relationship, but we see through the eye of the heart. As already mentioned, an understanding relationship not only develops the "soft" non-curricular areas (social skills, feelings of connectness); these are also directly bound to how we behave and perform in school. Our self-discipline, motivation, attention, and performance are tied to this relational domain. If we want to improve performance, especially among the most difficult students, then understanding and relationship are essential. Stuffing in more information or binding the student with more external controls, as in the typical modernist, objectivist prescription, does not address the heart of what vitalizes learning and engenders character. If teachers' and students' hearts are not in the room, there will be only superficial learning. Teaching for understanding means not only that we teach students to understand but also that our explicit task is to understand the student. It does not mean that the teacher must have a tear-evoking relationship with every student, but it does mean that the teacher is willing and available to meet and understand the student. This does not make "mushy" or overly sentimentalized teachers (or students); instead it invites them to meet the world and themselves directly, honestly, and openly. I remember attending a memorial service for Jim Dahl, a retired English professor. He was a slightly rumpled fellow who drove a beat-up car full of all sorts of debris, mostly old English papers, it seemed. He had an irreverent sense of humor and an extremely honest and playful presence; under it all, there was radiant warmth. A woman stood up at his memorial service and recalled her basic composition class with him many years before. He had failed her twice, and she wanted to express her gratitude. More than any other event in her academic life, it was this honest, unsentimental feedback, she said, that stretched her as a student and especially as a person. She passed the course with a "B," on her third try, and came on this day years later to thank him. Simply giving an "F" wasn't the key; it was giving it in the context of an honest relationship. The real function of a friend (and a teacher) is to be honest with us in a way that encourages our growth.

The most important capacity in a teacher may be his or her willingness and effort to understand and meet the student. Carl Jung tells us,

> An understanding heart is everything in a teacher, and cannot be esteemed high enough.... The curriculum is so much necessary raw material, but warmth is the vital element for the growing plant and for the soul of the child. (Jung, 1977, p. 144)

And Krishnamurti (1974) says it simply: "First of all you have to establish a relationship with the student... first have affection" (pp. 158, 138). Why not start our school year with an explicit goal of understanding? When we do, we cultivate an atmosphere "for developing the sensitiveness of the soul, for affording mind its true freedom of sympathy" (Tagore, 1961, p. 64). And like anything else we try to teach, first and foremost we teach by demonstrating it ourselves.

Feeling Into

And now here is my secret, a very simple secret: it is only with the heart that one can see rightly; what is essential is invisible to the eye.
— Antoine de Saint-Exupéry (1943/1971, p. 87)

Empathy, from the German *Einfuhlung*, originally meant "in feeling" or "feeling into." It has come to mean an understanding of the other's thoughts, feelings, and perspectives. When we empathize and understand someone, we often have a sense of making a connection and seeing through their eyes. We generally know or understand the other by a combination of inference based on our observations, along with an intuitive process that I have described in detail elsewhere (Hart, 1997, 1999). This process bridges the subject-object distinction in some way. Carl Rogers (1980) suggested that this involves "entering the private perceptual world of the other and being thoroughly at home in it.... It means temporarily living the other's life" (p. 142). Rogers suggests that this shift in knowing occurs as you "lay yourself aside" (p. 142). He describes seeing through the eye of the heart in this way: "It seems that my inner spirit has reached out and touched the inner spirit of the other. Our relationship transcends itself and becomes part of something larger" (p. 129). Husserl (1967) refers to "transcendental empathy," Watkins (1978) describes "co-feeling" and "co-understanding," Larson (1987), Rowan (1986), and Sprinkle (1985) refer to this more direct communication as "sympathetic resonance," and I have described it as "deep empathy" (Hart, 1999, 2000). For Martin Buber, this captures the experience of an "I-Thou" relationship in which feelings of deep connection, direct honesty, and even love are present. These experiences emerge naturally through the eye of the knowing heart.

While this knowing is not evoked by technique, it does correspond to certain qualities and activities. Empathy does not involve doing something to another person directly; instead a space is created in which we may meet and open to one another. Genuine meeting takes place in a kind of "clearing" as Heidegger (1977/1993) named it, or in "the between" (Buber, 1923/1958).

We open toward the other when we try to take the other's perspective. Simply trying to imagine what another person is experiencing (e.g., a new student in school, an orphan in Africa, an interesting character in a story) opens the door to empathic understanding. Ruth Shlossman (1996), the principal at a private elementary school, describes how empathy was intentionally cultivated in her school:

> When we had a new student who barely spoke English enter our school, I asked the students to imagine what it might be like for them if they suddenly had been placed in school in Thailand or Nigeria or Italy, and what they might have hoped for in the way of kindness and support from fellow students and teachers in that situation. After a lively discussion of their fantasies and fears, I asked them to apply that to the new student attending our school. They got it. (p. 20)

Empathy is awakened by *listening*. Listening is particularly powerful in the midst of hurt and conflict. When the parties involved in conflict or confusion are listened to with goodwill and fairness, most walk away with a sense of being understood. This allows all parties a sense of respect, regardless of whether they "win" the argument or not. When someone has been hurt (e.g., by a shove in the playground, an attack, a cold shoulder in a conversation, an intellectually sophisticated put-down in a class debate), we demonstrate the priority of care when we take time out from our curricular march to address the hurt. If it passes without consideration, we entrench a message of "everyone for himself or herself," where aggressiveness wins the day.

The technique of reflecting back what we hear is a useful way to begin practicing the basic skills of listening: "OK class, get a partner, describe your weekend highlights to each other, reflect them back to make sure you've heard them and then introduce your partner's weekend to another pair of students. And the topic can range from your favorite hero or your worst nightmare to your fantasy vacation or simply what you are aware of at this moment." We can stretch listening beyond the limits of our ears and of basic content when we ask students to pay attention to body language, feeling tone, and the meanings under the words. We invite intuition by trusting our guts, feeling into our own reaction, and then checking it out.

When we compare notes on our reactions with others, we open up intersubjective dialogue. This enables us to check out our own projections and refine our *awareness of subjectivity*. One of the keys to empathy is being able to sort out "what is mine and what is theirs." That is, making a distinction between our projection onto another and an accurate perception of the other. We can also reveal our subjectivity through various apperceptive experiments. For example, having students tell a story about a particular picture (any picture) and then comparing stories with other students helps to reveal how perception is constructed through our own subjective lens. Once we get over our concern for what the "right answer" is, this exercise opens us up to new ways of seeing. ("Oh, I didn't see or think of that.") In some of my classes I use an exercise adapted from Judith Brown (1996) in which students are asked to pick a positive and a negative card from a tarot deck (pictures cut out from a magazine or pictures of fine art would work just as effectively). They then are asked to take turns speaking as if they were the positive card and then the negative card to their partner (e.g., "I am a dark card; I have a sword and I am very dangerous..."). Then each person is asked to imagine and speak as if the negative and positive card were having a dialogue with each other. Once the initial hesitation is overcome, these dialogues quickly take on a life of their own. Next, all of the participants are asked to imagine that their positive card is negative and their negative card positive. This is followed by another round of dialogues ("I am now a positive card..."). This helps to reveal how subjectivity is projected onto the pictures. Switching the cards serves the additional function of bringing what was in the background into view, adding flexibility of perception. At the end, we process the whole experiment by asking what this experience was like, what was difficult and what was easy; and partners are invited to reflect on how similar or different their own perceptions of the other person's cards were. Subjectivity serves as a perceptual and interpretive filter; discriminative capacity is refined as we allow the feedback to inform the process of knowing.

Feeling into another requires a *range and depth of feeling*. We may speak of hating or liking something, but in daily usage our feeling vocabulary is usually quite limited. This is, in part, a reflection of the lack of attention paid to affective subtlety in our culture. Simply generating a list of feeling words, perhaps integrated into a vocabulary or spelling lesson, gives the opportunity to explore this firsthand. "Who can tell me what this word (e.g., betrayed, inspired, longing, courageous) means?" "Can you give me an example of when you experienced this?" We then explore the etymological origin of the word. This seemingly arcane academic exercise often reveals the deeply felt sense that the word originally tried to capture. Inspiration, for example, means to be filled with the breath of spirit or a god; courage has the same root as heart. The point is simply to stretch down into our deeply felt world so that we may be able to face our own experiences more fully and in turn understand another's experience. Simply knowing the vocabulary word is not sufficient. However, the word can serve as a sacred word, mantra, or doorway that may help us evoke the depths of the felt world.

Empathy involves both *reaching out* and *receiving in*. Husserl describes an "emotive and cognitive reaching out to the other in a self-transcending empathic understanding" (Kohak, 1984, p. 206). We use our intention to make contact and this willfulness to risk may move us near the other; but the shift to receive the other, to actually experience our interconnection, is more like a willingness than a willful intending or grasping. Receiving implies a shift in cognitive style from mental processing or computing to receiving or allowing the meeting to occur.

In empathy, one opens the self to the other and transcends personal boundaries. Boundaries may be thought of as being more or less permeable or, as Hartmann (1984) has called them, thick or thin. At the thin or more permeable end, there is increased sensitivity that enables empathy as well as vulnerability. There are individuals who find themselves particularly sensitive to the psychic distress of others, as well as those at the other end of the continuum who seem relatively impermeable, even impenetrable. Empathy requires and is a function of *permeable boundaries*. And boundaries are not only between ourselves and another person but also intrapsychic. Some rejected aspect of us may be "an other," a shadow, until it is empathized with and eventually integrated. Boundaries aren't always what they seem. That is, the tough kid may be masking vulnerability. As an example, an "impossibly unruly" child was given some chalk by his frustrated teacher. She asked him to draw a boundary around himself in the shape and size that was necessary for his comfort. He went around the entire paved area of the playground, around trees, around other children and teachers. He came back with a rather satisfied expression. "There!" he said. The teacher began to get a sense of how vulnerable and sensitive this child might be and also how violated he must feel when so much is within his perimeter. She then proceeded to work with him on establishing boundaries in other ways besides driving others out of his space with hostility or simply reacting as if he was out of control. It was soon revealed that he had been abused, and his need for exaggerated personal space symbolically reflected this. Ending the abusive living situation, learning basic assertion skills, constructing safe spaces in his artwork and his imagery, and working through the violation in therapy helped this boy gain new control of his defenses. Some time later, he asked if he could use the chalk again. He drew a line that went about three feet around him. Paradoxically, having adept control of our boundaries may enable intimacy; we may be willing to risk allowing someone in if we know we have the power to keep them out. Empathy can emerge because the other does not threaten the self as much; not that the self is invulnerable, but we can protect ourselves without resorting to isolation or attack. Ultimately, this vulnerability requires *courage*, a fullness of heart.

Empathy is natural and emerges out of an *impulse toward contact*, even toward oneness, to know and be known (Palmer, 1993). We see a dimension of the same impulse when we look at natural compassion (Dass & Gorman, 1996), which may spill into social interest (Adler, 1929) and prosocial or altruistic behavior. Empathy emphasizes knowing whereas compassion implies an impulse toward mercy or service. Both come from the same source, recognizing interconnection. And the "other" need not be a single person, but a group, a race, or even nature (see, e.g., Berry, 2000). The extent to which we are able to recognize and be moved by this impulse within us will be reflected in our willingness for meeting. Simply noticing and supporting children as they reach out toward contact is sufficient, whether their reach is toward a bug, a book, or a basketball.

Fundamentally, empathy serves understanding, and this enables the student to grow up to be

[a] different human being—one who cares, who has affection, who loves people.... Can you look at the beauty of the earth [and] have the quality of affection? And can you retain that? For if you do not, as you grow up, you will conform, because that is the easiest way to live. (Krishnamurti, 1974, p. 15)

Service as Understanding

To me, God and compassion are one and the same. Compassion is the joy of sharing. It's doing the small things for the love of each other—just a smile, or carrying a bucket of water, of showing some simple kindness.... The fruit of love is service, which is compassion in action.

—Mother Teresa (1990, p. 151)

One very direct way to experiment with empathy and understanding is through service. Service is important not just to fill the needs of the culture, or because it is the moral or good thing to do, but because it actually opens our consciousness, our ways of knowing. Service is a way of knowing our connection with a reality much larger than ourselves. It may serve as a direct path to the spiritual as spiritual pertains to the connected aspects of reality (see Deikman, 2000). Often our own heart opens through freely given service.

When a child takes the classroom bunny home for the weekend, it is primarily a lesson in service and responsibility to the bunny and to the class. When young children have plants to care for they are learning the lessons of service to the community of nature. When an older student helps a younger one, a bond is usually formed as the two come into relationship with one another and with the material at hand. A sense of pleasure and pride in the accomplishments of one another often emerge if the relationship takes root. This relationship develops between students of any ages. Third-graders help out in the kindergarten; eleventh-graders help with eight-grade math; many of my university students volunteer as tutors throughout the primary and secondary grades.

Assisting one another inside and outside the classroom develops the principle of "leaving no one out." This is an experiential curriculum of social justice, one in which *understanding* guides decisions about human affairs, and the goal is to leave no one out. This fosters an ecology of interconnection and a practice of compassion.

Understanding is an inclusive activity. When we understand, it is difficult to marginalize or otherwise exclude the other. In a classroom and in a school, children quickly notice who is on the outside and who is on the inside. Friendships develop, cliques form, and some students become outcasts because of their ability, their attitudes, their actions, their looks or family, or intangibles that are harder to name (e.g., cooties). Marginalization and scapegoating serve a purpose with social Darwinism as the backdrop. They reduce our own anxiety and allow us to demonize the other in order to make ourselves feel more right and righteous, or at least part of the in-group. Can we develop a classroom culture in which no one is left out or left behind academically or otherwise, one in which we share responsibility for the members of our group, in which the *modus operandi* is something other than social Darwinism, in which only the fittest socially, emotionally, and intellectually survive? If we cannot do this in the classroom, we most certainly cannot expect to do it in the world outside.

When we center on understanding, our attitudes and actions achieve an organizing principle that transcends purely individual accomplishment and recognition as the goal. Community, cooperation, and even communion can join with appropriate competition and necessary individuality.

Administrators often set the tone of a school community. Does the school embody a culture of fear or one of collaboration? I mention this briefly under service because the most helpful principle I have seen for administration is servant leadership (Greenleaf, 1977; Spears, 1998). This implies being a leader by being of service. The administrator's primary role may then be thought of as creating a clearing for teachers, encouraging teachers to develop as persons and as professionals, dealing with issues that infringe on classroom freedom, and serving as a buffer and an advocate for teachers. When leadership is confused with domination, control, emphasis on compliance, or bureaucratic imposition, the meaning of true leadership gets lost. The questions for administrators are: "What can I do to help create a clearing for teachers and teaching?" and "What are we doing to prevent the space needed from being created?" Anything other than this is a distortion of the role.

Serving the Task

Service may not only be to another person or the classroom bunny, but also to whatever task is at hand, serving the task (Deikman, 2000). When we notice the artist, mechanic, or even the engaged algebra student absorbed in their work, we see a deep relatedness and intimacy. The relationship looks like a love affair in the degree of commitment, care, and concern that are expressed. Just like the experience of empathy or of serving another person, serving the task involves a crossing of self-separateness; we "feel into" the task and it may even become us for a period of time. Heidegger (1977/1993) describes this:

> If he is to become a true cabinet maker, he makes himself answer and respond above all to the different kinds of wood and to the shapes slumbering

within the wood.... In fact, this relationship to wood is what maintains the whole craft. Without that relatedness, the craft will never be anything but empty busywork, any occupation with it will be determined exclusively by business concerns.... all humans' dealings, are constantly in that danger. The writing of poetry is no more exempt from it than is thinking. (p. 379)

This is how mastery of an activity (see chapter 3) stretches into understanding and passion. Somehow, we just end up loving the thing we do; it is in us and we in it. We develop sensitivity toward the work; the task may be accomplished with pleasure and appreciation, reverence and devotion. There is a certain deep resonance with the activity as we fall into harmony with it, as with the example of the child who lives for his or her favorite sport or activity. Hillman (1996) suggests that we should allow such "obsessions" as much freedom as possible, because they resonate with our character and calling so deeply. Following one's interest and sinking deeply into activity has been highlighted throughout this book. Instead of rushing just to "get it done" or find "the right answer" as efficiently as possible, educational activity and assignments can often invite us to see what the task really calls for.

Serving the task involves a conscious intention and commitment, but the activity of knowing is often shifted as we get into the "zone" or are absorbed in a state of flow (Csikszentmihalyi, 1990). In some moments, the sense of time abates, and a feeling of deep connection, even oneness or love, emerges. Serving the task can become a meditation.

Swedenborg, like so many mystics and sages, suggests that all things correspond with the spiritual. In his *theology of uses* he suggests that by investing ourselves fully in whatever task is at hand, we create the possibility of going beyond ourselves (see Van Dusen, 1992). And through this experience of commitment, we contact quality of investment and result, and ultimately we bring our awareness nearer the spirit. This argues for the importance of doing well, whatever our task. In this way, we look beyond ourselves. It would be a mistake to think of this as the Puritan work ethic, in which hard work is a moral precept by which one is supposed to earn credits toward the afterlife. In other words, to work hard is to be good, to do otherwise reflects moral bankruptcy. This is too hollow and moralistic as a guiding principle of work. Rather than simply working hard as a way to demonstrate worthiness and righteousness, serving the task invites us into the relationship with the activity in the present, with no expectation of moral gain. Serving the task is not about earning brownie points on some imagined holy ledger; instead it is an opportunity to free consciousness from the tangle of self-interest, which allows us to reach the "disinterested joy" (Tagore, 1961) that is the source and goal of creation.

There is a developmental progression in serving the task. Early in the practice of serving the task, it seems that you are simply trying to do the task better. Later it is as though the task is being done through you. You are closer to an observer watching something being done, even feeling yourself as a recipient vessel: "you feel like an awed spectator watching processes quite beyond your limits" (Van Dusen, 1992, pp. 14-15). Dante wrote, "I am one who, when love breathes in me, takes note, and I, in that manner in which he dictates within me, go setting it down" (Williams, 1982, p. 11). While we are in the midst of serving the task, the grasping, holding, and judging of normal consciousness shifts toward beholding. Distant observation becomes intimate participation; the separation between the knower and the known collapses, and we share pulse and breath.

Character, Violence, and Understanding

[Materialism] leads inevitably to a dead-end street in an intellectually senseless world.... Science can give us only physical power, which if not controlled by spiritual power, will lead inevitably to cosmic doom....The old evils continue and the age of reason has been transformed into an age of terror. Selfishness and hatred have not vanished with an enlargement of our educational system and an extension of our legislative policies.

—Martin Luther King, Jr. (1963, pp. 55, 56, 120)

Character is an embodied moral orientation or style. Part of education is to teach, shape, or evoke character. Knowledge demands character for its proper use, otherwise knowledge runs the risk of becoming dangerous and destructive; "knowledge is praiseworthy when it is coupled with ethical conduct and a virtuous character; otherwise it is a deadly poison, a frightful danger" (Universal House of Justice, 1987, p. 7). The contemporary backdrop of violence, greed, parental inadequacy, and everything from basic disrespect to poor manners invigorates the case for character development as being a legitimate part of public education. We all want students to be contributing community members who use knowledge well and wisely.

But from what center do we teach character? The statement of Martin Luther King, Jr., quoted above suggests that the dominant principles of the culture are a "dead-end" and have even led to an "age of terror." King's proposition gains support when we look at news broadcasts of the unthinkable horrors perpetrated in our world and even in our schools. Understanding gives counterweight to the impulse of objective science and materialism, and it provides an orientation guided by something other than mere self-interest.

The meaning of "character" in schools is often reduced to following rules and causing no trouble; character is mistaken for compliance. When we have a sense of belonging and mutual care, we tend to cooperate and participate; when we do not, we tend to resist. We must create safe environments, provide firm and consistent consequences, tolerate no violence or disrespect, remove students who are inordinately disruptive and provide alternatives when appropriate, and hold students and parents accountable. In some schools, this may mean metal detectors in the short run, but this does not make our society a safer place; it just adds another gated community. Law and order solutions do not address the violent or alienated heart that is the source of these problems. The overemphasis on external control has not led to more self-control or a society with greater character or caring.

How do we avoid reducing character to compliance or becoming overly moralistic, repressive, or simply embarrassingly superficial? Education for character involves more than following rules, posting commandments, or memorizing a few virtuous words. Such attempts to develop character do little more than appease the conscience of believers (legislators and others) and actually serve to distract us from more fundamental solutions. One of my daughters came home from school and declared that she had been selected for recognition in the character education program. "Great: what is this for?" I asked. "So that you can get an award from the principal," she said. "Yes, but why were you selected?" I asked. "I don't know," she responded. "Was there something in particular that you were recognized for?" I asked. "Oh, yeah, there was a word, 'op-something.' I don't remember." "Do you know what it means or why they selected you?" I asked. "No, not really. But we did get to go on the [closed circuit] TV."

Well, the word that she was recognized for was "optimism" and she is a good example of an optimist. But when character becomes just one more discrete bit of information to be memorized and one more curricular mandate added to teachers' already overstuffed schedules, we see how the information download model is insufficient not only to download information but also especially to cultivate anything that resembles character. The word simply becomes another commodity.

At the foundation of education for character is the heart of understanding, which cannot be reduced to particular words to be memorized, or conveyed adequately in an assembly but is expressed in the way we relate to the world each day.

The consequence of a failure of character and community is violence of one sort or another. Gandhi used the term *himsa*, which can be translated as "the intent to do harm," as the basis for understanding the core of violence. While a particular action may be destructive, it is the willingness and desire to harm another that powers violence. Swedenborg (1974) also emphasizes that character is primarily about the inner intent one has toward another. Do we hope for the highest good for our neighbor, or do we seek something else? The good intent is not forced or contrived but emerges naturally from the connection engendered by understanding.

We easily recognize the intersocial violence of war and the interpersonal violence between two or more persons in a more limited conflict. However, violence also resides in more shadowy realms. First and foremost, it exists within us as the intent to do harm. With this as its base, violence knows no bounds. As St. Augustine (trans. 1961) wrote in his *Confessions*, "imagine that our enemies can do us more harm than we do to ourselves by hating them" (p. 39). The unresolved bitterness, the fear, and the raw drive for vengeance are vultures that pick at our bones and prevent genuine relatedness. The self divided, the child who has been battered in one way or another, who is bitter at the world, who hates his or her own limitations, who is an adversary to himself or herself, is the breeding ground for the bacterium of violence. We project our inner fears onto the outer world and create dragons and demons. We build a Maginot Line around the self to protect us and it is overrun in ways that we do not anticipate. Violence will not be significantly reduced until we look at the violence within us. We do this when we face and embrace (understand) our shadow, the disowned parts of ourselves. Our self-expression through art and writing and the ways we play and relate to others betray our inner struggles in symbolic form. If we want to know the students' struggles let them draw their struggles or write a story about someone they know, or simply ask them directly. When understanding of self is incorporated into the curriculum, we ask our students questions about their experience, their fears and aspirations, their heroes and hopes. In the alchemy of self-understanding, fear grows into courage and hostility into compassion.

When we live in a sea of violence it is difficult to stay dry. The deluge of media and marketing violence reflect and reinforce our inner violence. Violence perpetrated upon us by ideologies and institutions is equally insidious. Racism and classism, for example, perpetuate structural violence in the society. In some states, legislatures provide vouchers for private schools. The result in Mississippi has been to create public schools that teach mostly black and low-income white students. Private schools, now state subsidized, teach mainly white children of some economic means. What is the lesson that is being modeled? It is not "leave no one out." Instead, the message is "take care of yourself and take care of your own." In this case at least the result of vouchers is a widening gulf, the "have-nots" lose ground that they hardly possessed in the first place, and an underclass becomes more entrenched. Fundamentally, there is a lack of understanding and generosity.

Character is shaped in large part by the modeling of adults, by stories and by the media, and from the institutional practices that students encounter. The teacher, parent, legislature, or organization that acts with integrity, fairness, honesty, and charity transmits this to the child:

> Good example still remains the best pedagogic method ... the methodological teaching of the curriculum is at most only half the meaning of school. The other half is the real psychological education made possible through the personality of the teacher. This education means guiding the child into the larger world. (Jung, 1977, p. 56)

Just as quickly, and perhaps more dramatically, the hostile, violent, prejudiced, and selfish images pass their imprints along. Significant models may take shape in the form of peers, parents and teachers, film or television characters, as well as through the power of autobiography, or heroic stories and myths. Of course, the student filters and selects, finds his or her own resonance with a particular image, but what we model through our stories, actions, and institutions has the biggest influence on character. Again, as teachers or parents mostly we teach who we are.

The most insidious sources of violence are ideologies of objectivism and materialism, which treat the other (person, object, the natural world, or even some disowned part of self) as an object to posses, measure, or control. Such "non-relational" knowing creates environments that lead to a basic sense of insecurity and isolation. Without a solid relational ground and basic sense of trust and security, basic anxiety develops and is manifest in personality strategies that include "moving away," "moving toward," or "moving against" others (Horney, 1950). Much of our social concern these days involves the level of violence, the "moving against" another; much of our educational concerns involves the "moving away," the isolation and numbness that stares back at us or simply drops out altogether. The "moving toward" implies an external dependence and lack of autonomy and individuation. The modernist milieu of objectification of the other, including the natural world (environment and body), contributes to these early experiences and to later ethical and educational failures. We never experience the other's subjectivity; the other remains merely an object for our consumer scrutiny and, thus, alienation and violence are more easily perpetrated. Knowing in isolation or illusory objectivity creates distance from the other; understanding or heartfulness offers an antidote and sets the stage for the growth of wisdom.

This intimate way of knowing leads to what the Greeks would call pursuit of *The True*, which is presumably what education focuses on, but also to *The Good* and even *The Beautiful*. And this is a profound clue that we are tapping into the depths of the world as the power of education begins to come to life. Thomas Berry (2000) says this knowing moves us from "experiencing the universe as a collection of objects" to "a communion of subjects" (p. 16). An ethic of care–for *The Good*–emerges organically from such communion. At a time where violence and virtue seem to be increasing responsibilities of schools, the valueless search for facts–the modernist goal of every science–is balanced and brought whole with the addition of a more intimate way of knowing. This approach will do more than metal detectors and the word of the month to cultivate The Good and represents an integrated approach to education for character.

Beauty also emerges from this quality of knowing and serves as both an outcome and a portal. We co-create beauty through the quality of our presence. As we dive in, like a great naturalist, we begin to see more richness, more depth, more subtlety and, ultimately, more beauty.

Beauty takes endless forms: a perfect pitch in baseball, a meal prepared with special attention to detail, a perfect lapis sky, the deep peace of an infant asleep in loving arms, the elegance of a mathematical formula, the heart of our neighbor. Beauty provides a doorway, gateway or bridge inviting us from one state to another, enabling us to expand our everyday reality and respond to something that is both greater than ourselves, and intimately part of us. By entering that doorway and opening into that communion, we are brought closer to the experience of the union between our inner and outer worlds, between the visible and the invisible.

Somehow beauty sends a "ping" into our own depths, a message of wholeness and possibility. We hunger for beauty; in and of itself beauty is nourishment and a necessity. Beauty, Dostoevsky wrote, will save the world.

CHAPTER 6

THE EYE OF WISDOM

Wisdom lies in human action which possesses both intellectual and ethical orienta-
tion; and the promotion of such wisdom is the task of education.
                                        —Douglas E. Lawson (1961, p. vii)

Wisdom is an activity rather than a static entity. That is, we do not possess wisdom, as if it were an object; instead, we act wisely. Wisdom is distinguished from technical mastery or intellectual acuity especially by its integration of the heart. Emerson says that true wisdom is a blend of "the 'intellectual' perception of truth and the moral sentiment of right" (Sealts, 1992, p. 257).

Acting wisely involves the capacity to listen and translate the power of the intellect and the sensitivity of the heart into an appropriate form (action, attitude, etc.). We might even say that wisdom is "the capacity of the mind to honor the wisdom of the heart" (Rodegast & Stanton, 1989, p. 28). Wisdom dynamically expands and integrates perspectives, seeing beyond what is visible from a stance of fear and self-interest. As Thomas Aquinas wrote, "Wisdom differs from science in looking at things from a greater height.... [it involves] *gnome*, or the ability to see through things" (quoted in Gilby, 1967, p. 364). Wisdom involves a degree of awareness that enables discrimination. This can include practicalities about when and how to linger and when to move on, which impulses should be followed and which may be interpreted and used for other purposes.

While the heart of understanding is universal and indiscriminate, wisdom brings this broad unconditionality to the particularities of a situation. For example, the wise response is not always "Just love"; it may be strategic, disruptive, confrontational. Jesus was said to have turned over the tables of the moneychangers who were doing business in a holy temple; Martin Luther King, Jr., organized a sit-in at a lunch counter in Montgomery; Gandhi's radical non-violence confronted the authority of the British Empire. We would not say that these actions were "smart," but they were wise. These examples reveal a central characteristic of wisdom; the wise person sees beyond immediate self-interest. In this way, wisdom does not simply serve individual growth but the growth in general. The actions of Jesus, King, and Gandhi helped to change their societies.

We know people who are brilliant intellectually but far from wise. Smart people sometimes act unwisely, falling prey to fallacies of invincibility or omnipotence or to narcissism. Some individuals may be able to navigate with "success" in the world. Such "fundamental pragmatics of life" are certainly valuable and have even been described as a component of wisdom (Baltes & Smith, 1990, p. 87), but they do not necessarily integrate the heart or see beyond self-interest; consequently, lives guided only by such pragmatics seem to be wanting in some very central way. Orwoll and Perlmutter (1990) recognize this missing dimension as a level of personality development that is necessary to transcend narcissism, personal needs, thoughts, and feelings. Without adequate development, people may see how to gain from the world but miss the opportunity to give to it at the same time.

On the other hand, we know people who are not intellectually brilliant but who are able to use their intelligence and their understanding to act wisely. We say they have character, virtue, or even goodness. They have insight into what is important and what is less so, and they act from this knowledge. They recognize both forests and trees and can discern the relative balance and the integration of each perspective. At times, they may tap into a vein of wise simplicity in the midst of perplexity. In fact, while knowledge and intelligence are often equated with complexity, wisdom often emerges as elegantly simple. This is not a simplicity born of ignorance but a simplicity that is close to what is essential in life; it cuts to the chase; it sees through the cloud of complexity.

Henry David Thoreau said that he would give first prize to the person who could live one day deliberately. Living deliberately means being "so centered that one becomes ultimately fascinated, ravished, and overwhelmed by the mystery that permeates and suffuses all nature, all people, all reality" (McNamara, 1990, p. 108). Thoreau's offer suggests how difficult such living really is. The deliberateness he refers to implies moving beyond habits of thought, perception, and deed to be fully centered and awake throughout the day. Education for wisdom and transformation is not about being taught but about waking up. Waking up requires a certain kind of energy, certain capacities for taking the world into our consciousness: "wisdom is not the product of mental effort. Wisdom is a state of the total being" (Richards, 1989, p. 15).

Waking up into the wisdom space is facilitated by what I refer to as centering: "centering is an act of bringing in, not of leaving out. It is brought about not by force but by coordinations" (Richards, 1989, p. 35). These coordinations are a "gesture of balance," according to Tarthang Tulku (1977), which provides our existence with a dynamic center. We do not accumulate wisdom so much as we develop our powers of centering and coordination so that we may act from the wisdom space. In this way, wisdom involves "assisting the mind in the powers of self creation" (Lawson, 1961, p. 8).

Centering may be thought of as a dialogue, "an unending dialectic" (Sternberg, 1990). M. C. Richards (1989) describes this dialogue through her experience as a potter:

> Centering: that act which precedes all others on the potter's wheel. The bringing of the clay into a spinning, unwobbling pivot, which will then be free to take innumerable shapes as potter and clay press against each other. The firm, tender, sensitive pressure which yields as much as it asserts. It is like a handclasp between two living hands, receiving the greeting at the very moment that they give it. It is this speech between the hand and the clay that makes me think of a dialogue. (p. 9)

Without this centering in pottery, as in life, our actions wobble, become distorted, and neither look nor feel right. We can learn from the wobble; it gives us feedback in the form of guilt, frustration, rejection, confusion, inflation, and so forth. If we do not tolerate and accept the inevitability of human wobble, we may be too anxious, in control, afraid of risking a mistake, or we may become puritanical, not permitting others their own wobble. Centering constantly incorporates the feedback of human experience (especially wobbles) and adjusts accordingly.

The heart of understanding serves as one of the coordinates for centering. As shown in the previous chapter, understanding breeds compassion, love, and communion fostered through empathy. This centers us first and foremost and often begins with a simple attitude of appreciation or curiosity.

Still borrowing from M. C. Richards' metaphor, to bring forth a pot or a life we must start at the center, at centering. T. S. Eliot in *Four Quartets* (1971) refers to this as the "still point of the turning world" (p. 16). This movement inward (in pottery and for wisdom) provides the basis for moving outward with integrity and symmetry, otherwise actions may spin out of control or into a lopsided mass. This chapter explores the process of centering for wisdom inside and outside of education.

The Wisdom Space

Be patient toward all that is unresolved in your heart.... Try to love the questions themselves..... Do not now seek the answers, which can not be given because you would not be able to live them—and the point is to live everything.
—Rainer Maria Rilke (1993, p. 35)

It is difficult to find any genuine consideration of wisdom in education. Why is wisdom so absent from educational aims and practice? Rorty (1979) suggests that the Cartesian shift marked the "triumph of the quest for certainty over the quest for wisdom" (p. 61). The goal thus became rigor, prediction, and control rather than wisdom or peace of mind. But this quest for certainty is a futile or delusional task since "what is really 'in' experience extends much further than that which at any time is *known*" (Dewey, 1929/1958, p. 21). To express it in another way, we simply cannot control or know it all; if we try to, our tight and focused grasping does not leave space enough for wisdom. This intolerance and fear of ambiguity and the unknown contributes to the sterilization and commodification of knowledge, where single correct answers, fear of making mistakes, and multiple-choice exams are the gatekeepers of certainty. Wisdom allows space for ambiguity. For teachers and especially administrators and elected officials, there is security in certainty; we can name it, even measure it, write reports with graphs about it, and hold others accountable to it. When we stretch away from certainty, we make ourselves (and the material) vulnerable. Few of us get past our personal need for control and predictability to risk the unknown and intentionally put our own vulnerability or that of the material on the line, in plain view. And yet vulnerability seems essential for our growth:

And all the while, deep inside, I know what I have always known: that the knowledge will never be enough. This is the secret we keep from ourselves. And the moment it is revealed, we become aware of a need for something else; for the wisdom to live with what we do not know, what we cannot control, what is painful—and still choose life. (Dreamer, 1999, p. 45)

The space, flow, and vitality of a classroom change when conscious vulnerability is present in the teacher. By moving out from behind the protection of certainty, curriculum, and role, the teacher invites the student to do the same. As Jung advised, "Please remember, it is what you *are* that heals [and educates], not what you *know*" (quoted in Johnson, 1998, p. 125). Vulnerability does not mean becoming passive or giving power away; it means being open to possibility, which opens the wisdom space. Vulnerability means tackling our fears head on. Ambiguity and vulnerability are the allies of wisdom.

Not every learning situation is appropriate for increasing ambiguity. When we ask for the correct answer to a basic mathematics problem, we want a particular answer. When we ask students to engage deductive reasoning to draw a straightforward logical inference, we are looking for less ambiguity, not more. In these examples we are using the tools of intelligence. But with most topics, there is an opportunity to create the dynamic tension of ambiguity and, in turn, open the wisdom space to engage the student at a very deep level. We do this when we lead off the lesson with an honest question that has no simple preset answer. We ask, "What are the causes of violence in our culture and in our school?" instead of truncating the wisdom space with "What are the five causes of violence that our text discusses?" Of course we want the student to know the text, but if our questions merely dead-end there, we have missed an opportunity for the growth of wisdom through ambiguity, vulnerability, and mystery. The text should be drawn on as part of a dialogue rather than as a diatribe.

Instead of grasping for certainty, wisdom rides the question, lives the question. "The wise person views himself and others as engaged in an unending dialectic with each other and the world" (Sternberg, 1990, p. 150). An unending dialectic is an activity that raises anxiety in the one-right-answer world of most contemporary schooling. When a question is treated primarily as a problem to be solved with certainty, the domain and goal of intelligence, the question is set up in opposition to the questioner. From the start, the question becomes something to beat, to conquer. This may be playful or deadly serious and represents the best of intelligent engagement. Wisdom treats the question differently. It seeks questions, as if looking for the best fruit on the tree. It then bites into the question, living it, allowing it to ful-

fill its purpose as nourishment. Whereas intelligence will cut, disman-
tle, and reconstruct the question in order to work toward certainty,
wisdom rides the question to see where it goes and what it turns into.
Recall Rilke's (1993) lines:

> Be patient toward all that is unresolved in your heart.... Try to love the
> questions themselves.... Do not now seek the answers, which can not be
> given because you would not be able to live them–and the point is to live
> everything. (p. 35)

Wisdom seeks and creates questions. Arlin (1990) describes "problem
finding," identifying the most salient problems, as being closely associated with wisdom. Problem finding allows us to move beyond conceptual limits (i.e., the problem as given) in order to reframe and
synthesize. We can encourage questions as much as answers in the
classroom by making a small but significant turn in what we ask for
and reward. For example, in an exam or in a class discussion, simply
asking for the questions that the students would ask about the topic,
what they are curious about, what they really want to know but have
been afraid to ask, serves to open up the wisdom space. Physicist
David Bohm (1981) explains, "Questioning is ... not an end in itself,
nor is its main purpose to give rise to answers. Rather, what is essential here is the whole flowing movement of life, which can be harmo-
nious only when there is ceaseless questioning" (p. 25). Pablo
Neruda's *The Book of Questions* (1991) provides a poetic and playful
hint of this "whole flowing movement" through the art of questioning:

> Is 4 the same 4 for everybody?
> Are all sevens equal?
> When the convict ponders the light
> is it the same light that shines on you? (p. 24)

In addition to attending to the question as posed, we are also conditioned to answer a question as soon as it is asked. This too reinforces the answer and leaves the question behind. There may be
hardly a breath between the question and our eagerness to answer it.
But it is from this gap that the wisdom space emerges. One simple
exercise invites students to generate questions instead of answers
about a particular event or idea (e.g., a Civil War battle, a science
demonstration, a story). These remarks can include students' own reactions and associations such as, "What does this have to do with my
life? or statements such as, "Something about this really excites (or
bothers) me, I wonder what it is." In one variation of this exercise,

students can anonymously write the questions on an index card to be shared out loud with the class by a designated reader. These are not immediately to be answered but just to be heard. We may place a "question chair" in the middle of the classroom and when there are questions we speak the question to the chair rather than to the teacher or another student. No one is allowed to answer the question directly; it is simply allowed to sit and simmer. Other questions may follow. Initially this is awkward and students fall back onto habits of looking to the teacher, forgetting to talk to the chair, or providing a quick response to the question. But with just a few reminders, space opens up in this situation because the emphasis is on welcoming questions without tidy answers. The feeling of competition or resistance in the typical one-right-answer classroom opens up into mystery: we don't know what will come, and I am always surprised by the deepening quality of questions and perspectives that I had not previously considered. The process is less like an assembly line and more like an artist's studio, the atmosphere gradually shifts, and I imagine that the space inside the student shifts and opens as well.

In a similar vein, the Quaker tradition provides a method of clarifying decisions called a "clearness committee" (see Livsey & Palmer, 1999, pp. 43-48). A member of the community can simply call upon other members of his or her choosing to sit together and ask questions about a concern or choice that is being faced (e.g., "Should I take this job?" "I am considering marrying this person." "What should I do with my life?"). The committee is not there to offer opinions or advice but simply to pose honest questions and listen. The point is to help one listen to one's inner knowing. We can use the spirit of the clearness committee when students are instructed to present, to a small group in the classroom or to the class as a whole, their topic for their term paper, or their understanding of some concept that they have been studying. Small groups can serve as mini-clearness committees. Given only minimal reminders about sticking to open and honest questions and acting in goodwill, the receiver of the questions regularly experiences an opening or clearing of awareness.

Wisdom asks questions about questions, not so much to close in and trap the answer but to see what the question has to tell us about our selves and our world. "What is the lesson here?" "What is the big picture?" "What can this teach me?" In this way, the question (as well as the universe) serves as a mirror and as a looking glass. Our reaction to the question, our feelings of superiority or inferiority, and our solutions themselves reveal the limits or edges of our seeing or insight. Often statements are embedded within questions. Sharing questions helps to expose those statements about who "I" am, what "my" perspective and projection is, and what "I" want. Wisdom acknowledges that we don't know, or at least that we know incompletely; once this is accepted, it frees us for true learning. In this way, "ambiguity potentiates learning" (Bateson, 1999, p. 137). Once we stop fighting the question and the situation and give up our quest for domination and certainty, we are really free to see what they have to offer. This is as true in meeting a person as it in meeting a question, and it is facilitated by understanding, as was elaborated in the previous chapter.

As we welcome ambiguity, attempt to balance an "unending dialectic," and "live everything," we open up, not to domination of the question, but to insight born of awe. In his study of the ancient prophets, Heschel (1972) concludes that wisdom comes through awe and reverence:

> The loss of awe is the great block to insight. A return to reverence is the first prerequisite for a revival of wisdom.... Wisdom comes from awe rather than from shrewdness. It is evoked not in moments of calculation but in moments of being in rapport with the mystery of reality. The greatest insights happen to us in moments of awe. (p. 78)

Awe, wonder, reverence, and epiphany are drawn forth not by a quest for control, domination, or certainty, but by an appreciative and open-ended engagement with the questions: this is why such qualities as the ability to listen, empathize, and comfort with ambiguity (Sternberg, 1990) are associated with wisdom. This is how understanding sets the stage for wisdom. Heschel (1972) writes:

> Awe enables us to perceive in the world intimations of the divine, to sense in small things the beginning of infinite significance, to sense the ultimate in the common and the simple; to feel the rush of the passing of the stillness of the eternal.... The beginning of awe is wonder, and the beginning of wisdom is awe. (pp. 75, 74)

We come to wonder, and in turn to awe and wisdom, through our vulnerability and openness. As we open up questions, a space is created, the wisdom space. The wisdom space opens to reveal a clearer view that is experienced not as a solution to a limited problem, as when intelligence solves a problem (although this is important), but involves being in rapport with the mystery. "Mystery sucks at our breath like a wind tunnel. Invites us into it. Let us pray and enter" (Richards, 1989, p. 8).

Wisdom as Defining Oneself Authentically and Spontaneously

The purpose of education is to show a person how to define himself authentically and spontaneously in relation to the world—not to impose a prefabricated definition of the world, still less an arbitrary definition of the individual himself.
—Thomas Merton (1979, p. 3)

Teaching for wisdom constantly asks who we are and who we are becoming. Wisdom seeks self-knowledge through the heart of understanding turned inward. This unfolding revelation is a movement toward an authentic life.

When the inner life is attended to on a daily basis, it does not breed narcissistic preoccupation or indulgence but the opportunity for depth and centering at the intersection of inside and outside. All the mystics and sages affirm the Delphic oracle's admonition, "Know thyself," and live true to your authentic nature. Inward awareness is not only important to provide balance but also because it reveals the intersection of our individual depth with a more universal depth. The universe lies not only about us but also within us; the outside can reveal the inside and vice versa. Emerson (1837/1968) tells us that

In yourself is the law of all nature ... in yourself slumbers the whole of Reason; it is for you to know all; it is for you to dare all.... Man is surprised to find that things near are not less beautiful and wondrous than things remote. The near explains the far. The drop is but a small ocean. A man is related to all nature. (pp. 47, 46)

The inside is completely bound to the outside in a dialectic of its own. With respect to perception, the inside co-constructs the outside. As outside and inside meet in awareness we begin to recognize our embeddedness in the physical, social, political, environmental, and linguistic worlds. Ideas, wrote Socrates, "never come out of me; they always come from the person I am talking with." "Nothing creates 'in and by itself.' When people and things interact, they are in a process of becoming 'for each other'" (McNiff, 1992, p. 37).

In addition, the inside-outside dichotomy is a false one, that is, a relative distinction. If our openness and connection are deep enough, our inside (i.e., consciousness, body, etc.) may no longer be distinct from the outside. When our consciousness opens and experiences deep interconnection, we do not experience the other as separate from us; experience arises without a distinct origin.

There is no need or no way to force this process of self-discovery. We open gradually through the small steps of authenticity, through being truly honest with ourselves. Polonius, Hamlet's intended father-in-law, offers him the formula for transformation: "This above all, to thine own self be true." Authenticity begins as a courtship with our interior and ends as communion with the world. Martin Buber (1975) recounts an old Hasidic tale that captures the central importance of being true to oneself. As an old man, Rabbi Zusya said, "In the coming world, they will not ask me: 'Why were you not Moses?' They will ask me: 'Why were you not Zusya?'" (p. 251).

One of the ways we discover who we are is by asking: "What do we love?" "What brings joy and wholeness?" In this way each student's emerging self is the curriculum (Hopkins, 1970). Krishnamurti (1974) says, "Right education is to help you to find out for yourself what you really, with all your heart, love to do.... Then you are really efficient, without becoming brutal" (p. 76). This provides inspiration, as Patanjali (1989) has called it. To define themselves authentically, children (and adults) must listen not only to the voices of parent and teacher and text, but especially to those of their own hearts.

The educator's role includes helping to find the song that sings in the student and helping him or her learn to sing it. This may come through questions in the spirit of: "Who are you?" "What have you come to learn and to teach?" "What is your offering, your gift, your work?" And foremost: "What do you love?" Instead, we often do not ask and so the child has trouble knowing what to ask him or her self. Mostly we say: "Here is what you are to know; it is the truth; be prepared to be tested on it." With such an orientation, one's own knowing is, at best, subordinate to prepackaged knowledge; at its worst, it is entirely dismissed. This squelches spontaneous and intuitive response to experience and thereby squelches the person, demanding that the person define himself or herself inauthentically, off center. The "Gospel according to Thomas" warns us that the consequences are dire:

> If you bring forth what is within you, what you bring forth will save you. If you do not bring forth what is within you, what you do not bring forth will destroy you. (in Pagels, 1979, p. 126)

However, when our knowing heart is welcomed, the educational orientation changes: "Here is what you need to join the feast of culture; here are some tools. Now what will you bring to the meal? What questions and knowing have you to add?"

Asking what we think or feel about something is the same as asking who we are. When students share perspectives with one another, they have an opportunity to see who they are in relation to others. Self-reflection can be evoked very simply, as when we ask eighth-graders to draw and/or write about what they are like on the inside and what they are like on the outside.

Our values betray the silhouette of ourselves. So questions such as "What would you die for?" "What would you have done if you were in the situation offered by today's lesson?" "What would your hero have done?" provide a chance for values to rise to the surface. A simple exercise such as "Sit quietly, write down five adjectives or words that describe you, share one at a time with a partner including explanations" sets a tone of self-reflection, community, and intimacy in a class. We can add another level of reflection in the same exercise by asking, "What feelings and thoughts popped up during the exercise?" "How much did you hold back?" "How risky or honest were you?" "How has your impression or sense of the person you spoke with changed due to your conversation?" I sometimes ask class members to write a poem that is intended to hint at some class lesson or experience, or write a haiku that captures an instant of existence. And nearly always, for every age, drawing is a direct route to express the inner life, giving the artist and the observer something tangible, a point of contact, to reflect on.

Asking about who we are can also come from asking what we hate, fear, or love in another person. We project our shadow, those aspects that we have not incorporated or owned, onto others. These are often revealed by our strong feelings or abject avoidance toward someone or something. When we fall deeply in love, we may be recognizing part of our shadow and projecting it on the other person. As Robert Johnson (1998) says, we unconsciously ask the other person to hold our "alchemical gold," those special and sacred parts that we have trouble owning within ourselves. We may also demonize another to hold those "negative" parts that we cannot own.

Wisdom helps to lead us to insight and epiphany, as James Joyce called it. Education then becomes not just about information or even intelligence but also equally about inspiration. Inspiration is not merely an emotional response or simple motivation but a way of knowing (Hart, 1998b). One student describes how epiphany occurred through a simple, honest act:

> My teacher asked me what I thought, what was important to me; he actually
> thought this was important, that I was important. And after years of getting
> the message that what they thought was all that was important... I began to
> trust and listen to myself. It was like being reintroduced to someone I forgot
> was there all along.

Perceiving that another person values and is interested in us sets off a profound ripple through our being, one that invites us to look at ourselves more deeply.

Our youngest students gain self-knowledge especially through their free play or experimentation with the world. Froebel (1887), the creator of the kindergarten, emphasized that play is the "self-active representation of the inner [nature]" (p. 55). For Froebel the purpose of the kindergarten is not to give the child a head start in information acquisition, although it has sometimes been co-opted to serve just this end. Instead, experimentation and play is an opportunity to bring out the inner nature, helping the student find and define him or her self accordingly. Without sufficient free space, especially psychological space, it becomes difficult to play out our inner natures. Without such experimentation, the self tends to be overly shaped from the outside, rather than drawn forth from within. Play and experimentation may reveal a sense of one's character and calling. Hillman (1996) takes up this question of calling in his exploration of the lives of many famous individuals, from Ella Fitzgerald to Eleanor Roosevelt, who seemed to demonstrate their calling from a very early age. Their genius or daimon pushed itself into embodiment. In this sense, "growing up" is actually better described as "growing down," bringing one's calling and character into the world. So self-discovery and definition are not merely a task of adolescence and adulthood, but they begin with the play of the youngest and extend to every age and level, even (and maybe especially) to the teacher. What is our calling as teachers? How do we define ourselves authentically and spontaneously?

Self-knowledge thrives when we are invited to listen to ourselves. When I was a first semester graduate student, I walked into my professor's office one day. The professor's name was Gunner and at some level I expected my ideas to be gunned down. I was sharing some half-baked idea and instead of correcting me or saying, "Yes, but..." he seemed to listen deeply and really try to understand what I meant. He asked probing but not attacking questions, reflected back his understanding, and shared some of his own ideas, not in a correction but in a mutual dialogue. I began to see my ideas in a new, less defensive way; even more significantly, I saw myself differently. I cannot fully describe the impact this has had on my life. I felt like a new person; I was heard and validated. All those years of trying to conform to someone else's "right answer" or way of being had been internalized into a very loud self-critic who drowned my own knowing to the point where I did not trust or listen to myself. Previously, most of my schooling had been drudgery. After this conversation, my motivation exploded; something was freed in that moment. I remember reading more in the one course I had with him that semester than I had in my previous four years of college, and I loved it.

As I became a therapist and a teacher I discovered that this moment in Gunner's office shaped my approach to working with others probably more than any other event; it provided a practice of centering. Specifically, I saw my most sacred task as opening and holding a space for understanding and deep meeting to occur. When we genuinely invite the other's perspective and establish a trusting and respectful relationship, a space is created. Even the space that is created by the configuration of our classroom furniture may symbolize openings and limits, private and public spaces, and direct the flow in one way or another.

Some time later, I discovered that a similar revelation had occurred in Gunner's own education many years earlier. As a high school student, he was a troubled, talented underachiever who, along with a group of others, was periodically taken by bus to visit the nearby Princeton University campus for presentations by distinguished scientists of the day, Einstein among them. One day, after a long dry talk by a physicist on a panel, a young girl wryly asked these men of science what they thought of ghosts. Two of the physicists quickly and precisely dismissed the possibility, citing a lack of hard scientific evidence. When they were finished, Robert Oppenheimer, who was instrumental in the development of the atomic bomb and later a staunch critic of its use, paused and offered a different response. He said, "That's a fascinating question. I accept the possibility of all things," and suggested that "it is necessary to find one's own required evidence" before accepting or rejecting a possibility. For Gunner, this was a revelation. Instead of closing down and accepting the world as prepackaged, Oppenheimer's perspective opened it back up to mystery, to the possibility of all things, and to one's responsibility to discover it for oneself. Gunner's "way of being" began to shift as he came to define himself from the center of his own direct experience. More than fifty years later, he remembered Oppenheimer's response as clearly as I remember Gunner's generous and genuine reply to me in his office many years ago. Since then I think have tried to stay open and honor mystery and possibility, listen, and seek my own required evidence. Essentially, these encounters opened us to ourselves and to the world.

This is often how teaching goes; we pay back and pass along the gifts given to us mostly by living them out honorably. For all of us who teach in one form or another, who were those teachers (formal or informal) who made the difference? What were those moments that opened the world up? What do we still hold dear from those epiphanies? And how well do we live and teach from the heart of those lessons learned?

Dancing with Authority

Defining oneself authentically involves rejecting authority. On the surface this, of course, appears to be a basic threat to the teacher, text, and the assistant principal. This is not to be misunderstood as thwarting the basic rules of community, established for safety, efficiency, and harmony. Instead, it means turning inward to rely on our own knowing rather than on someone else's. Remember Oppenheimer's invocation to Gunner: "Find your own required evidence." He said essentially, "Do not rely on these experts before you to find your truth. Use them, but find it yourself." This does not discard theories and experts, information and ideology, instead it dialogues and dances with them. The locus of evaluation moves inward, toward our center. It is easier to make the case for this internal movement with older students, but I suggest that we develop the capacity for ethical and intelligent choices and wise action when we ask students at every age to overcome the intimidation of authority in order to dialogue and dance with it.

There have been meaningful challenges to institutionalized authority. We have come to recognize the disproportional influences of power-knowledge-economic-discursive amalgams on our ideas (e.g., Foucault, 1980). Yet in education, we have not overcome the habit of looking primarily outside for authority, to the teachers, texts, sciences, leaders, and so forth. Unless children are weaned from this suckling on external authority, their internal decision-making and discernment skills do not mature. We teach obedience at the cost of insight and wisdom. "Being as little children" (the biblical injunction for entering heaven, a wisdom space) comes to mean compliance rather than openness to experience. When educational practice perpetuates this overdependence on external authority, students (and teachers) remain developmentally delayed in their abilities to form ethical choices, evaluate information, and understand themselves. The evaluative capacity becomes undernourished from lack of stimulation and practice. Instead of developing a capacity for discernment, we may become skilled at imposing beliefs or judgments on others because this is what has been modeled for us.

A culprit in our contemporary moral difficulties is not the lack of moral guidance (good ideas abound; God is in the bookstore) or the over-stimulation of the information age. It is, instead, in part, our habit of relying on external moral or intellectual authority, which has caused us to retard our children's skill in actively discerning value and virtue. The flood of options and images, diversity and dialogue, that comes with the postmodern era has not caused this difficulty but has exposed our weakness. Some have tried to stop the world by anchoring themselves in some doctrinal or fundamentalist-literalist solution and imposing layers of doctrine and rules upon others. Such solutions provide, at best, a moral sunscreen, a superficial response, one that does not address the underlying difficulty, the cause of the hole in the moral ozone (as my friend Mike Arons called it). The cause is our inability to center ourselves; instead, we train students to rely on institutionalized authority for their centerpoint.

It is ironic that in a society that prizes democratic values and self-determination, we have not developed a democratic-experiential approach to values in schools. The calls from our leaders are most often for imperialistic solutions driven by fear (and sometimes mere political opportunism) instead of insight. The imposition of Truth becomes an act of imperialism that, in time, breeds repression and revolution of one sort or another. It is not that the information is damaging, it is just that it is inevitably incomplete and its imposition as truth or fact is oppressive. We practice authenticity through changing the way we make choices. Teaching people how to make centered choices, like teaching people to fish instead of just giving them fish, makes ethical decision making an ongoing growth process. When we rely on the authority of some form, theory, or person, we give away the intimate experience and responsibility of choosing. When we are forced to swallow ideas whole, without question, we end up doing just that, or spitting them out entirely. When this occurs, the rift between the "moral" and the "amoral," us and them, the smart and the dumb, the obedient and the troublemakers, will grow wider.

Since the 1930s, Alfred Korzybski's dictum, "The map is not the territory," has cautioned us about relying on "maps" by themselves. However, as our ability to make all kinds of maps improved and our faith in an objective, scientifically knowable world grew, we came to rely increasingly on maps or theories as our guiding truths and became less inclined to create our own views through direct experience. The concept or map was elevated, from its position as mediator or representation of experience, to the experience itself. We became enamored with our concepts and discounted direct experience, and in so doing lost the sensitivity to and trust in experience as a valid way of knowing.

As the process of reliance on external authority becomes personally internalized, it takes the form of a dependence on theories or doctrine as opposed to dynamic experience, accepting the authority of form rather than the authority of experience. We learn to look for one right answer rather than to ask good questions, and we develop a habit of attaching ourselves to and depending on theories or externally generated forms that then shape our perceptions and experiences. The trouble comes when we replace our openness to experience with these maps or theories, failing to encounter the other in a way that keeps our maps open-ended and dynamic. Contact with the other is instead used to reinforce our theory, and "dogmatism ensues where hypothesis hardens into ideology" (Thurman, 1991, p. 59). When our theory becomes preeminent, we lose the chance to experience diversity and consequently prejudge individuals and ideas. Meacham (1990) suggests that the most significant feature of wisdom is "to hold an attitude that knowledge is fallible and to strive for a balance between knowing and doubting" (p. 181).

We help students define themselves authentically and spontaneously by helping them develop the art of dialoguing with authority. This can be approached through a balance of critical analysis and radical openness. Critical analysis and questioning (discussed in chapter 4) accepts nothing at face value. Its starting point is a kind of rejection of the surface proposition. This allows us to bounce perspectives around to see how they respond. The opposite and balance to critical questioning is what W. B. Yeats called "radical innocence." At times, in order to really understand the other (i.e., idea, person), we may need to suspend our disbelief, take a leap of faith, and uncritically steep ourselves in the other. Sometimes we have to believe (or suspend disbelief) before we can see. Such accommodation requires a profound sense of security, courage, and flexibility. But neither radical openness nor critical analysis is a final resting place for wisdom; "truth" is worked out in the dialogue between them.

Discernment also grows from centering. Judgment is the skilled use of the analytic mind to evaluate the relative merits of one thing over another. It draws largely from analysis of the present situation in light of past experiences. As valuable as this is, it remains only a partial way of knowing. Another "eye" of knowing comes more directly and quietly. The sages and mystics described it as an inner knowing, inner voice, inner guidance. Discernment involves a shift from being guided primarily by logical analysis of past experiences and by one's senses to allowing "inner guidance" to enter the dialogue. Discernment uses analysis but also includes this inner, more intuitive source. This goes beyond categories and systems of thinking to take into account the dynamic morality of the heart. Whereas the deep end of understanding frees us from our narrow prejudices, wisdom uses our inner knowing and the art of dialoguing with authority to enhance our ability to make refined distinctions.

Inner Wisdom

Wisdom is the process by which we come to know that the limited thing we thought was our whole being is not.
—Nathaniel Needle (1999, p. 12)

The consideration of self-knowledge and self-definition begs the question: What is the self that we are to know? In other words: What is the nature of our being? Educational practice follows from our assumptions about the nature of the student. If we assume the student is a blank slate or empty container, we will download upon "it"; if he or she is seen as merely the consequence of stimulus, then we will emphasize behavioral controls and external rewards and punishments; if the child is seen as a chaotic mass of unbridled irrationality, then we will seek to bridle and "rationalize" it. Yet what would practice look like if the child was seen as a spiritual being and an unfolding soul?

The self is too nebulous a concept for behaviorists; therefore they do not care much about the self but instead are interested in what we do, our behavior, stimulus and response. Cognitive behaviorists are interested in how we construct understanding and perception in the "gap" between stimulus and response. Most conventional assumptions about the self, embedded during this century in psychoanalytic psychology, equate self largely with ego, an independent rational mediating influence that navigates between a shadowy and primal unconscious (id) and the internalized moral imperatives of society (super conscious). However, just as the early maps of the globe underestimated the world, Freudian and behavioral maps underestimate the human. As these maps became dominant, especially in our educational philosophy, they served to institutionalize the underestimation of human nature.

Many traditions recognize the significance of the egoic self, but it is understood as one facet of the human, not mistaken for our whole being. For example, in Buddhism this dimension is recognized as the "lesser self." By its nature, it is insecure and may vacillate between feelings of superiority and inferiority; it attaches itself to desire, possessions, and itself. It seeks its own fulfillment at the expense of others because it views itself as separate from others. Humanistic psychology emphasizes a self that is not oriented merely by drive reduction or conditioned response, but a self that is necessarily pulled forward by creativity, compassion, and growth. Many postmodern writers suggest that the whole notion of self is a social construction and that our concern with personal identity and continuity is misplaced. For many of these thinkers, the self is better explained as a historical and cultural artifact, rather than possessing any inherent nature of itself. This critique decenters the author and fragments the self, deconstructs the subject and displaces the ego. The postmodern critique is useful and smudges the conventional maps of self, but these critiques have tended to leave us adrift in an uncharted sea.

Turning to the most holy book of the Hindu tradition, the *Bhagavad Gita*, we hear about something that is more than a singular self. Two distinct layers of the person are identified: "One should lift up the self by the [S]elf, And should not let the self down; For the [S]elf is the self's only friend, And the self is the [S]elf's only enemy" (ch. 6 v. 5, trans. 1944, p. 32). What is meant by self and Self exactly and what significance does it have for an education for wisdom? Most agree that the self represents the ego, the personality, while the Self is more encompassing; it stretches toward the universal, the One. This "big" Self is said to "lift us up," which implies a source of energy and Wisdom. At its most expansive, this is described as *atman* by Hindus, and Christ Consciousness by Christians. Many mystics and sages report the discovery of this larger Self or some facet of it. It has been called psychic being by Aurobindo, Over Soul by Emerson, Inner Man (Eckhart, 1958), inner teacher, Higher Self, and so forth. Roberto Assagioli (1973) maps layers of this realm that extends beyond the limited ego. He refers to these levels as Higher Self, Transpersonal Self and the Universal. Jung, in trying to capture the larger Self in psychological terms, refers to the Self as that part that is at once both the center and the circumference of the personality, embracing both the conscious and the unconscious (Johnson, 1998, p. 58).

The notion of a personal self, so much embedded in and reflective of modern rational-egoic consciousness, was apparently not a major concern among the ancients. They recognized and named their inner source of wisdom in a different way: as a personal guide, a Daimon, a genius, later personified as guardian angel. The task of the guide was to help one grow into the world; guides might provide insight, direction, inspiration, or warnings, as they did for Socrates. Ultimately, it may not be important whether we personify the source of this inner wisdom as a personal daimon, inner teacher, Higher Self, soul, divine immanent, or psychic being, or simply recognize it as expanding awareness. Each description may represent a facet of the Self and a way of naming the connection to inner wisdom.

Answers do not necessarily flow from opening to this awareness (remember Rilke's idea that we have to live the questions), but a sense of direction, a posture toward the world, and insight may be provided. The insight is often described as an opening of awareness that is sometimes described as a remembrance; Plato called this *anamnesis*– the soul's remembrance of truth. Rumi (trans. 1995) offers an image of this inner source of wisdom:

> There is another kind of tablet, one
> already completed and preserved inside you.
> A spring overflowing its springbox. A freshness
> in the center of the chest. This other intelligence
> does not turn yellow or stagnate. It's fluid,
> and it doesn't move from the outside to inside
> through the conduits of plumbing-learning.
> The second knowing is a fountainhead
> from within you, moving out. (p. 178)

The Wise Child

I was surprised to learn of my young daughter's untrained access to her inner wisdom, what she calls her angel. It was a typical bedtime and my daughter was settling in after a story. As I was saying good-night she noticed the cover of a book in my hand which had a picture of a child on it. She asked why I was reading a children's book and I said that it was not a children's book but a book about children, about all the ways that they see and think about the world. "Oh, you mean like seeing angels?" she said. That was not what this developmental psychology book was about, but I said, "Well, yes, I guess it could be about things like that." "I see my angel" she announced. "Do you see her now?" I asked. "Just a minute" she replied. With her eyes closed, she started to breath more deeply and initially wiggled her spine gently back and forth as if trying to find just the right spot; she seemed to be entering a gentle trance. After four or five minutes she said, "OK, I can see her now." She proceeded to describe both a visual and feeling sense of "her." I asked if I could speak with "her" and my daughter's initial reply was "Why?" After I explained my interest, she then went on to say that her angel knows my angel. An overwhelming sense of warmth came over me and I then began to pose various questions and my daughter served as a "go-between," offering sound and mature, even remarkably wise answers to my questions. When asked what her angel does for her she replied it, "It lets me know I'm loved and it helps me see better." "See clearer?" I asked." "Yes", she said. After several minutes of questioning the angel seemed to fade a bit and it seemed time for this little girl to go to sleep (see Hart, 2003).

There had been no prompting and no training; she had never been taught meditation, and we had not spoken of angels. I now think of her "angel" as perhaps a dimension of her wise Self, an aspect of innate wisdom and centeredness that is an aspect of that Self that the *Bhagavad Gita* names. It does not matter what we call it, daimon, genius, angel, Higher Self, and so forth. What does matter is that it represents a rich center of awareness, a source of loving comfort and insight, even in young children. The measure of its value and validity is the quality of the information provided and the impact it has on one's life. For her, this provided profound comfort and counsel.

Insight emerges without a personified source as well. Mary, aged forty-one, describes a moment that took place when she was eight years old:

> I was in church praying or thinking about praying. Suddenly, in a flash, I understood that I should be praying for love and wisdom. I suddenly "got" that this was the appropriate way to use prayer. This was never suggested to me or even really talked about, but this insight came to be my regular way of praying. Whenever I prayed, I prayed for love and wisdom. This was

my special secret. Even up until this moment I have never told anyone about it. Up until my late twenties I continued this style of prayer. Around the time of my marriage it changed somewhat. I started to pray to have my heart opened and ... this seems like a different version of the same theme.

Thirteen-year-old Llael accessed what she calls her guides, who provide insight, including specific information about the world or other people. We might call Llael highly intuitive. When I first interviewed her, she gave me information about me that she could not possibly have known through conventional means. She asks her guides for guidance and direction through simply listening. Kim claims to hear the internal dialogues of others in a form of deep empathy. At eight, Denise asks profound metaphysical questions and then answers them with astonishing wisdom; an award-winning sixteen-year-old writer, Michelle, describes her "most special" writing as "automatic." She says it comes "from some deep place within me" (see Hart, 2003).

As we tap into the realms of Self, we may gain access to a wide range of sources of information and guidance. Instead of cultivating repression of early profundity, openness to this inner wisdom invites refinement. Nearly all of the children (and former children) I have spoken to about these kinds of experiences were quite certain, often after a disappointing first disclosure or just a general fear, that they should keep their angles and epiphanies to themselves, lest they be humiliated or dismissed. Therefore, the deep interiority of their lives is repressed and denied or simply held forever private, ultimately without the benefit of dialogue and comparison. The result is often that the relationship with the interior world is no longer intimate but distant and strained. The firsthand directness of one's own questions and experiences are replaced by external standards, doctrines, and answers. The child's task is to swallow these and adapt to them. "Truth" and morality are imposed from the outside, doled out in the cafeteria line of values, prepackaged and processed rather than grown organically from our deep roots in dialogue and exchange with the outside. When our own profundity is not permitted space, we do not learn to center ourselves in its wise counsel. When we recognize that children have a rich spiritual life and a capacity for innate wisdom, we may no longer think of the task of education as simply downloading "truths"; instead we may recognize the task as helping to bring forth the wise Self.

Listening to Inner Wisdom

The inner voice lives in shadows and symbols, paradoxes and passions. It may send its messages not only through an angel, guide, or brilliant insight but also through a physical symptom, a serendipitous meeting, a feeling (ranging from guilt to ecstasy), a fleeting thought or image, a song that does not seem to go away, a book that jumps off the shelf, or a problem or a passion. These are offered to whomever will listen. And sometimes, it is the teacher's job to listen *for* the child.

Over a period of twenty hours a while ago, I put my shirt on backwards three times; then a tire shattered the windshield on my car as I was driving on the highway. "What is trying to get my attention?" "What am I not seeing?" I wondered. Once I paused and asked myself, I knew that I was avoiding dealing with my ailing and aging father and my feelings about him. It is not necessary or possible to prove the ultimate source of the tire or my backward shirts. We can use whatever is given as a reminder to listen and pay attention. Listening of this sort is a kind of divination that requires a dialogue with the message. We have to interact with it, work it out.

Sometimes our wise Self speaks to us through the symbolism of a dream. Jungian analyst Robert Johnson (1998) offers one of his own:

> I am standing next to a one-hundred-story building. There is no earthquake, but the building begins to collapse of its own weight. The building has been built up far higher than the underlying structure is capable of supporting. I can see the building begin to tremble, and people on the ground floor begin streaming out of the front door to escape. Then the second floor collapses downward, becoming the new ground floor. One by one, the floors come crashing down on top of the one below, in each case leaving just enough time for the people to get out safely. (p. 80)

For Johnson, this dream represented a "clear signal that my overblown psychic structure was in danger of collapsing" (p. 80).

In a classroom, I have found it powerful and playful to invite students on a search for their wise Self through the gateway of the imagination. All kinds of activities help, from journal writing to creating stories, to meditation.

When we ask, "What would your favorite wise person do in this situation?" we are seeking wise counsel. When the question is posed honestly and deeply, it can activate the energy of wisdom. Children do this all the time when they try to imagine the "right" or "cool" response in a situation. They are naturally trying to locate a source of guidance from their bank of experience; part of what occurs is that they project their inner wisdom on an outside figure as a way to see their wisdom more clearly. Wise historic figures can serve as touchstones, powerful sources with which to dialogue and activate our own internal wisdom. If we do not provide lively and viable guides through living examples or biographies, we leave students in dialogue with professional wrestlers, politicians, and other media creations that may lack substance or sufficient depth to resonate all the way to the wise Self.

Children have an innate capacity for philosophy, that is, for asking the big questions about life and being, about ethics and values, reality and death. They have a capacity for perplexity. As discussed in chapter 4, Matthews' (1980) work challenges Piagetian limits on children's cognitive capacity by suggesting that subtle and sophisticated reasoning is possible, even children of early school age. Children's openness, vulnerability, and tolerance for mystery enable them to entertain questions regarding existence and being, radical metaphysical questions. By encouraging and taking seriously the "big questions" of little people, we invite the growth of inner wisdom.

If a student possesses the capacity for inner wisdom, then a teacher does too. Aurobindo tells us that when a teacher listens to and trusts his or her Self in the service of the student's development, there occurs a meeting of psychic beings (see Marshak, 1997). This is, perhaps, the most powerful and graceful "method" that a teacher can employ. And I suspect that the great teachers do this regularly and spontaneously. They may describe it as "tuning into" or listening to or sensing what the child needs, even if it goes against common practice. They have a feeling for the soul of the child (see Hart, 1999, 2000, for a discussion of this as a form of empathy). In practice, this is a delicate act since distortion can occur through the teacher's projection or lack of accurate attunement with the child. But much of the potential danger is reduced by gently testing out hunches with the child.

These concepts of inner wisdom and the wise Self are found throughout the wisdom traditions and in the closets of our personal experience, but they are not entertained in mainstream education largely because of the underestimation of the Self. Hillman (1996) says "It is impossible to see the angel unless you first have a notion of it; otherwise the child is simply stupid, willful, or pathological" (p. 108). The point of these past few pages is to give a notion of that angel, that wise Self.

MindScience

Our thoughts first possess us. Later, if we have good heads, we come to possess them.

—Ralph Waldo Emerson (quoted in Sealts, 1992, p. 257)

Wisdom and self-knowledge involve the use of our mind and the comprehension of our heart. In order to use the mind wisely, it helps to have an idea of how it operates and how to access it. In this section, I first consider how the mind operates in two general processes. This is followed by an exploration of the relevance of the contemplative mind in the classroom. The section concludes with Experiments with Knowing, a variety of down-to-earth secular practices that can be safely applied in the classroom.

The dominant Western approach to knowledge for the last several hundred years has been largely a quest for control, predictability, and comprehension of the external and material worlds, from the atom to the atmosphere. But for some, the quest for knowledge went internal and delved into consciousness (i.e., exploring subjective experience). These interior explorers have developed maps and "inner technologies," what the Dalai Lama calls "MindScience," technology for using the mind rather than being driven by it (see Goleman & Thurman, 1991). Through such approaches, we come to possess our thoughts, rather than being possessed by them.

Typically, daily consciousness seems to function in two general modes. The most easily noticed is a steady stream of thinking composed of chronic evaluation and judgment. It deals with issues of survival and practical necessity and operates as a stream of internal dialogues. "Is this a good decision?" "Why did he say that to me?" "Can you believe she is wearing that!" "I wish I looked like that." What's in this for me?" This is the normal waking state, which involves self-protection, self-interest, and navigation through daily tasks; but it is not the only way our minds operate. All of us have had moments in which this chain of thinking abates and another process arises. This other mode involves a more free-flowing, receptive, open-ended, intuitive, nonlinear awareness. Perhaps this occurs when we are entering or waking from a dream, during a good workout, when we experience an intuitive flash or during a moment of love or appreciation, when we are absorbed in an issue, or when nature, art, or beauty grabs our attention. Wilber (1997) describes this shift in witnessing art:

Great art grabs you, against your will, and then suspends your will. You are ushered into a quiet clearing, free of desire, free of grasping, free of ego.... And through that opening or clearing in your own awareness may come flashing higher truths, subtler revelations, profound connections.... When we look at a beautiful object we suspend all other activity, and we simply are aware, we only want to contemplate the object.... We cease the restless movement that otherwise characterizes our every waking moment (p. 135).... Great art suspends the reverted eye, the lamented past, the anticipated future: we enter into the timeless present.... it suspends our desire to be elsewhere, releases us from the coil of ourselves. (p. 134)

This general kind of process has been described as receptive (Deikman, 2000), free-flow thinking (Pransky, 1998), or simply flow (Csikszentmihalyi, 1990), and is contrasted to an instrumental (Deikman, 2000) or ego-generated (Washburn, 2000) mode. Both states of mind are natural, but evaluative brain chatter in the course of daily activity generally overwhelms the non-linear state. The receptive mode seems to require our energy and awareness for it to emerge frequently. Part of us hungers for nonlinear consciousness because it is so satisfying, but we are not always sure exactly what it is or how to welcome it.

Wise people seem to find points of entry into a wisdom space. Walks in the woods, prayer, meditation, service to others, music, and so forth are common ways to invite a shift of knowing. These activities may shift attention from the normally dominant chatter of the small self and open the possibility for intuition, insight, and imagination. When this happens, awareness seems to become more spacious.

For the first-grader or the "lifelong learner," centering for wisdom involves the ability to understand and consciously use the mind. Wisdom involves awareness. We discussed the development of observational sensitivity (e.g., fully and carefully noticing an object or a scene) as a skill of intelligence. When we stretch this same skill inward and toward the center of the present moment, we cultivate an interior sensitivity, one that involves "a mindful reflection that includes in the reflection on a question the asker of the question and the process of asking itself" (Varela, Thompson, & Rosch, 1993, p. 30). This process "begin[s] to sense and interrupt automatic patterns of conditioned thinking, sensation and behavior" (p. 122); "the practices involved in the development of mindfulness/awareness are virtually never described as the training of meditative virtuosity but rather as the letting go of habits of mindlessness, as an unlearning rather than a learning" (p. 29). This involves "keeping one's consciousness alive to the present reality" (Hanh, 1975, p. 11). This is accomplished by what

Thich Nhat Hanh calls "pure recognition," which is recognition without judgment. That is, we can welcome equally all thoughts, sensations and feelings that arise by simply recognizing the presence of these things without judgment or attempts to chase them away. The result does not disengage the mind from the world; it enables the mind to be more present within the world. The point is "not to avoid action but to become fully present in one's action" (Varela, Thompson, & Rosch, 1993, p. 122). In addition, we do not replace the receding ground of the environment with the ground of the mind. That is, cognition is not reduced to being molded and shaped by an independent environment or to merely the internal generation of mind. It is instead the result of interaction, "enacted" in a dialogue, a constant interplay that does not posit an absolute ground in either the environment or the self.

As awareness develops, something else happens. The new degree of openness to experience not only encompasses one's own immediate sphere of perception but also enables one to appreciate others. An open heart, awareness of suffering, and deep compassion are regularly described as arising naturally out of the process. As we simply and honestly observe and tolerate our own reactions, we may also gain a tolerance for others. Gebser (1991) says, "Anyone with a sense of detachment from himself also gains a detachment from the world, including a sense of tolerance" (p. 531).

Opening the Contemplative Mind

How do these workings of the mind relate to the classroom? As suggested previously, contemporary education is dominated by an approach to knowing that emphasizes both the rational, which involves calculation, explanation and logical analysis, and the sensory, characterized by observation and measurement. Together this knowing forms the rational-empirical approach that has set the standard for knowing across most disciplines. However, contemplation adds a third way of knowing–a missing link–that both complements and enhances the rational and sensory. The contemplative mind is opened and activated through a wide range of approaches–from pondering to poetry to meditation–that are designed to shift states of mind in order to cultivate such capacities as deepened awareness, concentration and insight. Historically, the contemplative has been used throughout the wisdom traditions as fundamental for developing interiority and uncovering the most essential knowledge, yet it is almost entirely absent from contemporary education.

What the contemplative offers education is not a different set of knowledge so much as an expanded approach to knowing, one that engenders:

- An *epistemology of presence* that moves past conditioned habits of mind to stay awake in the here and now.
- A *pedagogy of resonance* that shapes our graciousness and spacious-ness toward meeting and receiving the world non-defensively.
- A *more intimate and integral empiricism* that includes in the consid-eration of the question a reflection on ourselves and on the ques-tion itself.

There is a long and rich history of cultivating the contemplative throughout the wisdom traditions. Contemplative practices have in-cluded meditation that has endured for thousands of years in Bud-dhism, various forms of yoga from Hindu traditions, contemplative prayer in Christianity, such as that of St. Theresa of Avila or Thomas Merton, radical questioning through dialogue such as that expressed by Plato or the self-inquiry of Ramana Maharsi, metaphysical reflec-tion of the Sufi tradition which leads to the deeper intuitive insight of the heart (*qalb*) or the deep pondering suggested in the Jewish Kab-balah. Each of these practices, and many, many more, offers an ap-proach to interrupt habitual thought routines and deepen awareness.

But in the West, the dominance of a largely Aristotelian emphasis in logic, the natural sciences and theology beginning at least by the twelfth and thirteenth centuries and consolidated in the reformation or scientific revolution helped push the contemplative out of favor (Stock, 1994). Among other influences, the industrial revolution and the modern western penchant for efficiency, speed, and productivity, as well as the race to keep up with increasing information have con-tinued to elbow the contemplative to the sidelines.

Despite (or perhaps as a reaction to) this modern bias, there is a surprisingly widespread use of contemplative practice outside of education. For example, in one recent random survey thirty percent of individuals indicated that they had meditated or tried yoga (Blum & Weprin, 2000). There also exists a large and growing body of evidence on the utility of contemplation in areas ranging from medicine (e.g., Benson, 2000; Kabat-Zinn, 1990) to spirituality (e.g., Finley, 2000;

Hanh, 1975). There is also some recent and growing appreciation of contemplative practice within higher education (Duerr, Zajonc, & Dana, 2003).

Before going farther I want to mention one concern that is sometimes seen as an obstacle to bringing contemplation to public education: Is the separation of church and state threatened by bringing approaches akin to those developed in spiritual traditions into secular education? I suggest that opening the contemplative mind in schools is not a religious issue but a practical epistemic question. It is about *how* we know, not about *what* knowledge we are giving others. Inviting the contemplative simply includes the natural human capacity for knowing through silence, looking inward, pondering deeply, beholding, witnessing the contents of our consciousness and so forth. These approaches cultivate an inner technology of knowing and thereby a technology of learning and pedagogy without any imposition of religious doctrine whatsoever. If we knew that particular and readily available activities would increase concentration, learning, well-being, social and emotional growth, and catalyze transformative learning, we would be cheating our students to exclude it. Contemplative knowing may provide just those potent offerings (Hart, 2004).

For consideration of its relevance to education, four consequences of contemplative knowing are explored below.

Presence

If you have ever found yourself having just read several pages in a book only to pause and realize that you had no idea what you just read, you know the importance of focus and attention to learning. Through such experience we understand that in learning, the *quantity* of time-on-task is subordinate to the *quality* of attention one brings to the task. If we are distracted, lost in our thoughts, or shut off in some way it is very difficult to absorb or learn well. An ability to focus, concentrate, and deploy attention is basic and essential to learning.

Nearly all contemplative practices train concentration–whether through such injunctions as repeating a mantra, focusing on love, watching the breath–in order to train the mind especially in quieting habitual internal chatter. The hundreds and even thousands of years of development of internal technologies in the wisdom traditions have something to offer contemporary learners. Without knowing another thing it would seem reasonable to explore technologies from contemplative practice if for no other reason than to help young people develop their capacities for attention and concentration, those capacities so central to learning. This may be especially valuable in a society where sounds bites, flashy images, streaming media, and living as perpetually accessible nodes on an information highway seems to be training minds for continuous partial attention (see Levy, 2006) rather than sustained and deep concentration.

Of course, such instrumental use of contemplative practice is not necessarily what the intention of a practice was originally designed for. Subtle inner changes that remain deeply personal and sometimes intangible are often described as a consequence of practice. Nonetheless, extending the application of such inner technology may prove reasonable and valuable for learning and living.

Attention, memory, learning and performance are largely state dependent–that is, the state of body, mind, and emotions are central to learning. Reading comprehension, performance on the tennis court or while playing the flute depends not only on skill level but also on state of mind and body. For example, boredom, illness, distraction, and anxiety can directly effect functioning. At a less transitory level, attachment theory shows us that over the long haul, a secure attachment to primary care giver(s) provides the emotional and neurophysiologic base or state to be eager learners, without that security our body, brain and behavior tend toward a fearful, defensive retreat (e.g., see Siegel, 1999).

One of the most well-established effects of contemplation is a change in physiological state, which in turn cascades into shifts in affect and cognition. This state change, especially as it relates to the autonomic nervous system, has been well documented for more than forty years. For example, if we ring a bell, close eyes, and focus on our breath or a sense of love we send a signal throughout the body-brain system that decreases blood pressure, lowers heart rate, reduces cortisol level (e.g., Murphy, Donovan, & Taylor, 1997). Such an immediate shift can have powerful influence on the ability to focus or be present in the classroom by reducing anxiety and helping to quiet the habitual chatter of the mind. This shift in turn allows us to either lock on to material or consolidate freshly learned material thereby avoiding retroactive interference to memory (muddling up memory with the next material). For a child who goes into vapor lock at the sight of a math problem, *"One train leaves Kansas City at 3:00 p.m. traveling eastbound at 70 miles per hour, a second train leaves Omaha at 1:30 traveling west at 45 miles per hour..."* shifts of state can dramatically change performance.

In a program twenty-five years ago I worked with students who had math anxiety. What we discovered was that their problem had little to do with deficit abilities in math and nearly everything to do with the state of mind as they approached the problem. They had a very low frustration threshold toward math and would either leap into panic or drift into a kind of dissociative fog, "spacing out." What resolved their difficulty in a few sessions was teaching some basic contemplative skills and helping them find the right state to avoid "locking down" in an anxious reaction and then providing some very basic math instruction as needed. In this sense much of education may benefit from simultaneous training in both the right *skill* set and the right *mind* set.

Detachment

William James made a distinction between the "I" and the "me." The "me" represents the contents of our consciousness—the thoughts, feelings, and sensations that rise and fall throughout our waking life. The "I" is that part of us that can watch or witness those contents. What are you aware of right now? What thoughts, feelings, and sensations do you notice? If you are able to notice then some aspect of you was doing the noticing—what James called the "I" and others have referred to as the witness or observer.

Many contemplative practices commonly describe enabling a type of detachment from the contents of our consciousness (e.g., Eckhart, 1958). This detachment is most often described not as a distant objectivism but instead as a non-defensive attitude of interest and curiosity. Several approaches instruct the practitioner to avoid reactive attachment by just being mindful of whatever thoughts or feelings emerge. This allows us to observe the activity of our minds rather than simply being absorbed by feelings or thoughts. Such arms-length distance allows us to recognize and therefore potentially interrupt usual patterns of thinking and impulsivity, freeing the mind to notice unexpected insights. For example, instead of just seething with anger, the contemplative mind may allow a little more space between the anger and us. We might both have our anger and also notice it: "Look at me being angry, what's that about?" rather than simply being lost in the anger. To notice, accept, embrace and thereby transform our anger may have significant impact on behavior. For example, in a recent study involving the effects of a meditation practice on forty-five inner-city African American adolescents, the meditating group was found to have significantly fewer rule infractions, a decrease in absenteeism, and fewer suspensions (Barnes, Bauza, &Treiber, 2003).

Being aware of the content of our consciousness is not only an important element in emotional maturity but also a marker of deepened cognitive functioning, a developmental step beyond basic abstraction. Self-observation and reflection help to expose and deconstruct positions of role, belief, culture, and so forth in order to see more deeply or from multiple perspectives. This allows students the conceptual flexibility to see beyond the information given and beyond their own presuppositions.

Creativity

In addition to developing the ability to hold and deploy attention and to witness our selves more clearly, some contemplative practices invite a kind of opening and receptivity that may result in a flow of new ideas, breakthrough insight or clarity. (Practices of silence may also lead to a deep sense of peace and spaciousness without any form or content.)

Clarity and insight come unbidden, you cannot will them exactly. *"Okay, let me have a creative breakthrough now."* But they can be wooed and welcomed and this often involves a kind of interior emptying, a sense of surrender, openness, and receptivity. Ancient Athenian philosopher Philo described his own inspirational breakthroughs in this way, "I have approached my work empty and suddenly become full, the ideas falling from a shower from above and being sown invisibly" (cited in Heschel, 1962, p. 333). Accounts such as this are quite common in the experience of creativity and inspiration (e.g., Hart, 1998, 2000). A variety of contemplative invocations from poetry, radical questioning, and certain meditations create both an opening and, as Suzuki (1970) called it, the "soft-mind" or as M. C. Richards (1962/1989) named, "a soft spot to sprout it" (p. 63). Going to the university curriculum committee or to the School Board and saying we want to develop "soft mind" might be met with a little skepticism, but this open, flexible, divergent, receptive, "soft" consciousness so essential for discovery and creativity balances the "hard" critical intellect important for verification, deduction and analysis.

Whereas breakthrough and clarity may be an outcome, silence and stillness may hint at the process. Silence helps allow the small chattering mind to settle down and recede a bit, in turn opening awareness of more subtle currents of consciousness. There is no need

to get into a metaphysical conundrum as to the source of these currents (e.g., God, our own mind, higher self, etc.) in order to recognize
their functional value. Especially as it relates to education, the value
lies in the quality of the material or insight as well as the more enduring shifts in being rather than in an attribution of source. And again,
sometimes there is silence with no content whatsoever. In some instances a subtle transformation of consciousness is claimed to take
place out of immediate awareness and without any identifiable form.
Rumi (1995, p. 109) said it this way:

> There is a way between voice and
> presence where information flows.
> In disciplined silence it opens.
> With wandering talk it closes.

The "disciplined silence" is not merely passivity or relaxation, it requires, as Rollo May (1975) said, "hold[ing]. . . [oneself] alive to hear
what being may speak. [This] requires a nimbleness, a fine-honed
sensitivity in order to let one's self be the vehicle of whatever vision
may emerge" (p. 91). Gowan (1977) makes the point this way, "When
Michelangelo did the Sistine Chapel he painted both the major and
the minor prophets. They can be told apart because, though there are
cherubim at the ears of all, only the major prophets are *listening*" (p.
250).

Resilience

Education has become increasingly involved in teaching for character,
health, and civility, reflecting contemporary societal needs. Young
people are growing into a world of unthinkable violence in schools,
where stress is implicated in the top six causes of death, where the
third leading cause of death for 10-14 year olds is suicide and the second and third leading causes of death for 15-24 year olds are homi-
cide and suicide, respectively (National Center for Injury Prevention
and Control, 2004), where millions of children are on psychotropic
medication, where constant electronic stimulation gives access not
only to dizzying amounts of information but also to sex, violence, and
sophisticated advertising.

The greater the complexity and demands, the external stressors,
the greater is the need for psychological and emotional balance and
resilience. In a state of chronic stimulation or low-grade anxiety it is
difficult to concentrate, step back and watch ourselves, be still and
silent, and maintain sensitivity toward one another. In other words,

our emotional state is significant not only for our well being but also for our capacity to learn.

Contemplative practices appear to help the individual return from and modulate a state of arousal and therefore may be valuable for emotional balance and resilience. During stress what has come to be referred to as the HPA axis (hypothalmus, pituitary, adrenal cortex) coordinates autonomic nervous system response that gets us ready for fight or flight in part by increasing levels of cortisol. But in an age of constant stimulation designed to grab our attention, shock or arouse us, not to mention the accelerated pace of the day, we may not return to an optimal baseline state. The hyper arousal of the HPA axis and elevated levels of cortisol have been related to obesity, memory deficit (Raber, 1998) even the neurobiology of suicide (Lopez, Vazquez, Chalmers, & Watson, 1997). Chronic stress or corticosterone treatment induces dendritic atrophy in the brain, which is paralleled by cognitive deficits. The good news is that contemplation reduces the level of cortisol during non-stressful events, increases response during stress and quickens the return to baseline levels (e.g., Maclean et al., 1997).

In a randomized controlled study in which participants were trained in an eight-week training program in their work place centered on mindfulness meditation (Davidson et al., 2003). Two measures were employed: 1) brain electrical activity was measured before, immediately after, and four months following the training program. 2) An influenza vaccine was given to both the experimental group and the control.

Those trained in the eight-week program showed a greater relative activation of left pre-frontal cortex (associated with "positive" affect). Additionally, there was a significantly increased immune response (antibody titers) to the vaccine among the meditation group compared with the control group. The magnitude of the increase in immune response was predicted by the magnitude in the increase in left side activation.

In addition to changes brain functioning, there is also recent research that suggests that brain structure (neuroplasticity) can literally be changed by long-term contemplative practice (see, e.g., Lazer et al., 2005; see Hart, 2009 for some summary material on brain, mind, and contemplation in education).

In the face of incredible stressors, helping students develop simple life long practices to shift consciousness and balance their emotional states, may increase their resilience, which in turn impact one's capacity to learn.

Experiments with Knowing

What we know about education is that one shoe does not fit all; students' varying learning styles, interests and capacities require variation in teaching. The same may be true in contemplation. Different paths may work better for different people. Various contemplative approaches also focus on different goals, for example, calming versus insight-oriented contemplation, each dividing into critical and creative types (Thurman, 1994). Translated into classroom goals, various approaches may evoke creative imagination, critical reflection or concentration and may use the gateway of silence, poetry, the body, or other means, as we will explore.

As I have indicated above, the contemplative mind cannot be willed, as it arises spontaneously, but it can be welcomed. What follows is a sampling of simple, "bare bones" instructions that might be modified, combined or used *as is* in the classroom. Some can be integrated with various course content, others stand on their own. They may be thought of as *experiments with knowing.* In a similar spirit as Einstein's *thought experiments* or even Gandhi's *experiments with truth,* their intent is to expand awareness and push beyond our assumptions and our sedimented habits of knowing.

While our focus is directly on *student* learning, contemplation also can nourish the teacher's own "presence" (see Miller, 1994; Solloway, 2000) and in turn influence the quality of the classroom experience. A teacher who explores his or her own contemplative mind is better able to help his or her students to do the same. The teacher-student dynamic is enhanced through this mutual exploration and we know that ultimately the teacher's own growth transforms the entire space in which education happens.

Not Doing

What we know of effective learning is that the predominant factor is not merely time-on-task; it is the quality of attention brought to that task. If our attention is somewhere else, scattered or racing perhaps, we may have little capacity to be present. Paradoxically, we may need to *not do* for a few minutes in order be more available for *doing* the task at hand.

At the beginning of a class or at a transition time I might turn the lights off and ask students to: "Take a few deep, slow clearing breaths. Let your body release and relax; let any parts of you that need to wiggle or stretch do so. Now feel the gentle pull of gravity and allow the chair you're sitting on, and the floor beneath you to support you without any effort on your part. Just let go and allow yourself to be silent and *not do* for a few minutes. You may want to focus only on your breathing, allowing it to flow in and out without effort. If you find yourself thinking, distracted, working on a problem, don't fight it, don't get stuck in it. Just allow it and you to be and redirect your awareness back to your breath, and to *not doing*. Perhaps you can imagine those thoughts or concerns to float up like bubbles from underwater. When they reach the surface they simply burst and disappear." We might add a ring of a bell, perhaps three rings to begin and one to end, in order to add to the power of ceremony that helps students to recognize this as a special time.

The moment of transition from the depth of contemplation to the action of the classroom is significant. "As you gently come back to the room you may notice the sensations of peacefulness, a clearer mind, or perhaps a feeling of centeredness. As you move through your day, even and maybe especially when things get difficult, you can take a breath and find that center again."

Following this exercise, which might last from just two or three minutes to fifteen or so, we might ask them to notice any difference before and after "not doing." They might share their experiences with one another; students are often surprised by the stream of their own thoughts. They may experiment with longer periods of contemplation and often report explorations on their own in various situations outside of class.

Where Am I Now?

A slightly different focus can also nourish self-awareness and presence. "Where are you now?" we might ask our class. "Take a few moments and just relax. Take a few deep breaths. Close your eyes if you are comfortable doing so, and tune into where you are right in this moment. Are you thinking about the day ahead? Rehashing some past experience? Caught in an emotional hangover about a situation with a friend or family member? How much of you is in your body? In your head? Floating outside you? Do you feel out in front of you? Stuck in a painful nook? Just be aware for a few moments; just noticing where you are and how that feels." After a few moments we might ask, "Now take two minutes and share your awareness with the person next to you (or in your notebook)."

Like many of these exercises, this could be extended into a daily activity outside of class. "Where am I now?" might become internalized as a kind of personal check-in, inviting self-awareness.

Deep Listening

Passive listening involves casual attention; *active listening* involves intentional focus and skills like paraphrasing and summarizing what another has said. For example, a waiter may practice repeating someone's order in order to be certain they have heard correctly. A teacher might ask his or her students to write down the important points in a teaching video or to reflect what the teacher or a fellow student just said. These are important skills of attention, but not contemplation. A third kind of listening is what I will refer to as *deep listening*.

We can help students explore deep listening with the following exercise. "Take a few deep cleansing breaths, relax, and close your eyes if you feel comfortable doing so. Take a few moments in silence to just settle in. Now listen deeply to the reading (poem, story, idea, quote, famous speech, music, sounds). (We could just as easily have them focus on a picture or piece of art or nature, or sit quietly in front of another student.) Gently open to and receive the words (picture, person, etc.) without needing to do anything to it or figure it out. Just meet these words gently, allowing them to wash over you like a warm breeze. Observe the images that arise in your mind, the feelings in your body, thoughts, emotions, meanings, sounds, tastes, movement, symbols, shapes, or anything else that arises. How does your body want to move? How does this resonate within you? What do you want to do as you listen deeply? What story can you tell about this? Sit silently for several moments and just notice without judgment."

We might reread the passage. In a few moments we can invite students to describe to their neighbor something that emerged for them—a feeling, image, question, etc. Comparing helps one notice both their own subjectivity and others' unique ways of perceiving. We might then ask, "How much came from within you and how much seems to be a common experience of the poem or picture?" As alternatives to sharing with a classmate, we could instead invite students to share out loud to the whole class or by drawing or journaling in

their notebooks or perhaps by moving their bodies as a kind of interpretive movement, and so forth.

Conventional rational empiricism trains us to pay attention to
some things and not to others, discounting hunches or feelings, for
example, in favor of certain appearances and utility–it focuses and
limits our field of awareness. Contemplation involves a softer focus
and lighter touch. The voice of the contemplative lives in these shadowy symbols, feelings and images as well as in paradoxes and passions. Understanding expands as we learn to listen to the unique
ways our inner life speaks to us and integrate the voices of the analytic and the contemplative.

I want to mention a special note about tuning into one another.
Some children are remarkably sensitive to the feelings that others are
experiencing. The ability to tune into another's inner world is very
powerful form of deep empathy (Hart, 2000). However, children (and
adults) who are empathically sensitive can get overwhelmed or lost in
others' emotions. Some students compensate by constructing a hard
exterior or find other means to try to shut off this sensitivity (Hart,
2003). Others remain overwhelmed and disoriented. However, when
we have the power of both experiencing this intensity and also witnessing it, we can take a deep breath, center ourselves, and distinguish between our own and others' experience. We then gain greater
freedom to appreciate their experience, perhaps sending them our
intention of compassionate caring, but we need not hold on to their
experience or confuse it with our own.

The Art of Pondering

The ancient Greek philosophers were bold in asking questions like
"Who are you?" "What are we here for?" Young children often naturally ask these big or radical questions as a way of trying to understand the world (Hart, 2003; Matthews, 1980). But in schools,
curricular demands and the emphasis on one right answer, often
works against depth of exploration. But pondering big and radical
questions, what Tillich (1951) named *ultimate concerns*, has the capacity of opening to unexpected insight. Using the intellect in this way to
go beyond intellectual understanding is described in a variety of traditions (see Rothberg, 1994). In the classroom we might pose and invite questions on:

• Big things. "What is life about?"

- Both local and distant influences. "What would make your school, the world, your parents, the universe better?" "What do you wonder about and worry about?"
- Ethics. "How do you know what's the right thing to do?" "What would you do if you were the president, the principal, the parent?"
- Identity. "What is the most important thing about being you? What's the most fun?" "What will your life be like in ten years?" "What would you like as your epitaph?" "Who are your heros?"
- New perspectives. "I wonder what the world looks like through an ant's eyes, a Martian's, a terrorist's?" "I wonder what your parents think about when you're not around?" "What if you had a week to live?"

In an exam or in a class discussion, simply asking for the questions that the student would ask about the topic, what they are curious about, what they really want to know but have been afraid to ask, serves as another means to loosen the lock of pre-determined answers on the process of knowing.

With most topics, there is an opportunity to create the dynamic tension of ambiguity that can lead to unexpected knowing. We do this when we lead off the lesson with an honest question that has no simple preset answer.

Holding paradoxical or contradictory perspectives long enough may frustrate and transform normal thinking. For example, we might invite students to ponder the idea that light operates both as waves and as particles, or the conflicting issues of fairness involved in a contemporary issue such as affirmative action. Could we take both the position of the disadvantaged youth as well as the privileged child who was denied admission to college in spite of his or her higher performance? The point is not to win an argument as in a debate; it is to see beyond the various sides in order to take in the whole of the issue and to synthesize a larger perspective. As mentioned previously, traditions ranging from Chinese and Indian philosophy to Heraclitus, from Hegel's dialectics to quantum physics and Zen Buddhism have used paradox to open knowing.

A Wisdom Walk

Guided imagery taps the symbolic or metaphorical aspects of the contemplative mind. Unexpected imagery and insight is often the result.

"Take some deep breaths, settle into your seat, close your eyes, and relax. Imagine yourself in a comfortable scene in nature, feel the soft breeze, notice the smells, the temperature on your face, the color of the sky, the feel of the ground beneath you, and the feeling in your body. Take a few moments to be still and sense all that you can in this pleasant and comfortable scene. Now off in one direction notice a well-worn path leading into the distance toward some woods. Follow the path and continue to notice the texture of the ground underfoot, the sounds near and far, the light, the vegetation, the wildlife, and the smells as you move further and further along the path. The path narrows as it winds its way deeper into the woods. You cross over a brook, perhaps pausing to listen and feel the water and then continue along the path. Soon the path emerges out of the woods and opens into a bright hilly meadow. Walk back into the bright light and notice a magnificent old tree on the hillside. Walk to the tree and sit under it for a few moments, appreciating its magnificence. The tree may have a message for you; listen and feel it's offering to you. Note the words, images, and feelings that arise. If you would like you can continue on around the hillside and discover that it becomes rockier, almost cliff-like on the far side. Among this rock you may notice a strong doorway. You approach and enter surprised to find a few steps leading to a gently lit curved room filled with other doorways. If you would like you can pick one and look inside. You don't need to go in. You can just observe from the opened doorway. Take a few moments in silence if you would like. When you're ready, consider if there is any lesson or knowledge that is offered. In a few moments it will be time to close the inner door, exit the way you came in back out onto the hillside. Return around the hill stopping back at the tree for a moment, listening. Then follow the path back the way you came, through the woods, crossing the brook and eventually back to the pleasant place where you started the journey. Know you can return to this place and to anywhere you visited on your own when you would like. Now it is time to come back fully. Give me a glance to let me know you have arrived back into the classroom. In a moment let's share some of our experiences (or write them in a journal). How many were able to find a place to start with? How many found a tree? Did the tree have anything for you? Who found a doorway? What did you see? Was there anything unexpected (scary, fun, confusing, helpful, etc.)? What did you take away?"

This can be a powerful experience for some and so it is important to follow up with anyone who seems unusually agitated. For a lighter version we could skip the doorway and simply linger with the tree. Alternative travels such as a journey to a wise woman or man, climbing a mountain (perhaps representing some struggle), visiting a special or sacred site or any number of images that can tug on our inner knowing.

Body Focusing

While knowing is most often associated with the head, both the ancients and contemporary neuroscience supports the idea of a body-wide mind. Researcher Candance Pert (1986) discovered that endorphins and their receptor sites, once thought to exist only in the brain, are present throughout the body. The reason, she suggests that we speak of gut feelings, is because the mechanisms for feeling in the gut are already in place. Research on energy cardiology and cellular memory in heart transplant patients, suggest knowing and memory may be contained in an energy-information system associated with the heart (e.g., Pearsall, 1999; Russek & Schwartz, 1996). Shifting awareness to the body may help to open to a state past the analytic.

One simple technique has already been employed successfully in schools. I'll paraphrase the instructions: "Take a few deep breaths and settle into your seat. As you relax bring your attention to the area of your chest, that place inside where you have experienced the feelings of love, care or appreciation. Pretend you are breathing slowly through the heart–five seconds in, five seconds out. Do this a few times and then breathe naturally, maintaining focus on your heart. Now remember a feeling of appreciation you have for someone now or from the past or focus a fun or joyful time in your life, bringing the feeling to you. Once you have felt this, you may want to radiate that appreciation to yourself and others. If distractions arise in your mind, simply bring the focus back to the area of your heart" (Childre & Martin, 1999).

Eugene Gendlin's (1988) focusing technique is another method for cultivating body awareness. Very briefly, his fundamental exercise begins by asking us to create a silent and relaxed space within us. I will condense and paraphrase some of his instructions:

1) "Pay attention inwardly, in your body, see what comes there when you ask, 'What is the main thing for me right now?' or 'How is my

life going?' Let the answers come slowly from this sensing. When some concern comes, rather than entering into it, stand back and just acknowledge it. Wait again and see if other concerns or topics arise.

2) From among what came, select one thing to focus on. Sense what the whole issue feels like without going inside it. Let yourself feel it all.

3) What is the quality of this unclear felt sense? Let a word, or image or whatever arise (e.g., tight, spacey, jumpy). Go back and forth between the felt sense and the word or image. Check how they resonate with each other. Is there a bodily signal that lets you know that it's a fit? Let the felt sense as well as the word change until they feel just right in capturing the quality of the felt sense.

4) Now ask yourself: 'What is it about this whole issue that makes this quality?' Sense that quality word or image again. 'What makes this whole problem so _____?' Be with this feeling until you sense a shift, a slight give.

5) Receive whatever comes gently and openly. Stay with it for a while; you may find other shifts; perhaps your first shift comes later" (pp. 43-45).

As a tiny way of shifting consciousness, my daughter's first-grade teacher had her students take off their shoes and let their feet feel and spread over the ground. She has them stand up to do some stretching and simple breathing exercises akin to martial arts or yoga, although her teacher had no background in these techniques and developed them quite spontaneously in response to what she felt her young charges needed. She will do this before exams and any time the classroom needs a little shift in energy or mood. While we might not consider this contemplation *per se*, it does shift awareness, discharge tension and help students be more present in their bodies. This is precisely the direction of body-centered knowing. By the way, her students love these interludes.

Concentrated Language

Within poetry lives the gift of metaphor and image. These words stretch out normal perception and can open surprising connections and unexpected depth even in young children. The play of rhythm, sounds and meanings of the concentrated language of poetry, both writing it and listening to it, can draw out the contemplative mind.

I have sometimes asked students to write a haiku poem, a 5-7-5 count, sixteen-word, three-line work that is intended to capture a moment. The open attention to that moment and the practice of capturing it in words can be a dramatic shift in normal thought and awareness. Most haikus: a) are acute observations of nature, b) use simple language, presenting objects rather than describing them, c) often contain an object, time and place, d) embody a sense of stillness or harmony by the blend of object, time, and place, e) often present a new discovery or insight in the third line (Inspirational, 2001). For example, a fifth-grade boy wrote,

> Butterfly awaits
> As it calls for another
> With a fountain of color. (p. 39)

Sometimes I'll change the rules and ask them to describe themselves or a particular issue using this format. But any form of concentrated language or imaging has the potential for practicing intensive awareness and opening the contemplative mind. We might invite students to write a poem about current events or their own life, or the world through the eyes of a terrorist or a historical figure that we happen to be studying. For other curriculum ideas, the *Language of the Awakened Heart* (Inspirational, 2001) offers a series of poetic exercises that have been refined in elementary and middle school classrooms. And Charles Burack (1999) describes his use of contemplation and poetry in his university-level courses.

Freely Writing

Writing involves two main processes: vision–inspiration, flow of ideas, etc. and revision–editing and crafting. These require two different and complementary cognitive operations. A process approach to writing (e.g., Elbow, 1998) may serve as a contemplative act in itself. For example, we might invite students to, "Take a few deep breaths, close your eyes, relax and then with eyes reopened, write everything you possibly can about a particular topic (perhaps a class assignment, a reaction to the day's reading assignment, a current event, their upcoming paper). Let the feelings, the wisdom, the struggle, or whatever emerges, flow onto your paper. Write the heart of what you want to say. Free write it, with no concern for spelling, grammar, judgment or logical coherence. Just go with the flow. If you are not sure where to start, write, "I'm not sure where to start" and keep writing, without putting down your pen. You have ten minutes."

Afterward, you might invite the students to share how they felt doing that task, or ask them to read one sentence of their writing to another student. Perhaps they take that sentence and write for another five minutes, seeing where they go next in a rhythm oscillating between flowing and focusing, diverging and converging.

Keeping a journal is another way to explore the inner world and build confidence in writing. We might ask students to reflect on a controversial problem discussed in class or a powerful speech or poem. "The invitation is to find a cozy space, take some deep breaths, and free write (or draw) about whatever arises from your reading or the topic at hand. Don't figure out what you're going to write but just let it flow as quickly and freely as you can." You might invite them to assume the voice of a character in a story, a historical figure, nature, or an animal.

There are also plenty of journal writing exercises designed explicitly for self-exploration, including questions like: "What would you like your life to be?" "What are the relationships like in your life? Write down names of each and then free write about each" (e.g., see Progoff, 1992). Visual journaling is another powerful way to move into the contemplative and past the confines of words (see Ganim & Fox, 1999, and Cameron, 1992). Adding a drawing or other artistic dimension can shift the perspective and potentially open the contemplative space in a great many learning situations.

The Natural World

Moments of ecstasy are most frequently reported as occurring in, or being "triggered" by nature (Laski, 1968). There is a resonance with the natural world that is particularly powerful in evoking moments of wonder, which involves opening the contemplative space. Louv (2005) suggests that the current generation of children may be on the verge of a kind of nature-deficit disorder as the result of over-scheduling, the seduction of electronic stimulation, and the loss of uncontrolled natural areas to explore and freely play in. This loss of touch with the natural world may have significant consequences for development.

Rather than offering an exercise here I want to simply name the power of a genuine encounter with nature as a source of contemplative opening and deep learning. I can think of no better way to do so than through Thomas Berry's own words. Berry is a pioneer in the field of spirituality and ecology. His work emphasizes human interconnection with the earth as recognized through a profound sense of reverence.

As a child of eleven Berry's awareness opened in some inexplicable way and formed a centerpoint for the moral orientation that he claims has endured throughout his life. His family was having a new home built at the edge of a small town. Downhill from the house was a small creek and across the creek was a meadow. Berry (2000) recalls:

> It was early afternoon in late May when I first wandered down the incline, crossed the creek, and looked out over the scene.
>
> The field was covered with white lilies rising above the thick grass. A magic moment, this experience gave to my life something that seems to explain my thinking at a more profound level than almost any other experience I can remember. It was not only the lilies. It was the singing of crickets and the woodlands in the distance and the clouds in a clear sky. It was not something conscious that happened just then. I went on about my life as any young person might do. Perhaps it was not simply this moment that made such a deep impression upon me. Perhaps it was a sensitivity that was developed throughout my childhood. As the years passed, this moment returns to me and whenever I think about my basic life attitude and the whole trend of my mind and the causes to which I have given my efforts, I seem to come back to this moment and the impact it has had on my feeling for what is real and worthwhile in life.
>
> This early experience, it seems, has become normative for me throughout the entire range of my thinking. Whatever preserves and enhances this meadow in the natural cycles of its transformation is good: whatever opposes this meadow or negates it is not good. My life orientation is that simple. It is also that pervasive. It applies in economics and political orientation as well as in education and religion. (pp. 12-13)

Inspired by Berry's work, *The Center for Imagination, Education and the Natural World* near Greensboro, North Carolina, is doing wonderful work with teachers and students in opening the contemplative mind through the natural world.

In using any of these exercises or in creating new ones, the contemplative mind in the classroom can be welcomed effectively with: a) *Ceremony.* We can convey a sense that this time is special perhaps by turning off the lights, using a slower, calmer voice tone, perhaps a bell or music. b) *Metaphor.* While the analytic lives in logic, the contemplative is invited through images, feelings, metaphor and stories. c) *Inner silence.* Providing an invitation to turn inward and just notice in silence is a dramatic contrast to the outward focus of the typical school day. Silence creates gaps in our normal thought and activity routine and can coax the contemplative to surface. *d) Intention.* The clarity of intention that is brought to an experiment–for example, "not doing," seeking clarity on an issue, simply beholding and appreciating, sending love and compassion, can help to concentrate the energy of contemplation. e) *Path*. Different students may respond to different approaches; one shoe may not fit all. f) *Community*. Contemplative experiments in a classroom have the advantage of drawing upon the energy of a group. Practitioners have both the chance to compare notes and also focus and feed off the energy of one another; often this nourishes empathy and in turn community. g) *Carrying forth*. If the body of contemplative practice is opening and centering the mind, the limbs are bringing this awareness to our daily encounters. Within contemplative knowing there is sometimes a sense of centering, clarity, "a still point of a turning world," as T. S. Eliot (1971, p. 16) named it or perhaps an inner source of wisdom and creativity. We can remind students that with a deep breath they can draw upon the nourishment and clarity of the contemplative mind as a touchstone throughout the day.

These handful of experiments mentioned above provide opportunities to activate, integrate, and normalize contemplative knowing in the classroom. Bringing contemplative practice to the classroom is not exactly bringing something new to children. Children–young children especially–are natural contemplatives. They ponder big questions, they daydream, they fall in wonder with nature, they reflect on their own existence, and find silence in their "special spot," perhaps under the arms of an old tree. However, the demands for constant activity, the habit of electronic stimulation and the production orientation of modern society make it very difficult to keep the contemplative alive, leaving children (and teachers) unbalanced in their ways of knowing and often losing touch with the inner landscape. Contemplative techniques offer both a portal to our inner world and an *internal technology*–a kind of *mindscience*–enabling us to use more of the mind rather than be driven by habitual responses or emotional impulsivity.

Long dormant in education, the natural capacity for contemplation balances and enriches the analytic. It has the potential to enhance performance, character, and depth of the student's experience. Perhaps most importantly, the contemplative helps to return the transformative power of wonder, intimacy, and presence in daily learning and daily living (Hart, 2004).

CHAPTER 7

THE PROCESS AND PARADOX OF TRANSFORMATION

We do not believe in a power of Education. We do not think we can call out God in man and we do not try.
—Ralph Waldo Emerson (1972, p. 290)

To transform is to go beyond current form. This means growth, creation, and evolution, an expansion of consciousness. When education serves transformation, it helps to take us beyond the mold of categories, the current limits of social structure, the pull of cultural conditioning, and the box of self-definition. We have the potential to "exist in such a way not only to comprehend the facts of our lives but also to transcend them" (Peden, 1978, p. 211), and this is where the deepest moments in education lead.

Transformation manifests as both an outcome and a process; it is the push and the pulse that drives self-organization and self-transcendence. As Jantsch (1980) states,

> Self-transcendent systems are evolution's vehicle for qualitative change and thus ensure its continuity; evolution, in turn, maintains self-transcendent systems which can only exist in a world of inter-dependence. For self-transcendent systems Being falls together with Becoming. (p. 11)

Drawing from Zen master Sasaki Roshi, Puhakka (1998) summarizes the transformative impulse: "All things that arise are incomplete but have in them the character of striving for completeness" (p. 139). Transformation is a movement toward increasing wholeness that simultaneously pushes toward diversity and uniqueness, becoming more uniquely who we are, and toward unity, recognizing how much we have in common with the universe and even recognition that we are the universe. In this way, self-actualization and self-transcendence do not contradict one another; instead they form part of the same process. We actualize our ever-expanding potential by transcending current self-structure. Thus, Maslow (1968) preferred the active term self-actualizing, which depicts an ongoing process, as opposed to self-actualization, which implies an end-state.

Transformation emphasizes liberation, fluidity and flexibility, movement and freshness, destruction and creation. However, these seem far from contemporary education's emphasis. Instead, "conventional schools work primarily for the purposes of limiting consciousness and reality to the current norms and defining power relations among the next generation" (Marshak, 1997, p. 215). Today's schooling largely trains for adaptation to the status quo (as does much of psychotherapy); we seek to produce well-adjusted students (and clients) who can "fit in" and fulfill our expectations of them in the workforce and the classroom. And while adaptation has its place, it is incomplete and confining: "If your ideal is adjustment to your situation ... then your success is likely to be just that and no more. You never transcend anything. You grow but your spirit never jumps out of your skin to go on wild adventures" (Bourne, 1977, p. 334).

Transformation is the process of creation, regeneration (a task of personal re-formation, as Swedenborg [1985] describes it), and liberation or freedom (Tagore, 1961) to undertake that re-formation consciously. We might even call it a process of resurrection, a "migration into newness... and a revealing of what truly exists" (Pagels, 1979, p. 12), as the gnostic Christians implied. This refers to an opening up of consciousness, "waking up" in Gurdjieff's words (see Tart, 1987).

The dynamic of personal transformation creates energy that often catalyzes growth extending beyond the individual. Interdependence at all levels reminds us that social structures (e.g., slavery), cultural beliefs or values (e.g., prejudice), and consciousness of the universe as a whole may be changed as the ripple of individual transformation grows to a wave. Gandhi's personal awakening to injustice led to the transformation of a society; when a drunk driver killed one mother's child, she began an organization, Mothers Against Drunk Driving (MADD), that has helped to change attitudes and legislation about driving and sobriety. When enough women gained "liberation" individually, the momentum helped a great many more to overcome gender oppression, and this has helped to shift oppression of the feminine even within the cultural unconscious. In this way, the microgenetic arc that I have outlined in this book serves ontogenetic development (the development of the individual) and phylogenetic development (the evolution of the species and the world). And this movement starts with a shift in consciousness. As Vaclav Haval, the playwright who became the first democratically elected President of Czechoslovakia understood, "Consciousness precedes being... without a global revolution in the sphere of human consciousness, nothing will change for the better in the sphere of being as humans" (quoted in Palmer, 1998, p. 21).

Personal transformation comes both from earthquakes in our worldview and from tiny sparks that offer a glint of insight. Form is transformed through an infinite number of events that might include:

- A child learning to spell her first words;
- Facing and overcoming a fear of speaking in public, asking someone out for a date, or resisting the pressure to conform when it does not seem right;
- Expressing ourselves successfully through writing or dancing;
- Speaking a "true word," not just an accurate or self-serving one. Perhaps this happens as we point out and do not participate in some small unkindness that diminishes another, speak clearly in the face of some injustice;
- Loving someone and receiving the love of another;
- Facing our personal limitations squarely and honestly, even loving and accepting them for their offerings of humility and compassion;
- Learning about a foreign country or how birds fly;
- Sitting with conflict just long enough for it to yield it's fruit;
- Saying "no," for example, when we assert our conscious power over something or someone that drags us down;
- Saying "yes" to life, implying a willingness to be here fully;
- Giving anything freely;
- Being present.

The question is not whether transformation happens: it does. We change and grow. Instead, the question is whether we can help it along. Can we create an education that invites, even nudges transformation? Can we listen for that impulse of creation or that inner teacher that orchestrates growth?

In and of itself we could claim that the act of creation (in art, of the universe, of the thought and quality of our life in this moment) is synonymous with transformation. It is the current that moves us along: the fire that burns within us, as Krishnamurti (1974, p. 47) described it.

Whitehead implied that creation is the category necessary to understand all other processes. That is, creation is the basic process of existence.

Creativity is a tangible and reproducible symbol of transformation, transcendence, and creation. We might even recognize it "as the humble human counterpart of God's creation" (Arieti, 1976, p. 4). The creative wave of transformation is not confined to paint and poem but involves who we are and how we live. In other words, this includes one's own self-creation. Education for transformation is about "train[ing] the individual in the process of creative self-sculpture" (Gokak, 1975, p. 145). We can both reach toward oneness and also become embodiments of the divine expression, in each moment:

> Beauty is life when life unveils her holy face.
> But you are life and you are the veil.
> Beauty is eternity gazing at itself in a mirror.
> But you are eternity and you are the mirror. (Gibran, 1968, p. 76)

Creative activity provides a touchstone for the act of teaching/learning. Any activity is creative that involves freshness of thought or perception, offers provocation and opportunities to stretch our selves, or helps develop tools of the mind. The most straightforward assessment for transformative learning may simply be the degree to which the student's creativity is engaged and current limits (of skill, thought, values, expression, etc.) are challenged. In addition, since we know that the teacher teaches not just a subject but especially who the teacher is, does the teacher's own expression of creativity and personal challenge express itself in some way? As teachers, do we nourish our own growth? If we do, it is likely that we are setting a wave of transformation in motion that will affect our students as well as ourselves. We deny transformation and creation by not paying attention to the inner significances of our lives.

Transformation is a dialectic of expression and reception, contraction and expansion, self-separateness and union, autonomy and interconnection, intention and surrender, initiating and allowing, control and flow, structure and freedom, and so forth. These are the yin and yang, or the masculine and feminine principles that underlie human growth throughout the lifespan. The dynamic interplay gives transformation its energy. For example, genuine creativity involves both perspiration (hard work, preparation, intention, etc.) and inspiration (receptivity and communion with some vision). One moment or one era (e.g., see Kegan, 1982) may be dominated by agency and independence and the next by receptivity and relationship. In the microgenetic moment, we may leap from one instant of willfulness (e.g., intending to meet another person or idea as directly as we can) to willingness (e.g., letting go of our defensiveness and preconceptions in order to commune deeply with the moment). The energy for growth is activated by this dynamic interplay. From a limited perspective these appear bipolar, but from another point of view they emerge as different aspects of the same wave, an undivided unity.

In this final chapter I examine the dialectic of will and willingness as a basis for transformation. This is followed by an exploration of how freedom is tied to facing fear, self-discipline, responsibility, and the transformation of time and space through a curriculum of inner significances.

Will and Willingness

The problem of personal mastery and self surrender exists in every moment of choice.... Willingness and willfulness become truly possible every time we truly engage life. The alternative is apathy, a dulled state of existence, a cloud of semiconsciousness responding reflexively and automatically—barely even noticing that we are alive.

—Gerald May (1982, p. 5)

Will and willingness provide the active or functional principles of autonomy or agency on the one hand and communion on the other. Transformation involves holding a space or engaging in a dialectic between will and willingness. Ignatius Loyola, founder of the Jesuits, captured part of the paradox of these dimensions: "We must pray as if all depends on Divine Action, but labor as if all depended on our own effort" (quoted in May, 1982, p. 208). How do we balance these directives both to surrender (prayer involves both intention and surrender) and to labor, and how do we cultivate each in the service of transformation?

Will represents the power of intention that throws or holds back our weight, our heart, and our effort, in one direction or another.

Without sufficient will, we lack the self-discipline that allows us to move, or to stop moving, at our own bidding. Will or agency involves standing on our own and taking care of ourselves through the choices we make. Will involves directing and coordinating energies in such activities as tying a shoe, asking a question, or writing a sentence. It also involves self-control, as when we refrain from leaping out of our seat in anger or indulging in a destructive whim. Will involves not only what we do on the outside but also and especially how we hold ourselves on the inside.

Will can seek mastery, self-assertion, self-protection; it sets boundaries, setting oneself apart from another. It allows us to direct our focus and our effort instead of simply being buffeted by inner impulses or reacting to external circumstances. It serves creativity and transformation because it allows us to throw our effort toward our vision and coordinate our activity.

> The true purpose of the will is not to act against the personality drives *to force* the accomplishment of one's purposes. It has a *directive* and *regulatory* function; it balances and constructively utilizes all the other activities and energies of the human being without repressing any of them. (Assagioli, 1973, p. 10)

Alone the will has no values; it can dominate another or direct a kind action. However, the will can turn willful, becoming the will to power and domination, as Nietzsche and others have shown. Understanding, love, and compassion temper the will; will without love becomes manipulation. This is why the development of understanding (chapter 5) is essential, otherwise we grow to be personally powerful manipulators. Jung (1916/1963) argues that where love is preeminent, the will to power disappears, but when love is lacking, power predominates.

Assagioli (1973) tells us that the awareness of the Self and the will becomes easily submerged by the constant surge of drives, desires, emotions, and ideas. He suggests that there are three stages toward the activation of will. The first is recognition that the will exists; the next is the realization that one has a will; and the final stage is the awareness that one *is* a will, a living subject who is responsible and powerful. Recognition of the will is unpredictable. On the one hand, we may make a choice against the impulse of some desire, saying "no," or on the other hand, we may move fully toward some conscious goal. We sometimes can feel the energy of will rising within us as we express determined action and make physical or mental effort, as when we work past our frustration or comfort zone, whether in working on a mathematics problem or jumping off a diving board. This is part of the reason why students must be appropriately challenged. If we can pitch our assignments just above the edge of their grasp they will be challenged to stretch and activate the will. Some years ago, I regularly took groups of high school students on a hiking trip in the High Peaks of the Adirondack Mountains. It provided an enjoyable weekend in the wilderness for some. But for others, those who had to really struggle and push themselves past their comfort zone in one way or another, a new degree of personal power was gained. This was not power over another person or even over the mountain but over a sense of limitation. This is one key item of learning that Outward Bound programs foster. Athletics, problem solving, even having to write a term paper or complete some other project, when pitched just at the right level, provide challenge and an opportunity to coordinate the qualities of will: energy, mastery, concentration, determination, persistence, initiative, and organization (Assagioli, 1973, p. 19).

Employing the will to regulate expression is the practice of wise control; it is not restrictive or prescriptive but spontaneously and situationally determined. In one situation, withholding one's impulse to respond angrily may be most helpful; at another moment, the use of anger as moral fire may serve as a catalyst to nudge a situation. Sometimes our will arises when something or someone pushes us to a limit. Stella, eleven, lived with her mother and stepfather. The stepfather would regularly beat the girl, often severely. After one such beating, Stella sat down on the living room couch next to her stepfather. As they both looked straight ahead, she calmly asked, "Do you know the big knife in the kitchen? I want you to know that if you ever touch me again that I will get that knife and will kill you with it in your bed at night." The stepfather never touched her again. The girl has grown into a successful professional helper and healer. In that clear moment, she discovered and expressed power through her will. But it is difficult to say exactly where that impulse emerged from; why did she take control of her life at this moment? While the will was the powerful vehicle for this expression, the impulse emerged from some small voice within her.

There is closeness between the will and the Self. As we come to understand ourselves as not merely having a will but even being a will, we come to see ourselves as responsible for our lives, "this culminates in the existential experience of pure self- consciousness, the direct awareness of the Self, the discovery of the 'I'" (Assagioli, 1973, p. 11). This helps to tease apart the "I" and the "me" as William James (1950) put it. That is, one recognizes the "I" (which comes very close to the understanding of "being a will") as distinct from the contents of consciousness (e.g., emotions, feelings, thoughts, impulses). As we center ourselves in the "I," we gain the ability to see more clearly and dis-identify with reactions, drives, and desires (e.g., I may have an emotional response or thought, but I am not that thought or feeling). Thoughts, feelings, and so forth can then be claimed as ours, but they are not us.

The power of will alone is insufficient to sustain transformation. In our modern egoic-rational consciousness, there is a sense that if I only will enough, strengthen myself enough, work hard enough, learn enough, I will take complete charge, mastering my destiny and controlling my situation. We may become obsessed with control, get anxious and angry when the unexpected happens, or, on the other hand, abandon any attempt at control altogether and hide from re-sponsibility. Personal will is essential but incomplete; it allows us to engage in the battle but does not show us how to give up the struggle. It seems other forces operate in creation that carry us this way or that, open some doors and close others. Whatever we name these forces (chance, synchronicity, evolution, karma, fate, God, chaos, etc.), they do not seem to bend very well to our will. As Gerald May (1982) ex-plains, "the fundamental problem with the act of surrender is not knowing how the individual will relates to the will of mystery" (p. 35).

Will defines us as self-separate from our world; its highest func-tion comes from providing a sense of detachment, not only from the world but also from the contents of our own consciousness. Willing-ness or surrender, on the other hand, says "yes" to belonging; it joins life as we give ourselves over to a certain flow. This leans toward communion and unity. The wise use of the will can move us to the edge of aligning with these currents, but joining with them occurs as a consequence of surrender. This has been described as aligning with the Tao, the life force, mystery, God's will, the divine will, transper-sonal or universal will, the Over Soul, and so forth. It is explained with such paradoxical phrases as "choiceless willing" or is named as impersonal, implying not some cold sterile detachment but a choice that takes us beyond the merely personal and individual. Eckhart (1981) says that such "detachment compels God to love me" (p. 286).

Gerald May (1982) writes that the desire for surrender provides the wellspring of our deepest hope. Surrender is an act of faith and a statement of hope. It arises out of both deep trust and also great desperation, when we are brought to our knees to ask for help. In either case, we let go of control for a moment.

Our normal waking ego-centered consciousness accustoms us to seeing before believing; however, at times it appears necessary to believe before we can see. This means letting go of preconceived assumptions and suspending disbelief. When we suspend self-doubt for a moment, we accomplish the impossible. When we forget why we hated our neighbor, we may see him as worthy of our appreciation. When we accept the possibility of all things, as Oppenheimer said (chapter 6), then all things become possible. Trust builds a bridge between the known and the unknown and then allows us to temporarily cross into the other world. Faith does not manifest itself as acceptance of some dogma; instead it involves a willingness to go past the current limits of our knowing. The new world (i.e., that yielded by transformation) may not be revealed or reached without surrender and faith.

As a simple example of the play of will and surrender, let me confess one of my unintended mantras; it emerged spontaneously—one of those phrases that popped up one day and stuck around for several months. In a period of particularly strong self-doubt, confusion, and lack of direction with regard to a project (an enterprise I tried to muscle my way through but succeeded only in making myself more frustrated), I paused, sat quietly, and asked for a way out. There was no bargaining, just a genuine request for help born of exhaustion and frustration. Almost immediately a phrase popped into my mind: "Sing the song that sings in you." For me, this became a mantra that served as an antidote to the density of worry, doubt, confusion, and the struggle to "figure out" my way through a problem or through my world. When I listened, what emerged was a feeling of "settling in" and trusting, instead of willfulness and worry. While extremely simple and perhaps even a little corny, this feeling entirely transformed both the project and my relationship to it. During the next couple of months, I would find myself regularly falling back into a sense of being blocked, confused, and doubtful, but as soon as I settled in and asked for help, this same mantra would emerge and almost instantly my awareness would open and the block and fog would clear. In a sense, this was engaged by my will, I asked the question in my mind, but a subtle and humble release occurred, a giving up that allowed a shift in consciousness to take place.

Letting go is paradoxical in the sense that we must be intentional (involving the will) as we move toward it, but we release control in the moment of surrender. Heidegger (1966) referred to this as "releasement," and Taoism calls it *wuwei*. It occurs subtly, unexpectedly, often with a "give." However, our overly willful, in-control cultural norms often exclude the possibility of constructive surrender.

Willingness is often associated with a kind of cleansing and clearing. Swedenborg describes the cleansing of his own mind in the following way: "This meant that my head was being put in order, and is actually being cleansed of all that might obstruct these thoughts" (Blackmer, 1991, p. 17). This is a profound reorganization of being, a clearing of the baggage obscuring the heart and mind. Underhill (1911/1961) describes this activity as self-knowledge or purgation, the second stage preceding illumination in the typical development of the Christian mystics she studied (e.g., Teresa of Avila, Eckhart, Boehme, Dante). This cleansing and awareness is also described in her fourth stage, the dark night of the soul or surrender, which represents an even more profound purification leading to mystical union. The normal rhythm of human development, including spiritual development, involves regularly shedding our snakeskin of knowledge, attachments, and identity to make room for expansion into a larger perspective and identity. Wisdom treats the self as a shell, a costume, a transitional object, a vehicle but not a driver, a lease, not a purchase for eternity. The mystics and many sages encourage us not merely to defend our position and our self but regularly and naturally to clean house, sloughing off rigid identify, reworking knowledge, refining intellect and understanding, transcending and including aspects of the self. (This includes developing appropriate ego strength but without ego fixation.) Transformation requires conscious alignment with this rhythm, which is very different from the amassing of armaments of information and the one-sided fortifying of self that characterizes our culture.

Embedded in this activity of creation is destruction. The old way, form, limit, concept is often destroyed and used as rich compost for creation. Something is lost and something gained in transformation and we are not always willing to give up our security, whether it is a cherished idea about the world or a perception of ourselves. In this sense, surrender may even be thought of as a mini-death. "Consult your death," Thomas Merton (1974) advised, because when we deeply experience impermanence we may wake up and stop wasting time defending and propping up the identity and the "stuff" (e.g., status, possessions) that inevitably pass away. Levoy (1997) writes:

> We all owe God a death, Shakespeare once said, so we owe it to ourselves to practice for the occasion whenever possible. One way we do so is by tending to the small surrenders that come our way almost daily: letting go of a bad mood, making a choice or a compromise, forgiving someone, parting with fear and saying the truth in a moment, spending time with our children instead of working late again. (p. 11)

Letting go and openness are directed not only toward some ascendant revelation but also to the shadow of our unconscious; as Jean Cocteau put it, "I do not believe that inspiration falls from heaven ... the poet is at the disposal of his night" (quoted in Ghiselin, 1952, p. 81). This willingness to explore the "night," the hidden recesses of self and shadow, can serve this knowing. We let go in order to be fully present; by holding nothing back, we surrender to mystery:

> The first requirement for even a partial encounter with mystery, then, is to be willing to surrender to one's habitual tendencies to either solve or ignore mystery. Second, one must be willing to risk some degree of fear. [One must have] willingness and courage to open oneself to mystery. (May, 1982, p. 32)

The capacities of intellect and intuition (elaborated in chapter 4) help to develop the skills of will and surrender. Logical-analytic functions develop interdependently with the will. Intuition, a knowing that arises more openly and spontaneously than ego-generated thought, involves the movement of reception. Experiences of hope, trust, and cooperation also nurture the fundamentals of surrender. Willingness comes especially as we develop the heart of understanding that recognizes interconnection. In this way, love serves surrender. The student can be welcomed into the natural interconnection of will and surrender as he or she feels the rhythms of effort and relaxation, holding on and letting go, contracting and expanding, separating and joining of ideas and individuals. These serve as experiments and metaphors for separation and rejoining. If we only dissect an animal or an idea, separating out its components, we only train half of what is necessary for transformation. If we can also rejoin, mend, blend, and unite, we experience both autonomy and communion. As will and surrender move from oppositional forces to interconnected ones, aspects of the same wave, we gain the ability to align with the rising current of creation. In this spirit, M. C. Richards (1989) advises:

> Let us ride our lives like natural beasts, like tempests, like the bounce of a ball, or the slightest ambiguous hovering of ash, the drift of scent: let us stick to those currents that can carry us, membering them with our souls. Our world personifies us, we know ourselves by it. (p. 7)

Freedom

The universe exists in order that the experiencer may experience it, and thus become liberated.

—Patanjali (1971, p. 130)

Discipline, Responsibility, and Fear

Transformation involves the growth of inner freedom, as ideas, actions, and self are liberated from present form. Tarthang Tulku (1977) describes the general process leading toward inner freedom:

> By learning to contact the essence of our being, we can discover an un-bounded freedom that is not only a freedom from some external restraint, but is itself the dynamic expression of the meaning and value of being hu-man. Once this intrinsic freedom becomes a lived reality, then all other free-doms follow naturally. (p. xxxv)

Emphasizing inner freedom does not mean underestimating the value of external freedom (e.g., rights and liberties). However, it suggests that the heart of transformation is an inner freedom that may, in turn, ripple toward the outside, into culture and society. Science frees us from some problems but it does not provide fulfillment; liberty allows us to choose our action as we wish, but it does not mean we choose in a way that frees our soul or deeply satisfies. In fact, sometimes we hear stories of radical freedom in the midst of complete external re-striction. Aurobindo found inner freedom during his year in solitary confinement in the Alipore jail, Baha'u'llah spent two years in a cave on his way to inner liberation, and St. Catherine cloistered herself in her room for three years. Some disciplines of growth are intentionally structured to evoke an opening or freeing of the inner space in part through controlling outer conditions. For example, a Zen Dai-sesshin provides almost complete imposed external control and regulation.

> The regulation of body and action ... is nearly complete. From wake up to bed time, one's posture and movement is expected to conform to a meticu-lously prescribed form. Eyes are always to be downcast, hands in a pre-

scribed mudra position when sitting, pressed together in gasho when bowing, and at all other times folded against the chest in sasho. The silence is broken only by the sounds of various bells and clappers that announce the beginning or end of a sit, a walk.... The pace is fast thus curtailing the time left for hesitation or enactment of whatever feeling or attitudes may arise toward what is going on. (Puhakka, 1998, p. 144)

This structure intentionally limits one's typical choices so that one can then notice all the ego-generated resistance, compliance, or other reactions. This can lead to exposing and dissolving a fixated self (and even dissolving a fixation on no-self) that generates such reactions. In other words, "it gives us an opportunity to get unstuck" (p. 145). So while sufficient external freedoms are crucial in education, as has been discussed previously (e.g., Froebel's free play for kindergartners, opportunity for independent expression, making one's own choices as a practice of developing values and discernment), it is inner freedom that serves as the axis of transformation.

"The task of a University [I will stretch this to mean all of education] is the creation of the future" (Whitehead, 1938/1958, p. 233); school age is a time for developing the tools of mind and the habits of heart that will serve and shape a life and a future. Seneca captures a desirable outcome of education when describing "a mind which is free, upright, undaunted and steadfast beyond the influence of fear and desire" (in Baskin, 1966, p. 641). Education for transformation does not to try to impose, force, or even teach liberation but provides liberating (transformative) habits and tools that include strength of will, clarity of mind, compassion of heart, and power of critical dialogue. Through their appropriate use, one may gain the personal power, depth of vision, and understanding to achieve transparency of the world and the self. Transformative education enables us to avoid getting caught in our own little whirlpool of existence, so that we may live in the whole river of life. This is the whole function of education, cultivating the whole being, the totality of mind, and the "sensitiveness of soul" as Tagore (1961, p. 64) named it.

Freedom then requires the kind of discipline that allows us to overcome habitual tendencies. Goethe (1829/1949) said, "whatever liberates our spirit without giving us mastery over ourselves is destructive" (p. 184). The student's power to direct and sustain attention, as well as the ability to stop and watch the flow of thoughts or feelings, to avoid fixation in a perspective, the will to say "no" to an impulse, and also to say "yes," involves discipline.

The hidden curriculum even of basic skill training can foster inner discipline and thus become a tool of liberation. It is not necessary to set up a Zen practice in the schoolroom; the point is to recognize that self-discipline is practiced not simply to achieve skill competence or conformity but to afford inner freedom. Learning to write words frees us to express ourselves in new ways. Learning geometric formula allows abstract, representational thought to complement concrete measurement (for example, we no longer have to build the triangle in order to measure its angles or length of its sides, or "eyeball" the correct pitch for building a roof; we can calculate it). The goal is not a controlled classroom or curricular compliance but inner control. We may see discipline as learning or mastering skills, understanding and directing emotional responses, focusing attention as in problem solving or gymnastics, developing concentration through meditation, practicing the analytic tools of deconstruction, or coordinating hands and eyes and aesthetic form, as when Japanese children work on calligraphy and, to a lesser extent, when children in the United States work on handwriting. On the surface, these activities cultivate particular skills, but looking below the surface, the work develops powers of discipline and mastery. The skill practice, say of handwriting, becomes a meditation; the gymnastics routine or even the practice of reasoning skills becomes yoga. We remind students of the inner freedom that is the deep goal of self-discipline when they are offered the chance to use the tools of discipline for autonomous expression and experimentation, whether in a class debate or an art project. Without such reminders, demands for compliance may mechanize the work and dull the impulse for inner freedom.

Beyond discipline, freedom involves assuming responsibility for our own growth. This means that we have no one else to blame and no one else to tell us the truth. And the greater the depth of our development, the greater is our freedom and simultaneously our responsibility.

The notion of change as merely a vague possibility deludes us into believing that change is optional. We are a creative process in action; change is inevitable, as is our responsibility for our growth. The opposite of responsibility is avoidance, which apathy and fear often engender. Perhaps more than any single attitude, our unwillingness to notice the inner significances of our lives and to understand and care about another serves as the portent of stagnation of person and society. On the other hand, the greatest ally of freedom may be imagination. Archibald MacLeish (1959) writes as follows:

> The real defense of freedom is imagination, that feeling life of the mind which actually knows because it involves itself in its knowing, puts itself in the place where its thought goes.... That man who knows with his heart knows himself to be a man, feels himself, cannot be silenced. He is free no matter where he lives.... The man who knows with his mind only, who will not commit himself beyond his wits, who does not feel the thing he thinks— that man has no freedom anywhere. Slavery begins when men give up the human need to know with the whole heart, to know for themselves, to bear the "burden," as Wordsworth called it, "of the mystery." (p. 46)

Freedom inevitably involves working directly with fear. Fear may engender some low-grade anxiety and lead to avoidance. Fear holds us back from the embrace of spirit, of creation and communion, and from the responsibility to reach toward it. Contemporary schools often embody a "culture of fear," from fear-based reform to the fear engendered in students who must produce one right answer, to the teachers who must deal with extraordinary demands from others and their own limitations, to the fearful separation inherent in the dominant objectivist ways of knowing (see Palmer, 1998, pp. 35-60). Fear says you cannot trust the mystery, you cannot let love or joy guide you, but you must above all remain self-protective. Fear says, "Stay low; grab what you can; do not take the risks necessary for understanding or freedom; fortify and concretize the small self at all costs." But fear cannot be ignored or swept away. It is a sign showing us where to pay attention. It gives itself away, saying "Look here, I have something for you. Here is where you need to look and work." Yet we do not often think to partner with fear but instead tend to resist and avoid it, creating a labyrinth of hiding places for ourselves. The good news is that all that is required to unbuckle ourselves from the seat of fear is to be still and awake in the face of it:

> We are transformed, not by adopting attitudes toward ourselves but by bringing into center all the elements of our sensation and our thinking and our emotions and our will: all the realities of our bodies and our souls. All the dark void in us of our undiscovered selves, all the small light of our discovered being. All the drive of our hungers, and our fairest and blackest dreams. All, all the elements come into center, into union with all other elements. And in such a state they become quite different in function than when they are separated and segregated and discriminated between or against. (Richards, 1989, p. 36)

In a climate of fear and pressure we may protect ourselves by shutting down, avoiding conflict, being compliant, or dropping out altogether. And while this may describe many students, it is even more disturbing that it also describes a great many teachers. Teachers are currently radically disempowered, often squeezed with oppressive curricular demands and subjected to an overemphasis on competition and standardized testing. They are de-professionalized, having lost both autonomy and adequate support for personal and professional development.

The organizations designed to empower the profession, teachers' unions, seem to have served less as a sensible voice in a meaningful dialogue about the best way to educate our children and more as a tool to try to get a bit more money or security for their constituents. While such advocacy is certainly a legitimate and important part of the role, as the primary focus it misses the opportunity for serving as genuine catalyst for transformation. The result has been a question about the credibility for teacher's organizations, even among teachers themselves.

If the professional organizations are inadequate to empower teachers, can individual teachers or small groups find their own voices? Currently, beginning teachers are in the same position that many beginning composition students find themselves in; they have some skills and some issues to speak about, but they must find their own authentic voice if their craft and their profession as a whole is to be potent and transformative. For many teachers, facing fear and finding one's own voice these days may include questioning the top-down demands on testing and curriculum, dialoguing with others (i.e., colleagues, parents, media) when something does not seem in the best interest of teaching, and being honest about what brings education to life and what relegates it to banality. Sometimes it may mean refusing to accept practices that diminish the teacher and the teaching. The status quo can even be challenged in the spirit of Gandhi's "experiments with truth" or Rosa Parks' decision to sit in the "whites only" section of the public bus. As just one example, when compulsory testing in Japanese elementary schools was legislated, teachers simply refused to take part. And this is a culture that is not noted for grassroots uprisings. Teachers were not adverse to new ideas or to more work for themselves, but they recognized that the mandated testing would simply not be in the best interest of students or of learning. Alfie Kohn declares that as a result of the integrity and clarity of their voices, there is no such testing in Japanese elementary schools (in Miller, 2000). Freedom involves facing our fears in order to find our voice.

Time-Freedom

The world seems to be spinning faster. We recognize it in the hurried pace of our day, the instantaneous nature of communication, the rate of change in the world, the time it takes for information to double, the blur of our life. Significantly, transformation involves freedom from time.

Time freedom involves living our questions more knowingly and honestly; we accomplish this by being present with them in the moment. As Whitehead wrote, "The present contains all that there is. It is holy ground.... The communion of saints is a great and inspiring assemblage, but it has only one possible hall of meeting, and that is the present" (Whitehead, 1967, p. 4). The nexus of the decent and ascent of spirit lies in this moment. So the invitation reads ... "once an hour ask yourself softly, 'Am I here?'" (Rodegast & Stanton, 1989, p. 28). To be present allows us to consciously and freely engage in our own transformation and the growth of others.

In contemporary modern (rational-egoic) culture, time is viewed as continuous, sequential, quantifiable. (Gebser, 1991, and Wilber, 1995 among others, suggest an evolutionary model for humans that parallels the development of an individual through the life span [ontogeny recapitulates phylogeny]. Basically, the levels include the archaic, magic, mythic, rational-egoic, integral, and beyond. Contemporary culture is embedded in the rational-egoic but the front edge stretches farther; Gebser suggests that we are pushing that front edge of culture into integral consciousness.) From a rational-egoic perspective, time is generally seen as a sequential march into a future. However, the "magic" thinker (e.g., a three-year-old) has little sense of clock time; a "mythic" point of view sees time as rhythms and cycles, such as another full moon, another spring, and so forth. Most of us "moderns," fixed in linear time, may notice when time, normally perceived as quantity or progression, is instead experienced as quality and intensity. We recognize how time becomes condensed in dreams; ecstatic and unitive events are represented as outside of time, timeless; important events seem to distort time. The cyclical or the linear nature of time does not disappear; our watches still work, the sun and the seasons still pass, but our anxiety in relation to our watches may shift. Gebser (1991) tells us that

> Everyone today can become aware of the various temporal forms which all point to origin, and everyone can experience timelessness in conjugal love, the timelessness of nightly deep sleep, the experience of rhythmic comple-mentarity of natural temporicity which unites him in every heart-beat and rhythmic breath with the courses of the universe; and everyone can employ measured time.... The hours and days are to be spent not only purposefully but also meaningfully. What is today called "free-time" must not be squan-dered leisurely but employed to acquire time-freedom. (p. 531)

The rational modernist knowing looks to the future, the mythic world looks to the past, but in "time-freedom" we live in the now. Time-freedom involves transparency to time and thereby unhitches us from its control. For me, this is the shift that T. S. Eliot (1971) alludes to when he writes "to be conscious is not to be in time" (p. 16). Essen-tially this means being present. Presence involves an ability to prac-tice grateful satisfaction, "to absorb it [the world] thoroughly in each bite, each sip, each breath, each dose of fully experienced reality" (Needle, 1999, p. 11). This requires an inner self-sufficiency. It takes only a few moments in front of the television or at the store to see how contemporary advertising challenges self-sufficiency. "I want that" rings through our heads and perhaps through our houses (espe-cially if we have children) when the advertisement tantalizes and thus tries to establish an insufficiency within us. Many of us go from one desire or longing (diet, relationship, idea, car, etc.) to the next, seeking the illusive satisfaction that is promised. It is always just ahead and rarely right here and now, precisely because we are often not in the here and now. We may not be sufficiently present to suck the marrow from the bone of the moment. Too often we lick, chew a bit, and then quickly move on, looking for the next satisfaction. Communion and creation occur only in the present. Heschel (1996) writes:

> Man's true fulfillment depends upon communion with that which tran-scends him.... The most urgent task is to destroy the myth that accumula-tion of wealth and the achievement of comfort are the child's vocations of man. (pp. 31, 32)

We can be brought nearer the now through a variety of ap-proaches that have been addressed throughout this book. These in-clude using awareness strategies, owning projections, and reorienting from a quest for certainty to one of openness to mystery (chapter 6), dismantling unchecked assumptions, including emphasizing immediate experience and reflecting upon that experience. This can be initiated simply by asking, "Where are you now?" (Chapters 5 and 6), seeking understanding, appreciation, or "pure recognition" by meeting the other directly (Chapter 4), settling for nothing less than a first-hand encounter with truth, with the world (Chapter 3), and presenting material that engages relevance and resonance which rivet attention to the now (Chapter 2).

Space-Freedom

Modern transportation has made the world smaller (the other side of the planet can be reached in a few hours); satellite communication and the Internet collapse space (and time) and create a virtual space; quantum phenomena such as nonlocal influence, in which objects separated in space remain in some kind of connection or communication, alter the significance of space. While these phenomena affect our relations with and presuppositions about the space around us, the space that is most profoundly transformed is the place where we stand and from where we look, that is, our perspective.

Typical rational-egoic consciousness allows events to happen "out there," in a space apart from us. The rational mind enables objectivism, allowing us to stand separate from enmeshment with nature, and allows the detachment of contemporary science. It also supports the centrality of the self as the subject that observes an object.

When an instant of transformation occurs, it brings a kind of freedom from spatial limitations and perspective. When some belief gives way through an insight or an opening, our point of view changes. One student says, "It is like a veil being lifted. I suddenly could see what was there all along." Usually, we experience this as an expansion or an opening up. Our self becomes more fluid and may even seem to recede altogether. One student describes it this way: "The whole scene came into focus for me when I got out of my own way and let go of how I was looking at the problem. When I changed, it [the problem] did too." What we look at (e.g., a problem, the world) and the place from which we look at it alters in some way. We are freed from space as subject and object lose their fixity.

When individual development proceeds far enough, for example, beyond the limits of formal operational thinking, other kinds of space open up. Gebser (1991) describes post-formal operational thought as integral-aperspectival; Wilber (1995) calls it vision-logic. Using this capacity, perspective (and space) moves from a single vantage point

to multiple perspectives, to aperspectival space. We move from having a perspective to being able to move into many perspectives, to
holding multiple perspectives simultaneously, to seeing through their
presuppositions to awareness. This involves an openness in which
one is not fixed in a single location or even in multiple locations but
perceives from within and without simultaneously. This means that
there is not a subject seeing an object, nor identification with one
point of view or another. We develop the ability to transcend dualistic
perceptions. In this sense, "seeing" is not identification with the seer
("I see what is happening here"), or identification with the object (e.g.,
complete absorbtion in emotions or dream content); it exists in the
aperspectival space "between" the two. This becomes awareness
rather than perspective. The inherent nature of mind may require a
subject-object perspective for daily operations; however, perspective
can shift and open into awareness. This shift begins simply by honoring diversity, "taking up space" in a variety of perspectives, imagining possibility, and unpacking the presuppositions of any one
position. When we view students as relatively uniform commodities
to be molded in fairly homogenous ways, we reinforce perspectival
consciousness, both ours and theirs. A teacher begins to shift to a
more multi-perspectival awareness simply by genuinely honoring
and understanding the uniqueness of each child, that is, by uncovering and giving space to their perspectives.

Enduring aperspectival awareness may be reserved for a very
few; however, momentary breakthroughs occur whenever we experience a loosening of the grip of perspective.

An Education of Inner Significances

Throughout this book I have advocated an education of inner significances as well as one of outer concerns. A curriculum of inner significances focuses on value, quality, virtue, resonance, and relevance, all
of which tend to emerge from the inside out. It does not require that
more information be added to the contemporary curriculum, but it
invites us to the inside of the subject matter, the other and the Self.
This is a curriculum where the largest questions sit alongside the
smallest, and all are fair game.

Education for transformation is inherently a spiritual endeavor as
it involves the fundamental impulses of spirit: creation and communion. Spirituality in this sense is the consciousness that enables us to
perceive deeper levels of being, meaning, values, and purpose. But

suggesting a spiritual approach to education does not mean advocating a religious curriculum for our schools or adding on more information to the curriculum. Parker Palmer (1998-99) reminds us that

> the spiritual is always present in ... education whether we acknowledge it or not. Spiritual questions, rightly understood, are embedded in every discipline.... Spirituality–the human quest for connectedness [and I would add creation]–is not something that needs to be brought into or added onto the curriculum. It is at the heart of every subject we teach, where it awaits to be brought forth. (p. 8)... We can evoke the spirituality of any discipline by teaching in ways that allow the "big story" told by the discipline to intersect with the "little story" of the student's life. (p. 9)

Knowledge, intelligence, understanding, wisdom, and transformation can be activated with any student from any meeting at this intersection. It is a question of whether the meeting of education is used as an opportunity to open and deepen consciousness. This opening does not take away from the information exchange but makes it richer, gives it context, and brings it alive. We work toward this depth when we invite students to directly and openly meet their world and themselves. This is enabled when we, as educators, meet ourselves, ideas, and our students directly, openly and honestly; in this way, teaching primarily becomes a way of Being. Then the aims of education reach beyond information exchange to transformation.

When the heart of the discipline and our own hearts and minds are plumbed, information serves as currency for learning; knowledge brings an economy of interaction; intelligence gives power, precision, and critical reflection to our enterprise; understanding opens the heart; and wisdom balances heart and head, leading us to insight and right action. Transformation culminates and animates this opening as it endows us with the force of creation and communion. In education and in life in general, we activate the power of transformation simply by making a choice to open ourselves to the depths. When this becomes central to schooling, education moves toward becoming a wisdom tradition itself.

REFERENCES

Adler, A. (1929). *The practice and theory of individual psychotherapy* (2nd ed.). London: Routledge & Kegan Paul.

Anyon, J. (1980). Social class and the hidden curriculum of work. *Journal of Education, 162* (1), 67-92.

Arieti, S. (1976). *Creativity: The magic synthesis.* New York: Basic Books.

Arlin, P. K. (1990). Wisdom: The art of problem finding. In R. J. Sternberg (Ed.), *Wisdom: Its nature, origins, and development* (pp. 230-243). New York: Cambridge University Press.

Assagioli, R. (1973). *The act of will.* New York: Penguin Books.

Augustine, St. (1961). *Confessions* (R. S. Pine-Coffin, Trans.). New York: Penguin Books.

Azar, B. (1997). Defining the trait that makes us most human. *APA Monitor, 28* (11), 1-15.

Baltes, P. B., & Smith, J. (1990). Toward a psychology of wisdom and its ontogenesis. In R. J. Sternberg (Ed.), *Wisdom: Its nature, origins, and development* (pp. 87-120). New York: Cambridge University Press.

Barnes, V. A., Bauza, L. B., & Treiber, F. A. (2003). Impact of stress reduction on negative school behavior in adolescents. *Health and Quality of Life Outcomes 1:10* http://www.hqlo.com/content/1/1/10

Baskin, W. (Ed.). (1966). *Classics in education.* New York: Philosophical Library.

Bateson, G. (1980). *Mind and nature: A necessary unity.* New York: Bantam Books.

Bateson, G., & Bateson, M. C. (1987). *Angels fear: Towards an epistemology of the sacred.* New York: Macmillan.

Bateson, M. C. (1999). In praise of ambiguity. In J. Kane (Ed.), *Education, information, and transformation: Essays on learning and thinking* (pp. 133-146). Upper Saddle River, NJ: Prentice Hall.

Benson, H. (2000). *The relaxation response.* New York: HarperTorch. (Original work published in 1975).

Berendt, J. (1991). *The world is sound: Nada Brahma: Music and the landscape of consciousness* (F. Edgerton, Trans.). Rochester, VT: Destiny Books. (Original work published 1983).

Berry, T. (2000). *The great work: Our way into the future.* New York: Random House.

Bhagavad Gita, The . (1944). New York: Harper Torchbooks.

Blackmer, C. (1991). *Essays on spiritual psychology: Reflections on the thought of Emanuel Swedenborg.* New York: Swedenborg Foundation.

Bloom, B. (Ed.). (1956). *Taxonomy of educational objectives: The classification of educational goals.* (Handbook 1). New York: McKay.

———(1981). *All our children learning: A primer for parents, teachers, and other educators.* New York: McGraw-Hill.

Blum & Weprin Associates. (2000, May 10). The inner life of Americans: Views on spirituality, identity, sexuality, anxiety, and more. *New York Times Poll.* Retrieved July 15, 2003, from http://inic.utexas.edu/~bennett/__310/Wolfe-poll.htm

Bohm, D. (1981). Insight, knowledge, science, and human values. In D. Sloan (Ed.), *Toward the recovery of wholeness* (pp. 8-30). New York: Teachers College Press.

Bourne, R. (1977). *The radical will: Selected writings, 1911-1918.* New York: Urizen.

Bransford, J. D., Brown, A. L., & Cocking, R. R. (Eds.). (1999). *How people learn: Brain, mind, experience, and school.* Washington, DC: National Academy Press.

Brown, J. R. (1996). *The I in science: Training to utilize subjectivity in research.* Oslo, Norway: Scandinavian University Press.

Bruer, J. T. (1997). Education and the brain: A bridge too far. *Educational Researcher, 26* (8), 4.

Bruner, J. S. (1963). *The process of education.* New York: Vintage.

Buber, M. (1958). *I and thou* (R. G. Smith, Trans.). New York: Charles Scribner & Sons. (Original work published 1923).

———(1975). *Tales of the Hasidim: The early masters.* New York: Schocken Books.

Burack, C. (1999). Returning meditation to education. *Tikkun, 14* (5), 41-46.

Cameron, J. (1992). The artist's way: A spiritual path to higher creativity. New York: Tarcher.

Campbell, D. (1997). *The Mozart effect: Tapping the power of music to heal the body, strengthen the mind, and unlock the creative spirit.* New York: Avon Books.

Carter, F. (1986). *The education of Little Tree.* Albuquerque, NM: University of New Mexico Press. (Original work published 1976).

Casey, E. S. (2000). *Imagining: A phenomenological study.* Bloomington: Indiana University Press.

Childre, D., & Martin, H. (1999). *The heartmath solution.* San Francisco: HarperSanFrancisco.

Crain, W. (2000). *Theories of development: Concepts and applications* (4th ed.). Upper Saddle River, NJ: Prentice Hall.

Csikszentmihalyi, M. (1990). *Flow: The psychology of optimal experience.* New York: Harper & Row.

Dabrowski, K. (1964). *Positive disintegration.* London: Little, Brown.

Dass, R., & Gorman, P. (1996). *How can I help? Stories and reflections on service.* New York: Alfred A. Knopf.

Davidson, R. J., Kabat-Zinn, J., Schumacher, J., Rosenkranz, M., Muller, D., Santorelli, S. F., Urbanowski, F., Harrington, A., Bonus, K., & Sheridan, J. F. (2003). Alternations in brain and immune function produced by mindfulness meditation. *Psychosomatic Medicine, 65,* 564-570.

Davis, A. (1992). *The logic of ecstasy: Canadian mystical painting 1920-1940.* Toronto: University of Toronto Press.

deBono, E. (1985). *Six thinking hats.* Boston: Little, Brown.

Deikman, A. (2000). Service as knowing. In T. Hart, P. Nelson, & K. Puhakka (Eds.), *Transpersonal knowing: Exploring the horizon of consciousness* (pp. 303-318). Albany: State University of New York Press.

Dennison, P. E. (2006). *Brain gym and me.* Ventura, CA: Edu-Kinesthetics.

de Saint Exupéry, A. (1971). *The little prince* (K. Woods, Trans.). San Diego, CA: Harcourt Brace Jovanovich. (Original work published 1943).

Dewey, J. (1958). *Experience and nature.* New York: Dover. (Original work published 1929).

— — —(1963). *Experience and education.* New York: Macmillan. (Original work published 1938).

Dreamer, O. M. (1999). *The invitation.* San Francisco: HarperSanFrancisco.

Duerr, M., Zajonc, A. & Dana, D. (2003). Survey of transformative and spiritual dimensions of higher education. *Journal of Transformative Education, 1*(3), 177-211.

Eckhart, M. (1958). *Meister Eckhart: Selected treatises and sermons* (J. M. Clark & J. V. Skinner, Trans.). London: Faber & Faber.

———(1981). *Meister Eckhart: The essential sermons, commentaries, trea-tises, and defense* (E. Colledge & B. McGinn, Trans.). New York: Paulist Press.

Einstein, A. (1979). *Autobiographical notes* (P. A. Schilpp, Ed. & Trans.). La Salle, IL: Open Court. (Original work published 1949).

Elbow, P. (1998). *Writing with power: Techniques for mastering the writ-ing process.* New York: Oxford University Press.

Eliot, T. S. (1971). *Four quartets.* New York: Harcourt, Brace, and World.

Emerson, R. W. (1968). The American scholar. In L. Mumford (Ed.), *Ralph Waldo Emerson: Essays and journals.* Garden City, NY: Dou-bleday. (Original address delivered 1837).

———(1972). Education. In R. E. Spiller & W. E. Williams (Eds.), *The early lectures of Ralph Waldo Emerson Vol. 3.* Cambridge, MA: Belknap Press of Harvard University Press. (Original work pub-lished 1883).

Feige, D. M. (1999). The legacy of Gregory Bateson: Envisioning aes-thetic epistemologies and praxis. In J. Kane (Ed.), *Education, infor-mation, and transformation: Essays on learning and thinking* (pp. 77-109). Upper Saddle River, NJ: Prentice Hall.

Feuerstein, G. (1987). *Structures of consciousness.* Lower Lake, CA: In-tegral.

Finley, J. (2000). *The contemplative heart.* Notre Dame, IN: Sorin Books.

Foucault, M. (1980). *Power/knowledge.* New York: Pantheon.

Freire, P. (1974). *Pedagogy of the oppressed.* New York: Seabury.

Froebel, F. (1887). *The education of man.* (W. N. Hailmann, Trans.). New York: D. Appleton.

Gackenbach, J. (Ed.). (1998). *Psychology and the Internet: Intrapersonal, interpersonal, and transpersonal implications.* San Diego, CA: Aca-demic Press.

Ganim, B., & Fox, S. (1999). *Visual journaling: Going deeper than words.* Wheaton, IL: Quest Books.

Gardner, H. (1983). *Frames of mind: A theory of multiple intelligences.* New York: Basic Books.

———(1991). *The unschooled mind: How children think and how schools should teach.* New York: Basic Books.

———(1993). *Multiple intelligences: The theory in practice.* New York: Basic Books.

Gardner, J. (1996). *Education in search of the spirit.* Hudson, NY: An-throposophic Press.

Gatto, J. (1993). *The exhausted school: The first national grassroots speak-out on the right to school choice.* Oxford: Odysseus Group.

Gebser, J. (1991). *The ever-present origin* (N. Barstad & A. Mickunas, Trans.). Athens: Ohio University Press. (Original work published 1949).

Gendlin, E. T. (1988). *Focusing* (2nd ed.). New York: Bantam Books.

Ghiselin, B. (Ed.). (1952). *The creative process.* New York: Mentor.

Ghose, A. (1924). *A system of national education.* Calcutta: Arya.

Gibran, K. (1968). *The prophet.* New York: Alfred A. Knopf. (Original work published 1923).

Gilby, T. (Trans.) (1967). *St. Thomas Aquinas: Philosophical texts.* New York: Oxford University Press.

Gilligan, C. (1982). *In a different voice: Psychological theory and women's development.* Cambridge, MA: Harvard University Press.

Goethe, J. (1949). *Wisdom and Experience* (H. J. Weigand, Ed. & Trans.). New York: Pantheon Books. Passage cited in text is no. 504 from *Maxims and Reflections.* (Original work published 1829).

Gokak, V. K. (1975). *Bhagavan Sri Sathya Sai Baba.* New Delhi: Abhinav Publications.

Goldberg, P. (1983). *The intuitive edge.* Los Angeles: Tarcher.

Goldhaber, D. E. (2000). *Theories of human development: Integral perspectives.* Mountain View, CA: Mayfield.

Goleman, D. (2006). *Social intelligence: The new science of human relationships.* New York: Random House.

Goleman, D., & Thurman, R. A. F. (Eds.). (1991). *Mindscience.* Boston: Wisdom.

Gowan, J. C. (1977). Creative inspiration in composers. *The Journal of Creative Behavior, 11* (4), 249-255.

Gray, J. G. (1968). *The promise of wisdom: An introduction to philosophy of education.* Philadelphia: J. B. Lippincott.

Greenleaf, R. K. (1977). *Servant leadership: A journey into the nature of legitimate power and greatness.* Mahwah, NJ: Paulist Press.

Grene, M. (Ed.). (1969). Towards a unity of knowledge. *Psychological Issues Monograph, 6* (2), 22. New York: International Universities Press.

Hanh, T. N. (1975). *The miracle of mindfulness.* Boston: Beacon Press.

Hanna, F. J. (1993). Rigorous intuition: Consciousness, being and the phenomenological method. *Journal of Transpersonal Psychology, 25* (2), 181-197.

Hart, T. (1997). From category to contact: Epistemology and the enlivening and deadening of spirit in education. *Journal of Humanistic Education and Development, 36* (1), 23-34.

———(1998a). A dialectic of knowing: Integrating the intuitive and the analytic. *Encounter: Education for Meaning and Social Justice, 11* (3), 5-16.

———(1998b). Inspiration: An exploration of the experience and its meaning. *Journal of Humanistic Psychology, 38* (1), 7-35.

———(1999). The refinement of empathy. *Journal of Humanistic Psychology, 39* (4), 111-125.

———(2000). Deep empathy. In T. Hart, P. L. Nelson, & K. Puhakka (Eds.), *Transpersonal knowing: Exploring the horizon of consciousness* (pp. 253-269). Albany: State University of New York Press.

———(2003). *The secret spiritual world of children.* Novato, CA: New World Library.

———(2004). Opening the contemplative mind in the classroom. *Journal of transformative Education, 2*(1), 28-46.

———(2009). Interiority and education: Exploring the neurophenomenology of contemplation and its potential role in education. *Journal of Transformative Education, 7*(1)

Hart, T., & Zellars, E. (2006). When imaginary friends are sources of wisdom. *Encounter: Education for Meaning and Social Justice, 19* (1), 6-16.

Hartmann, E. (1984). *The nightmare: The psychology and biology of terrifying dreams.* New York: Basic Books.

Hegel, G. W. (1955). *The phenomenology of mind* (2nd ed.) (J. B. Baillie, Trans.). New York: Macmillan. (Original work published 1807).

Heidegger, M. (1966). *Discourse on thinking* (J. M. Anderson & E. H. Freund, Trans.). New York: Harper & Row. (Original work published 1959).

———(1975). What is metaphysics? In W. Kaufman (Ed.), *Existentialism from Dostoevsky to Sartre* (pp. 242-264). New York: New American Library. (Original work published 1929).

———(1993). What calls for thinking? In D. F. Krell (Ed.), *Basic writings* (rev. ed.) (pp. 365-391). New York: HarperCollins. (Original work published 1977).

Heschel, A. J. (1962).*The prophets.* New York: Harper & Row.

———(1972). *God in search of man.* New York: Octagon Books. (Original work published 1955).

———(1996). *Moral grandeur and spiritual audacity* (S. Heschel, Ed.). New York: Farrar, Straus, & Giroux.

Hillman, J. (1988). *Archetypal psychology: A brief account.* Dallas: Spring Publications.

Hillman, J. (1989). *A blue fire.* New York: HarperCollins.

———(1996). *The soul's code: In search of character and calling.* New York: Warner Books.

Hoffman, M. L. (1990). Empathy and justice motivation. *Motivation and emotion, 14* (2), 151-172.

Hopkins, L. (1970). *The emerging self in school and home.* Westport, CT: Greenwood. (Original work published 1954).

Horney, K. (1950). *Neurosis and human growth: The struggle toward self-realization.* New York: W. W. Norton.

Huang Po. (1958). *The Zen teaching of Huang Po: On the transmission of mind* (J. Blofeld, Trans.). New York: Grove Weidenfeld.

Husserl, E. (1967). *The Paris lectures* (P. Koesternbaum, Trans.). The Hague, Netherlands: Martinus Nijhoff.

———(1970). *The crisis of European sciences and transcendental phenomenology* (D. Carr, Trans.). Evanston, IL: Northwestern University Press. (Original work published 1936).

Inspirational guide for a new language: Language of the awakened heart. (2001). Port Reyes Station, CA: Fund for Global Awakening (available at www.ffga.org)

James, W. (1977). *A pluralistic universe.* Cambridge, MA: Harvard University Press. (Original work published 1909).

———(1950). *Principles of psychology.* New York: Dover. (Original work published 1890).

———(1956). *The will to believe and other essays in popular philosophy.* New York: Dover. (Original work published 1897).

———(1967). *Essays in radical empiricism and a pluralistic universe* (R. B. Perry, Ed.). Gloucester, MA: Peter Smith.

Jantsch, E. (1980). *The self-organizing universe.* New York: Pergamon.

Johnson, A. (1992). The development of creative thinking in childhood. *Holistic Education Review, 5* (2), 25-34.

Johnson, R. A. (1998). *Balancing heaven and earth: A memoir of visions, dreams, and realizations.* San Francisco: HarperSanFrancisco.

Joshi, R. K. (1975). On education. *The Advent, XXXII (1).*

Jung, C. G. (1963). *Psychology of the unconscious: A study of the transformations and symbolisms of the libido* (B. M. Hinkle, Trans.). New York: Dodd, Mead. (Original work published 1916).

―――(1977). *The development of personality* (5th ed.). Princeton, NJ: Princeton University Press.

Kabat-Zinn, J. (1990). Full catastrophe living: Using the wisdom of your body and mind to face stress, pain, and illness. New York: Dell.

Kegan, R. (1982). *The evolving self: Problem and process in human development.* Cambridge, MA: Harvard University Press.

Keller, E. (1983). *A feeling for the organism: The life and work of Barbara McClintock.* New York: Freeman.

Khan, Z. I. (2000). Illuminative presence. In T. Hart, P. L. Nelson, & K. Puhakka (Eds.), *Transpersonal knowing: Exploring the horizon of consciousness* (pp. 147-159). Albany: State University of New York Press.

King, M. L., Jr. (1963). *Strength to love.* New York: Harper & Row.

Koestler, A. (1964). *The act of creation.* New York: Macmillan.

Kohak, E. (1984). *The embers and the stars: A philosophical inquiry into the moral sense of nature.* Chicago: University of Chicago Press.

Kolb, D. (1976). *Learning style inventory.* Boston: McBer.

Krishnamurti, J. (1974). *Krishnamurti on education* (Krishnamurti Foundation Trust Limited, Eds.). New York: Harper & Row.

Larson, V. A. (1987). An exploration of psychotherapeutic resonance. *Psychotherapy, 24* (3), 321-324.

Laski, M. (1968). *Ecstasy: A study of some secular and religious experiences.* London: Cresset Press.

Lawson, D. E. (1961). *Wisdom and education.* Carbondale: Southern Illinois University Press.

Lazar, S. W., Kerr, C., Wasserman, R. H., Gray, J. R., Greve, D., Treadway, M. T, McGarvey, M., Quinn, B. T., Dusek, J. A., Benson, H., Rauch, S. L., Moore, & C. I., Fischl, B. (2005). Meditation experience is associated with increased cortical thickness. *NeuroReport, 16,* 1893-1897.

Levoy, G. (1997). *Callings: Finding and following an authentic life.* New York: Three Rivers Press.

Levy, S. (2006, March 27). (Some) attention must be paid! *Newsweek,* 16.

Lifton, R. J. (1993). *The protean self: Human resilience in an age of fragmentation.* New York: Basic Books.

Lipman, M. (1993). Promoting better classroom thinking. *Educational Psychology: An International Journal of Experimental Psychology, 13,* 291-304.

Livsey, R., & Palmer, P. J. (1999). *The courage to teach: A guide for reflection and renewal.* San Francisco: Jossey-Bass.

Lopez, J. F., Vazquez, D. M., Chalmers, D. T., & Watson, S. J. (1997). Regulation of 5-HT receptors and the hypothalamic-pituitary-adrenal axis. Implications for the neurobiology of suicide. *Academy of Science, 29*(836), 106-34.

Louv, R. (2005). *Last child in the woods: Saving our children from nature-deficit disorder.* Chapel Hill, NC: Algonquin.

Lubar, J. F. (1991). Discourse on the development of EEG diagnostics and biofeedback for attention-deficit/ hyperactivity disorders. *Biofeedback and Self-Regulation, 16,* 201-225.

MacLean, C., Walton, K., Wenneberg, S., Levitsky, D., Mandarino, J., Waziri, R., Hillis, S. L., & Schneider, R. H. (1997). Effects of the transcendental meditation program on adaptive mechanisms: Changes in hormone levels and responses to stress after 4 months of practice. *Psychoneuroendocrinology, 22*(4), 277-295.

MacLeish, A. (1959, March). The poet and the press. *Atlantic Monthly.*

Maggio, R. (1997). *Quotations on education.* Paramus, NJ: Prentice Hall.

Marshak, D. (1997). *The common vision: Parenting and educating for wholeness.* New York: Peter Lang.

Martin, J. R. (1992). *The schoolhome: Rethinking schools for changing families.* Cambridge, MA: Harvard University Press.

Martino, R., Fromm, E., & Suzuki, D. T. (1960). *Zen Buddhism and psychoanalysis.* New York: Harper Brothers.

Maslow, A. H. (1968). *Towards a psychology of being* (2nd ed.). New York: Van Nostrand Reinhold.

Matthews, G. B. (1980). *Philosophy and the young child.* Cambridge, MA: Harvard University Press.

May, G. G. (1982). *Will and spirit: A contemplative psychology.* New York: HarperSanFrancisco.

May, R. (1975). *The courage to create.* New York: Bantam Books.

McCombs, B. L. (1996). Alternative perspectives for motivation. In L. Baker, P. Afflerback, & D. Reinking (Eds.), *Developing engaged readers in school and home communities* (pp. 67-87). Hillsdale, NJ: Erlbaum.

McNamara, W. (1990). Alive with God. In B. Shield & R. Carlson (Eds.), *For the love of God: New writings by spiritual and psychological leaders* (pp. 107-111). San Rafael, CA: New World Library.

McNiff, S. (1992). *Art as medicine: Creating a therapy of the imagination.* Boston: Shambhala.

Meacham, J. A. (1990). The loss of wisdom. In R. J. Sternberg (Ed.), *Wisdom: Its nature, origins, and development* (pp. 87-120). New York: Cambridge University Press.

Merleau-Ponty, M. (1962). *The phenomenology of perception* (C. Smith, Trans.). New York: Humanities Press. (Original work published 1945).

Merton, T. (1974). *A Thomas Merton reader.* New York: Harcourt, Brace & World. (Original work published 1938).

———(1979). *Love and living.* New York: Farrar, Straus & Giroux.

Miller, J. (1994). The contemplative practitioner: Meditation in education and the professions. Westport, CT: Bergin and Garvey.

Miller, R. (1992). *What are schools for? Holistic education in American culture* (2nd ed., rev.). Brandon, VT: Holistic Education Press.

———(2000). The compassion our children deserve: An interview with Alfie Kohn. *Paths of Learning: Options for Families & Communities, 3,* 31-39.

Montgomery, C. L. (1991, November/December). Caring vs. curing: It's not what we do, it's what we allow ourselves to become part of. *Common Boundary,* 37-40.

Montuori, A., & Purser, R. (1995). Deconstructing the lone genius myth: Toward a contextual view of creativity. *Journal of Humanistic Psychology, 35* (3), 62-112.

Morgan, H. (1997). *Cognitive styles and classroom learning.* Westport, CT: Praeger.

Morgan, P. A. (1999). The wrong question: Technology and the evasion of educational aims. *Encounter: Education for meaning and social justice, 12* (3), 39-50.

Morton. (1984, December 23). The story-telling animal. *New York Times Book Review,* pp. 1-2.

Murphy, M., Donovan, S., & Taylor, E. (1997). *The physical and psychological effects of meditation: A review of contemporary research 1991-1996* (2nd ed.) Petaluma, CA: Institute of Noetic Sciences.

Murray, B. (2000, March). From brain scan to lesson plan. *Monitor on Psychology, 31* (3), 22-28.

National Center for Injury Prevention and Control (2004). *10 leading causes of death, United States.* Retrieved January 16, 2007, from http://webappa.cdc.gov/cgi-bin/broker.exe

National Commission on Excellence in Education (1983, April). *A nation at risk: The imperative for educational reform.* Washington, DC.

Needle, N. (1999). The six paramitas: Outline for a Buddhist education. *Encounter: Education for Meaning and Social Justice, 12* (1), 9-21.

Neihardt, J. G. (1988). *Black Elk speaks: Being the life story of a Holy Man of the Oglala Sioux.* Lincoln: University of Nebraska Press. (Original work published 1932).

Neruda, P. (1991) *The book of questions* (W. O'Daly, Trans.). Port Townsend, WA: Copper Canyon Press. (Original work published 1974).

Noddings, N., & Shore, P. (1984). *Awakening the inner eye: Intuition in education.* New York: Teachers College Press.

Ochse, R. (1990). *Before the gates of excellence: The determinants of creative genius.* Cambridge, MA: Cambridge University Press.

Orwoll, L., & Perlmutter, M. (1990). The study of wise persons: Integrating a personality perspective. In R. J. Sternberg (Ed.), *Wisdom: Its nature, origins, and development* (pp. 87-120). New York: Cambridge University Press.

Pagels, E. (1979). *The gnostic gospels.* New York: Random House.

Palmer, P. (1993). *To know as we are known: Education as a spiritual journey.* San Francisco: HarperSanFrancisco.

———(1998). *The courage to teach.* San Francisco: Jossey-Bass.

———(1998-1999, December-January). Evoking the spirit. *Educational Leadership,* pp. 6-11.

Patanjali, M. (1989). *The yoga sutra of Patanjali* (G. Feuerstein, Trans.). Rochester, VT: Inner Traditions International. (Original work published 1979).

———(1971). *How to know God: The yoga aphorisms of Patanjali* (S. Prabhavananda & C. Isherwood, Trans.). Hollywood, CA: Vedanta Press. (Original work published 1953).

Pearsall, P. (1999). The heart's code: Tapping the wisdom and power of our heart energy. New York: Broadway Books.

Peden, C. (1978). Freedom and wisdom: The heart of Tagore. *Journal of Thought, 13,* (3), 210-216.

Pert, C. B. (1986). The wisdom of the receptors: Neuropeptides, the emotions, and bodymind. *Advance, 3*(3), 8-16.

Pestalozzi, H. (1951). *The education of man. Aphorisms.* New York: Greenwood.

Piaget, J. (1977). *The essential Piaget* (H. Gruber & J. Voneche, Eds.). New York: Basic Books.

Pintrich, P. R., & Schunk, D. (1996). *Motivation in education: Theory, research, and application.* Columbus, OH: Merrill Prentice-Hall.

Polanyi, M. (1958). *Personal knowledge: Towards a post-critical philosophy*. Chicago: University of Chicago Press.

Pransky, G. (1998). *The Renaissance of psychology*. New York: Sulzburger & Graham.

Progoff, I. (1992). *At a journal writing workshop: Writing to access the power of the unconscious and evoke creative ability*. New York: Tarcher.

Puhakka, K. (1998). Dissolving the self: Rinzai Zen training at an American monastery. *The Journal of Transpersonal Psychology, 30* (2), 135-159.

— — —(2000). An invitation to authentic knowing. In T. Hart, P. L. Nelson, & K. Puhakka (Eds.), *Transpersonal knowing: Exploring the horizon of consciousness* (pp. 11-30). Albany: State University of New York Press.

Raber, J. (1998). Detrimental effects of chronic hypothalamic-pituitary-adrenal axis activation. From obesity to memory deficits. *Molecular Neurobiology, 18* (1), 1-22.

Richards, M. C. (1989). *Centering in pottery, poetry, and the person* (2nd Ed.). Hanover, NH: Wesleyan University Press. (Original work published 1962).

Richards, R. (1996). Does the lone genius ride again? Chaos, creativity, and community. *Journal of Humanistic Psychology, 36* (2), 44-60.

Rilke, R. M. (1986). *Rodin and other prose pieces*. London: Quartet Books.

— — —(1993). *Letters to a young poet* (M. D. Herter Norton, Trans.). New York: Norton.

Robinson, J. (Ed.). (1977). *The Nag Hammadi library in English*. New York: Harper & Row.

Rodegast, P., & Stanton, J. (1989). *Emmauel's book II: The choice for love*. New York: Bantam Books.

Rodriguez, T. (Producer), & Hutchings, P. (Senior Director). (1987). *A world of difference: Eye of the beholder* [Motion picture]. Post-Newsweek Stations of Florida, Inc.

Roe, A. (1953). A psychological study of eminent psychologists and anthropologists, and a comparison with biological and physical scientists. *Psychological Monographs: General and Applied, 67* (352).

Rogers, C. R. (1980). *A way of being*. Boston: Houghton Mifflin.

Root-Bernstein, R. S. & Root-Bernstein, M. M. (2001). *Sparks of genius: The thirteen thinking tools of the world's most creative people*. New York: Mariner.

Rorty, R. (1979). *Philosophy and the mirror of nature*. Princeton, NJ: Princeton University Press.

Rosenberg, A. (1986). Creative contradictions. In D. Coleman & D. Heller (Eds.), *The pleasures of psychology*. New York: Mentor.

Rothberg, D. (1990). Contemporary epistemology and the study of mysticism. In R. Forman (Ed.), *The problem to pure consciousness* (pp. 163-210). New York: Oxford University Press.

— — —(1994). Spiritual inquiry. *Revision, 17* (2), 2-12.

Rousseau, J. J. (1957). *Emile* (B. Fosley, Trans.). New York: E. P. Dutton. (Original work published 1762).

Rowan, J. (1986). Holistic listening. *Journal of Humanistic Psychology, 26* (1), 83-102.

Rumi, J. (1995). *The essential Rumi* (C. Barks, Trans., with J. Moyne, A. J. Arberry, & R. Nicholson). San Francisco: HarperSanFrancisco.

Russek, L. G., & Schwartz, G. (1996). Energy cardiology: A dynamical energy systems approach for integrating conventional and alternative medicine. *Advance, 12*(4), 4-14.

Sagan, C. (1980). *Cosmos*. New York: Ballantine Books.

Salk, J. (1983). *Anatomy of reality: Merging of intuition and reason*. New York: Columbia University Press.

Schoenfeld, A. H. (1983). Problem solving in the mathematics curriculum: A report, recommendation, and annotated bibliography. *Mathematical Association of America Notes*, No. 1.

Schrodinger, E. (1945). *What is life? Mind and matter*. London: Cambridge University Press.

Schroeder, W. R. (1984). *Sartre and his predecessors: The self and the other*. Boston: Routledge and Kegan Paul.

Sealts, M. M. (1992). *Emerson on the scholar*. Columbia: University of Missouri Press.

Sheldrake, R. (1995). *The presence of the past: Morphic resonance and the habits of nature*. S. Paris, ME: Park Street Press.

Shlossman, R. (1996). Can you teach empathy? *Tikkun, 11* (2), 20-22.

Siegel, D. J. (1999). *The developing mind: How relationships and the brain interact to shape who we are*. New York: Aldine.

Sigel, I. E. (1993). The centrality of a distancing model for the development of representational competence. In R. Coching & A. Renninger (Eds.), *The development and meaning of psychological distance* (pp. 141-155). Hillsdale, NJ: Erlbaum.

Silverman, L. (1994). The moral sensitivity of gifted children and the evolution of society. *Rooper Review, 17* (2), 110-116.

Smith, H. (1993). Educating the intellect: On opening the eye of the heart. In B. Darling-Smith (Ed.), *Can virtue be taught?* (pp. 17-31). Notre Dame, IN: University of Notre Dame Press.

Solloway, S. (2000). Contemplative practitioners: Presence of the project of thinking gaze differently. *Encounter: Education for Meaning and Social Justice, 13* (3), 30-42.

Spears, L. C. (Ed.). (1998). *Insights on leadership: Service, stewardship, spirit, and servant-leadership.* New York: John Wiley & Sons.

Sprinkle, L. (1985). Psychological resonance: A holographic model of counseling. *Journal of Counseling and Development, 64,* 206-208.

Stace, W. T. (1955). *The philosophy of Hegel.* New York: Dover. (Original work published 1924).

Sternberg, R. J. (Ed.). (1990). *Wisdom: Its nature, origins, and development.* New York: Cambridge University Press.

Stock, B. (1994). *The contemplative life and the teaching of humanities.* The Center for Contemplative Mind in Society. Retrieved July 22, 2003, from http://www.contemplativemind.org/resources/pubs/stock.pdf

Storm, H. (1972). *Seven arrows.* New York: Ballantine Books.

Suzuki, S. (1970). Zen mind, beginner's mind: Informal talks on Zen meditation and practice. New York: Weatherhill.

Swedenborg, E. (1933). *The true Christian religion* (E. Rhys, Ed.). New York: E. P. Dutton. (Original work published 1771).

———(1974). *A compendium of the theological writings of Emanuel Swedenborg* (S. M. Warren, Ed.). New York: Swedenborg Foundation.

———(1985). Divine Providence. In G. Dole (Trans.), *A view from within: A compendium of Swedenborg's theological thought.* New York: Swedenborg Foundation.

Tagore, R. (1961). *Rabindranath Tagore: Pioneer in education.* London: John Murray.

Tart, C. (1987). *Waking up: Overcoming the obstacles to human potential.* Boston: Shambhala.

Teilhard de Chardin, P. (1975). *Toward the future* (R. Hague, Trans.). New York: Harcourt Brace Jovanovich. (Original work published 1973).

Teresa, Mother (1990). *For the love of God: New writings by spiritual and psychological leaders* (B. Shield & R. Carlson, Eds.). San Rafael, CA: New World Library.

Thurman, R. A. F. (1991). Tibetan psychology: Sophisticated software for the human brain. In D. Golman & R. A. F. Thurman (Eds.), *MindScience: An east-west dialogue* (pp. 51-74). Boston: Wisdom.

———(1994). *Meditation and education: Buddhist India, Tibet and Modern America*. The Contemplative Mind in Society. Retrieved July 22, 2003, from http://www.contemplativemind.org/resources/ papers/thurman.html

Tillich, P. (1951). *Systematic theology* (Vol. I). Chicago: University of Chicago Press.

Tulku, T. (1977). *Time, space, and knowledge: A new vision of reality.* Emeryville, CA: Dharma.

Underhill, E. (1961). *Mysticism: A study in the nature and development of man's spiritual consciousness.* New York: E. P. Dutton. (Original work published 1911).

Universal House of Justice (1987). *Baha'i education.* London: Baha'i Publishing Trust.

Valett, R. E. (1991). Developing creative imagination. *Holistic Education Review, 4* (1), 22-27.

Van Dusen, W. (1992). *The country of spirit.* San Francisco: J. Appleseed.

Varela, F., Thomson, E., & Rosch, E. (1993). *The embodied mind: Cognitive science and human experience.* Cambridge, MA: MIT Press.

Vaughan, F. E. (1979). *Awakening intuition.* New York: Doubleday.

Vogt, K. D. (1987). *Vision and revision: The concept of inspiration in Thomas Mann's fiction.* New York: Peter Lang.

von Bertalanffy, L. 1968. General system theory: Foundations, developments, applications. New York: Braziller.

Vygotsky, L. S. (1987). *The collected works of L. S. Vygotsky* (R. W. Rieber & A. S. Caton, Trans.). New York: Plenum.

Washburn, M. (2000). Integrated cognition. In T. Hart, P. Nelson, & K. Puhakka (Eds.), *Transpersonal knowing: Exploring the horizon of consciousness* (pp. 185-212). Albany: State University of New York Press.

Watkins, J. G. (1978). *The therapeutic self: Developing resonance—key to effective relationships.* New York: Human Science Press.

Webster's Universal College Dictionary (2001). New York: Random House.

Weil, A. (1972). *The natural mind.* Boston: Houghton Mifflin.

Welwood, J. (1996). Reflection and presence: The dialectic of self-knowledge. *Journal of Transpersonal Psychology, 28* (2), 107-128.

— — —(2000). Reflection and presence: The dialectic of awakening. In T. Hart, P. L. Nelson, & K. Puhakka (Eds.), *Transpersonal knowing: Exploring the horizon of consciousness* (pp. 85-111). Albany: State University of New York Press.

Westcott, M. (1968). *Toward a contemporary psychology of intuition.* New York: Holt, Reinhart and Winston.

Whitehead, A. N. (1958). *Modes of thought.* New York: Capricorn Books. (Original work published 1938).

— — —(1967). *The aims of education and other essays.* New York: The Free Press. (Original work published 1929).

Wilber, K. (1989). *Eye to eye.* Garden City, NY: Anchor.

— — —(1995). *Sex, ecology, spirituality: The spirit of evolution.* Boston: Shambhala.

— — —(1997). *The eye of the spirit: An integral vision for a world gone slightly mad.* Boston: Shambhala.

Williams, M. E. (1982). *Inspiration in Milton and Keats.* Totowa, NJ: Barnes and Noble Books.

Winnicott, D. W. (1996). *Playing and reality.* New York: Routledge. (Original work published 1971).

Wood, G. H. (1998). *A time to learn: Creating community in America's high schools.* New York: Dutton.

Zuckerman, H. (1977). *Scientific elite: Nobel laureates in the United States.* New York: The Free Press.

INDEX

Studies in the Postmodern Theory of Education

General Editors
Joe L. Kincheloe & Shirley R. Steinberg

Counterpoints publishes the most compelling and imaginative books being written in education today. Grounded on the theoretical advances in criticalism, feminism, and postmodernism in the last two decades of the twentieth century, Counterpoints engages the meaning of these innovations in various forms of educational expression. Committed to the proposition that theoretical literature should be accessible to a variety of audiences, the series insists that its authors avoid esoteric and jargonistic languages that transform educational scholarship into an elite discourse for the initiated. Scholarly work matters only to the degree it affects consciousness and practice at multiple sites. Counterpoints' editorial policy is based on these principles and the ability of scholars to break new ground, to open new conversations, to go where educators have never gone before.

For additional information about this series or for the submission of manuscripts, please contact:

Joe L. Kincheloe & Shirley R. Steinberg
c/o Peter Lang Publishing, Inc.
29 Broadway, 18th floor
New York, New York 10006

To order other books in this series, please contact our Customer Service Department:

(800) 770-LANG (within the U.S.)
(212) 647-7706 (outside the U.S.)
(212) 647-7707 FAX

Or browse online by series:
www.peterlang.com

COUNTERPOINTS

Studies in the Postmodern Theory of Education